Linguistic Variation as Social Practice

The Linguistic Construction of Identity in Belten High

Penelope Eckert

Stanford University

BLACKWELL
Publishers

Copyright © Penelope Eckert 2000

The right of Penelope Eckert to be identified as the author of this work has been asserted in accordance with the Copyright, Designs and Patents Act 1988.

First published 2000

2 4 6 8 10 9 7 5 3 1

Blackwell Publishers Inc.
350 Main Street
Malden, Massachusetts 02148
USA

Blackwell Publishers Ltd
108 Cowley Road
Oxford OX4 1JF
UK

Library of Congress Cataloging-in-Publication Data
Eckert, Penelope.
Linguistic variation as social practice: the linguistic construction of identity in Belten High / Penelope Eckert.
p. cm.—(Language in society; 27)
Includes bibliographical references and index.
ISBN 0–631–18603–4 (alk. paper).—ISBN 0–631–18604–2 (pbk.: alk. paper)
1. Language and languages—Variation. 2. Sociolinguistics.
3. High school students—Language. I. Title. II. Series: Language in society (Oxford, England); 27.
P120.V37E37 1999
306.44—dc21   99–22433
                                                                                CIP

British Library Cataloguing in Publication Data
A CIP catalogue record for this book is available from the British Library.

Typeset in 10½ on 12½ pt Ehrhardt
by Best-set Typesetter Ltd., Hong Kong
Printed in Great Britain by T. J. International, Padstow, Cornwall

This book is printed on acid-free paper.

In memory of David Mann

Contents

List of Figures

List of Tables

Preface

As a native of New Jersey who learned fairly young to spit out my accent along with my gum, I came to the study of sociolinguistics with an inalienable sense that variation is laden with interesting social meaning. When I was an adolescent, there was a kind of a knock-knock joke in our house. A close family friend, Jo Schilt, would ask me "Penelope, where did you learn to talk like that?", and I would say "Friends." My pronunciation of *friends*, with that particular lip-rounded and palatalized r, sent her time and again rolling with laughter. My parents thought this was pretty clever too, and I savored the opportunity to remind all those adults that I had a community of my own that had, among other things, its own way of talking.

In that community in Leonia High School in the late fifties, Irene Erianne brought in new ways of saying things, Judy O'Grady ratified them, and each of us picked them up more or less, depending on the degree to which we cast our lot with the aspects of the local Italian-American culture that they were tied to. Or that's how I remember it. Ethnicity, class, and local geography were embedded in social meaning and social practice within our crowd and within the school, linking our local high school concerns with the broader social structure. Standing in front of our lockers, walking up and down Broad Avenue, sitting in the park, or dancing over at somebody's house, we worked out our personal significance within our community of practice and in relation to our wider surroundings. I did not find Irene or Judy in Belten High, because human nature finds infinite variety. But I did find elements of each of them. I found personal characteristics and forms of social participation that license, and stem from, particular roles in making social meaning through the creation and deployment of styles. The very same uses of linguistic style that linked Irene to her wider networks both within and beyond school made her who she was in our crowd, and united the ephemeral with the enduring.

The research described in this book is a quantitative study of variation embedded in an ethnography. It grew out of my questions about the nature of social meaning in variation, its role in the spread of linguistic change, and its relation to class. It also grew out of my sheer enjoyment of adolescents and my interest in the adolescent life stage. We have known for some time that adolescents are the speakers who advance sound change, yet the discussions of class that predominate in the study of variation focus on adults. I'm embarrassed and compelled to say that I began this project with plenty of feminist ideals but a level of sophistication about gender that was barely above average in variation circles. My interest in gender developed in the course of this work, and has been responsible for my increasing focus on practice, on the construction of identity, and hence on very local and often ephemeral detail. I fear that my pursuit of the ephemeral has confused some of my more conservative colleagues, who believed that my concern with local meaning constituted a rejection of their interest in the "big picture." As I explored the local construction of gender and social class, some thought I was discarding global social categories as theoretical constructs. In fact, I have looked away from the "big" picture, to see how us "little" people use variation to both find and make our way in the world, and in the process connect to, and create, the big picture.

I began this study with the intention of using ethnography simply to replace adult class categories with adolescent "native" categories. I found these categories in the jocks and the burnouts, but gradually came to realize that in my search for the fabled structured heterogeneity, I was constructing homogeneity. Focused on the categories and on categorization, I found myself feeling threatened by, and resistant to, the richness of human experience both within and beyond the categories. And this is the very richness in which social meaning resides. I had to rediscover a fundamental principle of ethnography, which is to discover rather than impose, but this is a difficult principle to follow when one is under time pressure to procure a linguistic sample. My initial approach to this fieldwork grew out of established practice in the study of variation, but more crucially out of the constraints of academia and our funding structures, which make it more than difficult to pursue intensive, and certainly longtime ethnography, particularly while living at home. I pursued the ethnographic work that forms the basis of this study while teaching in the Department of Anthropology at the University of Michigan, driving 45 minutes to the suburbs and returning in the afternoon to my normal academic responsibilities. With this continual pressure, I went to school less often than I would have liked, and returned less often than I would have liked in the evenings and on weekends to attend functions or to hang out. Access to the situations and relationships that make participant-observation what it is depends on being in the right place at the right time, and on being a reliable participant. I point this out to emphasize that our work confronts us with many difficult choices. I generally made the sacrifices in favor of the ethnography, and I have continued to make ethnography a way of life and fundamental to my linguistic practice. While I have done this at considerable professional cost, I do not regret having followed my desires and my intellectual judgment, and I have come away with the luxurious feeling that my life and my work are my own.

The Belten High students who appear in this book are way beyond adolescence now and one of my regrets is that I have not been able to keep up with them. I frequently remind myself that they were much more important to me than I was to them, and that while I still remember each one of them vividly, they may well not remember that I was even there. But they're the ones who gave and I was the one who took – I enjoyed them beyond belief, I learned from them, and I'm grateful for their willingness to let me into part of their world. The teachers were phenomenally patient with my presence, and offered me a welcome into the adult world of Belten High that I would have enjoyed but could not accept. And the school and district administrators, who not only gave me access to their school but helped me gain access to more schools for my geographic sample, were perceptive, forward looking and generous. I know that it is taking a tremendous risk to allow a researcher into a school, and I am grateful to the students and personnel of Belten High and the schools in the geographic sample for their trust, and hope that I have done nothing to violate it.

However wonderful the people in school may be, fieldwork is stressful, and I was lucky to be able to return every day to a lab full of great people working on the other end of this project. A team of research assistants were responsible for much of the work that went into this study, and helped keep me going from day to day. I've lost track of some of them now, but I think of them often and thank them continually in my mind. Lynne Robins, Marcia Salomon, and Mary Steedly transcribed the interviews into text files; Susan Blum, Jane Covert, Larry Diemer, Alison Edwards, and Becky Knack did the phonetic transcription; and Leanna Tyler did all the data entry. They were loyal, supportive, fun, and extremely good at their work.

I owe a special debt to the community that is the Institute for Research on Learning, where I have spent the most important years and the most important moments of my intellectual life. This is the place where I have felt appreciated for my interdisciplinariness, and the first place where I have felt completely unafraid to show my personal and intellectual warts. It is the place, as a result, where I have learned the most, and where I have developed my confidence and my best ideas. It is also the place where I met Jean Lave and Etienne Wenger, who have been an enduring source of inspiration, love, and intellectual friendship that has extended far beyond IRL's walls. Their ideas are everywhere in this book.

A university is a very different kind of institution from a small interdisciplinary institute, offering the complementarity of vast intellectual resources, a constant challenge from both colleagues and students, and a strong disciplinary pull. I am fortunate to be able to divide my time between IRL and the Department of Linguistics at Stanford, which is an unusually congenial academic environment, particularly for a sociolinguist, and challenging in the most wonderful ways. I am grateful to my students and colleagues for their excellence, inspiration, and friendship, and for their apparent appreciation of my style of sociolinguistics.

As my interest in gender developed during this study, my casual friendship with Sally McConnell-Ginet turned into a very close and wonderful intellectual partnership. I have learned a tremendous amount from my joint work with Sally, and I have gained a lifelong friend in the process.

I can never write anything major without thanking Bill Labov. Looking at the big picture, I'm grateful to him for inventing the study of sociolinguistic variation for heaven's sake. And at the level of the ephemeral, I'm not sure I could have tolerated graduate school had it not been for him. I am forever grateful to Bill for his teaching, his brilliant example, his friendship and encouragement, and for his forbearance when I get mad at him.

In the course of this project, I made three job moves and I got married. Ivan Sag, with whom I engaged in the latter, has been my continual and ever-patient linguistic sounding board, and a gratifying fan of my work. The field of sociolinguistics has suffered vastly from Ivan's decision to do syntax instead of variation, and I really wish he'd do fieldwork with me. I have benefited immeasurably from his receptive and constructively critical ear, from his companionship and encouragement, and from all kinds of things that have nothing to do with this book.

Finally, I could not have done this work without the support of the Spencer Foundation, which funded the pilot project, and the National Science Foundation (BNS-8023291), which funded all of the analysis. Like many, many linguists, I am personally grateful to Paul Chapin for his work at NSF on the behalf of linguists and linguistics. I feel particularly indebted to Paul for offering me extraordinary help and encouragement when I needed it most.

Introduction: Variation and Agency

Judy slouches in her chair, lifts her right foot to her knee and toys with the fringe on her rawhide boot. "... we used to tell our moms that we'd, uh she'd be sleeping at my house, I'd be sleeping at hers, we'd go out and pull an all-nighter, you know. I'd come home the next day, *'Where were you?'* 'Joan's.' *'No you weren't'* because her mom and my mom are like really close – since we got in so much trouble they know each other really good."

Judy's tight laugh seems to match her tight jeans, her speed-thin body, her dark eye liner, and her tense front vowels. In everything she does, Judy embodies and projects her style: independent but strung out, on the edge, restless, fierce. Judy is a burnout. To the rest of the people in her class she stands as the prototypical burnout – a "burned-out burnout." Her dress, her manner, her actions, her speech are all extreme versions of burnout style. Her every move, her every utterance seems to thumb her nose at the school, at adults, at fear.

Our attention to sociolinguistic variation begins with observations like these. We notice people's clothing, their hair, their movements, their facial expressions, and we notice a speech style – a complex construction of lexicon, prosody, segmental phonetics, morphology, syntax, discourse. And we come to associate all of these with the things they do and say – with the attitudes and beliefs they project, and with the things they talk about. It is individual speakers who bring language to life for us, and whose behavior points us to the social significance of variables. But these observations, and many of the insights that they embody, rarely find their way into our scientific accounts of sociolinguistic variation. With our eyes fixed firmly on statistical significance and the global picture, we repackage individuals as members of groups and categories, and we speak of those categories in terms of the characteristics that their members share, losing the local experience that makes variation meaningful to speakers. Ultimately, the social life of variation lies in the variety of individuals' ways of participating in their communities – their ways of fitting in, and of making their mark – their ways of constructing meaning in their own lives. It lies in the day-to-day use and transformation of linguistic resources for local stylistic purposes, and its global significance lies in the articulation between these local purposes and larger patterns of ways of being in the world.

This book is a study of variation in Judy's Detroit suburban high school, Belten High. The people whose lives and language serve as material for analysis are members of a vast social network as initially defined by Judy's graduating class. Based on two years of ethnographic work in and around the school, this study aims to give reality to the identities being associated with linguistic data – to situate the sociolinguistic analysis in a rich social landscape, and to examine the linguistic behavior of speakers as they participate jointly and individually in that landscape. The study is an effort to get closer to the social meaning of variation – to understand the particular local meanings that this adolescent population associates with linguistic style, and to link it to larger patterns associated with such abstractions as class, gender, social networks, and linguistic markets. No community exists in a vacuum, and the social meaning of variation within Belten High, as well as the role of Belten High students in the spread of linguistic change, are to be found in their orientation to, use of, and contact across the wider metropolitan area. This study, therefore, includes shorter periods of linguistic ethnography in schools across the Detroit suburban area, placing the actions and orientations of the Belten High students within the context of the actions and orientations of their peers across the urban–suburban continuum.

I begin this book, as I will end it, with Judy, because she plays a crucial role in the sociolinguistic order of Belten High. She is a cultural and a linguistic icon – a local personage whose extreme embodiment of burnout practice and style serves as a benchmark of social meaning for her cohort – and it is her flamboyance that first led me to view personal style as the locus of this meaning. The examination of variation to follow begins with the highlighted and opposed social categories that dominate the social order in each of the Detroit suburban schools I studied: the jocks and the burnouts. I have examined these categories in depth in my ethnography, *Jocks and Burnouts* (Eckert 1989), showing that they are not random eruptions of adolescent stylizing, but the very means by which socioeconomic class is constructed in and for the adolescent population. The jocks and burnouts constitute middle class and working class cultures respectively – they are the instantiation of class in the adolescent life stage, and serve as trajectories to adulthood. Representing opposing orientations to school and to the local area, the jocks are an institutional, corporate culture while the burnouts are a personal, locally oriented culture. In offering class-based alternatives, these categories offer gender alternatives as well, embodying different ways of being male and of being female. The opposition between the jocks and the burnouts is fundamental to the social order of Belten High, and structures the lives of those who affiliate with one category or the other. And the fact that the many students who affiliate with neither are commonly referred to as "in-betweens", is an indication that these categories dominate the lives of even those who assiduously avoid them.

The burnouts and the jocks are not simply two visible social groups, but they embody opposing class-related ideologies, norms, trajectories, and practices of all sorts. From their attitudes to smoking to their ways of making friends, the jocks and the burnouts live very different lives, and as a result do very different things with language. It is no surprise, then, that this split frequently correlates with the use of sociolinguistic variables. The meanings of the variables are to be found not in a simple association of variation with social category, however, but in the meaning of being a jock and being a burnout, and the various meanings of being in-between. The jock–burnout split, therefore, serves as the background to the following discussion of variation. It is the point of departure, not the end, of an examination of social identity and meaning, and of the analysis of sociolinguistic variation. Ethnography can yield local ("native") categories, but an interpretation of the relation between these categories and variation requires going beyond categories to the practices that make categorization meaningful. Categories such as *jock* and *burnout* emerge around aspects of social practice that are sufficiently salient in the community to warrant a differentiation and separation between people on the basis of their participation in those practices. It is here that the difference between a theory of variation as structure and a theory of variation as practice arises.

A theory of variation as structure would take the categories *jock* and *burnout* as given, and would focus on Judy's use of variation as an indicator of her place in relation to them. A theory of variation as social practice sees speakers as constituting, rather than representing, broad social categories, and it sees speakers as constructing, as well as responding to, the social meaning of variation. This study, accordingly, will take the jock and burnout categories as a means by which kids deal with the situations they find themselves in, and will focus on Judy's style as part of the very constitution of these categories. It will view the social meaning of variation not just as a reflection of membership, or by extension as a way of claiming membership, but as related to the practices that give rise to and maintain those categories, and that make membership in them meaningful.

The study aims to treat the speaker as a linguistic agent, to treat speech as a building of meaning, and to treat the community as mutually engaged in a meaning-making enterprise. Based on a view of social meaning as constructed in use, and of variation as a resource for that construction, it builds on the notion that the social meaning associated with variation is local – that it has to do with concrete places, people, styles, and issues. At the same time, these concrete local things are what constitute broad cultural categories such as class, gender, ethnicity, region. The correlation of a sociolinguistic variant with female gender or with working class status will indicate that the meaning of that variant is related to the lives of women or working class people. But it will not tell us what the variant actually means to the females or the working class people who use it frequently, or to the other members of their community who use it less. This can only be learned by examining communities up close enough to understand the local relation between these categories and social identity.

This book is not just about adolescents, but about adolescence, and the particular insights that the adolescent life stage can offer into the social meaning of variation. Adolescence is a crucial life stage for the study of variation, for it is the adolescent age group that has been found to lead all other age groups in sound change, and more generally in the use of the vernacular (Chambers 1995). This simple fact is sufficient to argue against any account of variation and change that does not foreground social agency. If sound change were, as Halle (1962) has claimed, solely a by-product of the process of acquisition, or if the social stratification of variation were, as Kroch (1978) has claimed, solely the result of differential social motivation to resist change, then the youngest age groups would lead the rest of the population in sound change. The only possible explanation for the adolescent lead in the use of the vernacular lies in that age group's positive motivations for the use of innovative and non-standard forms. This study, therefore, takes as given that variation reflects social agency, and that this agency involves the deployment and the construction of social meaning.

There is little doubt that the adolescent age group's lead in the use of vernacular variables is related to the particular juncture in life, and place in society, shared by the adolescent population. Adolescence marks the official transition from childhood to adulthood, and from the family social sphere to a peer-based social order, and the acceleration of the use of the vernacular is related to the identity work that takes place in the adolescent life stage.

The development of the peer social order, furthermore, inasmuch as it is dominated by the confined and segregated environment of the school, is fraught with conflict, competition, and emotional volatility. And with it comes an unequalled efflorescence of symbolic activity in all spheres. This heightened social activity offers a unique opportunity to examine the social meaning of variation. The grouping and confinement of the adolescent age group in school institutions also offer an opportunity to witness the social order in action. Adolescence does not have the relative segregation of social groups that characterizes much of adult life. Public schooling often brings together children and adolescents from a wide social spectrum under one roof for the better part of the day, obliging them to share an environment and activities on a long-term basis. Social groups of all sorts, therefore, can be seen together, avoiding or interacting with each other, reacting to each other. A hothouse for social development, the high school also constitutes a natural sociolinguistic experiment.

For this reason, the landscape to be studied in this book has the high school as its center. One of the most striking aspects of educational practice in the United States is the particular conception of secondary education as an all-encompassing social and civic as well as curricular endeavor. The US public high school has primary responsibility for the adolescent age group. Public resources (however skimpy) for adolescents' athletic, artistic, and social activities are funnelled into the high school, and in many communities the school is the only place where adolescents can pursue not only curricular activities, but sports, theater, music, arts, or community service. It is through the school that most psychological counseling services are channeled, and it is to the school that students must look for employment counseling as well. As a result, the adolescent's relation to the school is almost a defining fact. The school-age person who is not in school is overwhelmingly defined by the category "dropout." And those who are in school are expected to spend the better part of their days in the school, staying there when school is out to participate in extracurricular activities. Those who do not are deviant in the eyes of society, and certainly of the school. The norm of school participation, therefore, gives school the power to define people. Based in a school, this study does not include people who have left school, although the social networks defined by the school reach out to include many who have left, whether by graduation or by dropping out. Thus while the story I am about to tell about variation includes the possibility of dropping out, it only tells about the language use of those who have so far managed to stay in. Specifically, it tells the story of the various ways of staying in – of the communities of practice that arise in response to the school institution as kids engage jointly in making sense of their mutual lives in school, and in articulating their lives in school with their lives outside. It tells the story of kids' use of sociolinguistic variation as a resource for the construction of these communities.

1

Interpreting the Meaning of Variation

Studying the sociolinguistic dynamics of an adolescent community on its own terms requires rethinking aspects of our social theories of variation which by and large have been based on adult speech and adult social categories. Adult patterns of variation, therefore, are viewed, at least implicitly, as a finished product, and the target of development. The focus in the field of variation on adult social constraints in variation has led researchers to think of the child's development of the use of variation in adult terms as well. This view is implicit in variationists' speculations about the age at which children have "complete" control over patterns of variation. This adult focus is arguably a reflection of a general middle-aged bias in social science research (Baltes et al. 1980, Coupland, Coupland and Giles 1991, Eckert 1996b). More benignly, it is an artifact of the available data. Since the age span of adult working life is longer than the age span of children or of retired people, age-representative survey samples yield more sociolinguistic data on speakers in their "productive years" than any other group. And since measures of socioeconomic class are based on school-leaving, employment, adult consumption patterns (Labov 1966), and adult life style (Milroy and Milroy 1992), social theorizing related to variation is most complete for this age group as well. In the same way, to the extent that gender has been theorized in social science and in the study of variation, it too has been viewed in terms of adult experience and often in terms of relation to the means of production and specifically in terms of women's exclusion from the marketplace (Trudgill 1972).

Viewing development from an adult-centered point of view yields a view of development in which socialization is a matter of learning roles, with children sliding easily into the social positions to which they have been exposed (most likely by their parents). No variationist to my knowledge has actually embraced this view of development, but no explicit broadly developmental alternative has been proposed. A view of sociolinguistic development that allows the speaker more agency is more likely to view children as actively and creatively coming to terms with the situations in which they find themselves.

1.1   A Developmental View of Variation

Most developmental speculation about variation takes the acceleration of vernacular use as evidence that adolescence marks the point at which patterns of variation come into their own as socially meaningful (see Chambers 1995: chapter 4 for a developmental discussion of variation). I would argue, however, that adolescence is not a magical beginning of social consciousness, but a license and an imperative to begin acting on certain kinds of social knowledge that the age cohort has been developing for years. And while adolescent patterns of variation begin to fall into the kinds of global patterns found in the adult population, I would argue that this does not signal a sudden awareness of the social function of variation, but the adaptation of an already robust sociolinguistic competence to a new set of social meanings.

All of childhood is, among other things, about learning to be the next step older. Participation in kid communities requires a continuous learning of new age-appropriate behavior, and age-appropriateness changes rapidly. Social status among one's peers requires demonstrating new "mature" behaviors, a continual move beyond the childish – a need to be age appropriate that amounts to a *developmental imperative* (Eckert 1994). As a result, kids are continually trying on new behaviors and styles, in a continual and conscious production of a new self. This imperative continues throughout life, but is more noticeable in childhood and adolescence, since by adulthood one has learned to be more subtle in one's efforts at self-reconstruction. Linguistic style is an important part of age-appropriate behavior, and sociolinguistic development is a continuous process. But if adolescence has been pinpointed as a turning point in the speaker's sociolinguistic competence, little is known about the development of patterns of variation in childhood that lead up to adolescence.

There has been a relatively small amount of research on children's patterns of variation, at least in comparison with research on older populations, and there has emerged no consensus about the development of sociolinguistic variation. Much of the work on children's patterns of variation has abstracted away from the social, focusing on age limits for the acquisition of new dialects, on the one hand, and for the development of internal constraints in variation on the other. Since variation affects word classes, locally appropriate patterns of variation depend on locally appropriate underlying forms in the lexicon. Studies that focus on children moving into new dialect areas offer evidence that certain phonological patterns cannot be learned after a fairly young age. Payne's work (1980) in the Philadelphia suburb King of Prussia showed that children moving in from a different dialect area before the age of eight or nine picked up simple local vowel shifts. They did not have the same success, however, at developing the Philadelphia short-a pattern, which required complex knowledge of word-class assignment. It appeared that this had to be learned very early, as only children whose parents were from Philadelphia developed this pattern completely. Payne's conclusion was that while children may be able to add lower-level rules until adolescence, they cannot restructure their grammars as readily. Chambers' study (1992) of six Canadian children moving to Britain provided similar evidence of a developmental cutoff. Coming from a Canadian dialect area in which /oh/ and /o/ (*caught* vs. *cot*) are merged, they needed to learn the appropriate lexical assignments to develop the opposition as in the British dialect. In this case, Chambers found a close to perfect development of the opposition in the speech of a nine-year-old, and a sharp decrease in success for speakers over the age of 13.

While these studies tell us important things about phonological development, they do not say much about the kinds of dynamics that are the major preoccupation in studies of adult patterns of sociolinguistic variation. Studies correlating phonological variables with social factors do not deal with word-class assignments, but with phonetic processes that affect those word classes. There is recent evidence (Labov 1989, Roberts 1997, Roberts and Labov 1992, Wolfram 1989) that these processes begin quite early, and that children as young as three exhibit internally systematic patterns of variation in the use of both stable sociolinguistic variables (such as -*ing*, and t/d deletion) and in the use of patterns of local variation representing change in progress (such as the raising of short a in Philadelphia). These patterns show internal constraints similar to those in the speech of the adult population in their community. Thus variation is built into linguistic competence from the very earliest stages – a finding that is not at all surprising since, as Labov (1989) points out, the input for acquisition is variable.

An understanding of sociolinguistic development requires an understanding of how children come to recognize and produce socially meaningful patterns of variation, and ultimately to alter the rates of this variability over the life course. For kids to recognize that variation carries social meaning requires that they have the social knowledge necessary to distinguish social patterns of variation. There has been little study of the nature of this knowledge in children.

It is clear that very small children are stylistically active (Andersen 1990). And the well-established fact that kids' major dialect influence is their peers rather than their parents (e.g. Labov 1972b: 304–7) suggests that the development of sociolinguistic competence is not a simple matter of exposure, but that the actual source of the exposure matters. Kids spend plenty of time interacting with their parents and other adults, but it is their peers' patterns that they attend to. From an early age, then, children appear to recognize language patterns as related to their own social possibilities. In order to study the earliest development of sociolinguistic variation, then, it is crucial to understand what would constitute a sociolinguistic variable in a childhood age group, for the focus on adult social practice in the study of variation may well obscure age-specific use and interpretation among children. This requires merging a *developmental* perspective with a *mature-use* perspective (Eckert 1996b) for all age groups. That is, to understand the social use of language, we have to recognize that people are developing language skills throughout life, and that the skills that they exercise at any time in life are geared to that life stage. A child's language is not simply a manifestation of an effort to develop "real" language, but a fully mature linguistic form for that stage of childhood. In the study of variation this is crucial as well, for in view of the importance of the developmental imperative in childhood, issues associated with maturation, and the relation between age-appropriateness and social status at all early ages, are likely to be the ground on which children begin to develop a sense of the relation between linguistic features and social identity and status.

A study of the development of variation might do well to begin with phonological features of baby talk, for baby talk both marks a developmental stage and constitutes an important register (Andersen 1990, Ferguson 1977, Gleason 1973) for a wider age group. Baby talk is clearly linked with small children's social identities, and moving away from being a "baby" is a central social concern for kids. The transition from baby talk as one's sole competence to baby talk as a stylistic device would no doubt tell us volumes about the development of variable communicative competence. It is important to recognize, furthermore, that features of baby talk are not just a kids' resource, but a broader community resource whose value is related to the meaning of childhood in the community. Features of baby talk are not only part of a register for speaking with small children; they are also used among speakers of all ages, including adults, when no children are present. Many adults use baby talk, for example, when teasing about fear or low pain tolerance, expressing sympathy, talking to animals, or in intimate talk to a lover. These features have clear social meaning, derived from the community's view of children, as aspects of child identity and social relations endure in the linguistic strategies of older people. Rather than look for adult variables in children's speech to assess sociolinguistic competence, then, one might begin a developmental study of variation with a focus on children's linguistic resources, social identities, and strategies, asking how these patterns are transformed into adult strategies. An adult orientation leads the variationist to search children's speech only for variables that have been studied in the adult population, but it is quite clear, as shown by Andersen (1990), that the beginnings of social awareness in language variability lie in other, childhood-specific, linguistic material.

It is also likely that at least some variables studied in the adult community have childhood meaning. If one is to trace an awareness of the social function of variation to the earliest stages, it is important to pull back some from the concentration on peers. Labov has speculated (1990: 219) that mothers play a particular role in the advancement of sound change through their role as primary care-giver. While Labov is focusing on the advancement of female-led sound changes, one might extend this speculation to inquire about mothers' role in kids' learning about the social meaning of variation. The fact that women have a greater stylistic range in variation suggests that they make greater expressive use of variation, and it would be instructive to examine how mothers actually use phonological variables in interactions around children. It is possible that part of women's style involves a generally expressive use of variation, which would emerge in mothers' use of certain variables in phatic and affectionate communication with their children. In this case, very small children may come to recognize a relation between at least some adult phonological variables and certain kinds of social dynamics and relations – indeed, this could be the beginning of an association of certain variables with solidarity.

Because of a lack of studies of social variation among very small children, we so far know little about correlations of variables with social characteristics in this age group. Stratification according to parents' socioeconomic status shows up regularly in the speech of preadolescents (Wolfram 1969, Macaulay 1977, Romaine 1984, Reid 1978), the youngest age group normally included in class stratified samples. However, a distinction must be made between evidence of social variation among children that may reflect simple exposure, as in class or ethnic differences, and evidence of the social use of variation. Evidence of the social use of variation could be found in gender and in stylistic variation. While small children are commonly exposed to a population that is fairly homogeneous with respect to class and ethnicity, they are generally exposed to both male and female speech patterns and to stylistic variability. Stylistic and gendered patterning of variation, therefore, would indicate a socially based choice. Romaine (1984) provided non-quantitative evidence of stylistic variation in the use of (au) ([aw]~[u]) in the speech of six-year-olds in Edinburgh, and Biondi (1975) found stylistic use of despirantized (th) and (dh) among six-year-old Italian-American children between speech and reading style. Labov (1989) found stylistic variation in the use of t/d deletion and -*ing* by six-, seven- and nine-year-olds. The most robust data on stylistic variation in children, however, begins with the speech of preadolescents, around age ten. Reid (1978) showed variation in two speech styles among 11-year-old boys, in the use of -*ing* and in the use of glottal stop. Romaine's data from Edinburgh (1984) show variation in the use of the same two variables among ten-year-olds, between speech and reading style.

The most robust findings on gender differences in variation are also among older children, beginning at age ten. Romaine (1984) found gender differences in ten-year-olds in Glasgow and Edinburgh, and Macaulay (1977) found gender differences in Glasgow in ten- and 15-year-olds, with a considerably greater difference among the 15-year-olds. Biondi (1975), as well, found gender differences among Italian-American children in Boston. In all these cases, boys were using more non-standard forms than girls. Fischer's study (1958) of a small population of school children is particularly revealing, since it showed a correlation between the reduction of -*ing* (*walking*, *talking*) and aspects of kids' social practice. Specifically, he found that "model" boys (i.e. teachers' pets) reduced -*ing* less than "typical" boys as well as girls, showing clearly that variation has age-based social meaning for kids. The appropriation of stylistic variables for age-specific use can be seen as evidence that kids live also in the wider world, and are aware of social dynamics in all age groups around them. Purely anecdotal, but clear in its significance, is a quip made by my nephew, Michael Eckert, when he was seven years old. When I inquired how he felt about his family's recent move from an upper middle class suburb to Jersey City, he replied, in his lowest-pitch voice and with great gusto, "I'm the Jersey Jerk and I live in the sewer." This statement of his awareness of the social status of his new residence was delivered in a perfect New Jersey vernacular, completely with fortis (th), fortis word-initial (s), extremely rounded (u), final (r) deletion, and the palatalized retroflex syllabic /r/ in *Jersey* and *jerk* – a New Jersey variable that escapes popular stereotypes.

As kids move towards adolescence, they move from children's linguistic resources to adult resources. One might say that they lay claim to adult linguistic resources, just as they lay claim to aspects of adult identity and to adult prerogatives such as makeup, tobacco, and alcohol. Early on, this is clearly manifested in the increasing and daring use of obscenities and profanity, and adult vernacular expressions (e.g. *dude*). This linguistic behavior attracts adult notice and sanction, associated as it is with issues of control. More standard adult linguistic prerogatives go unsanctioned by adults, but can be sanctioned by kids. Kids' use of certain kinds of adult-like authoritative speech, prissy speech, or bossy speech is frequently riciduled by their peers for their presumption. Awareness of the social significance of standard speech, therefore, no doubt creeps into kids' linguistic practice quite early on. The notions of vernacular and standard may well emerge in a distinction between child and adult speech, and perhaps between affectionate and angry speech, gathering greater correspondence to global norms in school, where teachers' speech comes to be the ultimate adult speech. Thus while kids may not begin to display a recognition of standard norms in use until they are older (Labov 1964, Chambers 1995: 153ff), they may be developing an understanding of the linguistic market and the relation between linguistic variation and power, quite early on. In elementary schools with a diverse student body, as well, where more standard-speaking kids linguistically resemble the teacher, issues of standard and vernacular can be foregrounded quite early on in relations among kids, and viewed in terms of certain kids' alliances with adults. Ultimately it is relations among kids, and their mutual evaluation of the social significance of the different forms of language available in their environment, that will give rise to a peer-based linguistic market.

The notion *linguistic market* is particularly important to this discussion, because it focuses on the relation between variation and the production of a self in a symbolic economy. Bourdieu and Boltanski (1975) first introduced the notion of a linguistic market, in which the value of a speaker's verbal offerings – the likelihood that these offerings will be heard and heeded – depends on the linguistic variety in which they are encoded. The notion of a linguistic market has a particularly attractive explanatory power in the development of adolescent language, where the production of the self to maximize one's value in the marketplace is so clear. The linguistic market, in fact, is part of a broader symbolic market, and one can see the self as the commodity that is being produced for value in the market. Thus one is both agent and commodity. Bourdieu and Boltanski (1975) speak of only one market – the market controlled by global elites, whose linguistic variety comes to be known as the legitimate or standard language. This focus on the standard stems from their concern with the concentration of global power, and the control from above of societal material and symbolic resources. While there is a close relation between the linguistic market and class in capitalist industrialized society, it is not clear that class is what kids respond to initially as they develop a sense of the market. Rather, for instance, the power of adults over children may be an initial development of a sense of the relation between power and ways of speaking.

Part of going from being a child to being an adult involves moving from an ascriptive to an achieved place in the world. And part of developing an achieved place in the world is an increasing sense of the self as a commodity on the social market. In some very important sense, social development involves a process of objectification, as one comes to see oneself as having value in a marketplace. We take it for granted that adults see themselves as having value in the employment market, or in the academic market: résumés, transcripts, and letters of recommendation are easily recognized as part of the construction of value. Personal style is also part of this construction. Children begin to recognize the need to produce themselves for the market as they approach adolescence – as they come to see themselves as commodities whose value is determined in a peer-controlled "marketplace of identities." Most particularly, as they approach adolescence, kids find themselves thrown into a heterosexual market (Thorne 1993, Eckert 1997a), where their value is largely determined by their ability to command alliances with, and attention from, valued members of the other sex. They also find themselves in a related marketplace of popularity, where one's value depends on access to visibility and contacts. This market begins in late elementary school, where activity unfolds in a safe and stable classroom social unit, under the watchful eye of nurturant teachers. In secondary school, though, where the cohort suddenly expands and where heterosexuality is suddenly licensed, kids find themselves in a more public and competitive context. As they seek a place in the informal social sphere and the extracurricular sphere, and later as they prepare for the college and employment marketplaces, they will have to market themselves in an increasing variety of ways. To the extent that language is part of the packaging of a product for the market, one can expect an explosion of linguistic activity in secondary school.

Secondary school makes the exact dates of the transition from childhood to adolescence official, and provides the institutional structure and resources to organize the transition. In the US, children anticipate entrance into secondary school with a mixture of eagerness and trepidation, as adolescence brings greater freedom and new opportunities on the one hand, and makes new social demands on the other. One can list any number of changes that accompany the move from elementary school to secondary school – a move from an institution that takes responsibility for its students' development to one that views students' development as their own responsibility. Suddenly students' behavior is viewed as the result of personal choice, their activities are seen as the initiation of a trajectory to adulthood, and their actions are seen as having permanent consequences. Adolescence also brings greater freedom and mobility, and a legitimation, and institutionalization, of heterosexuality. Adolescence is the pivot between childhood and adulthood, between a place in society based on parents' place and one's own. Yet while it is supremely transitional, it is reified as a stage in itself. Adolescence is a way of life that kids fear and anticipate for its own sake, and that they experience very differently depending on their circumstances. Normative adolescence in the US entails engagement in school, a happy-go-lucky social whirl, innocent mischief, and independence from family and material responsibilities – a leisure that is unavailable to most members of the adolescent age group, and a way of life that is distasteful to many. Yet while the social circumstances of adolescence are a recipe for stress, experts commonly attribute the emotional turbulence that marks adolescence for many to biological processes. While the "raging hormones" of puberty may well be a source of difficulty, the social construction of this life stage is sufficiently elaborate to make the effects of biology seem trivial.

Adolescents are very much in the middle. On the one hand, they have pulled away definitively from childhood – on the other hand, they remain under adult control. The age cohort makes sense of itself by constructing difference within, on the one hand, and by opposing itself to the adult and child age groups on the other. The very status of adolescence, with its institutional supports, separates the age group from childhood once and for all. At the same time, the focus on autonomy sets up a new kind of opposition between adolescence and adulthood. Since institutional requirements prevent adolescents from affirming independence from their parents through engagement in the adult world, they must do so through engagement in the adolescent world. While one agenda of adolescence is laying claim to adult prerogatives, the only legitimate way to have a sense of autonomy is to elevate the peer community and culture as an independent form of membership and participation. And the value of such a claim to autonomy depends on the worthiness and autonomy of that adolescent culture. The elaboration of adolescent social practices stems from the need to create a viable alternative to adulthood, making adolescent life both short and intense – a social hothouse. Symbolic intensity facilitates the rapid social change of adolescence, giving rise to comparably intense preoccupations with clothing and other adornment, style of demeanor and motion, substance use and eating patterns, cars and other forms of consumption, and language use. It should be no surpise, therefore, that adolescents lead all age groups in linguistic innovation.

Ultimately, all of this symbolic activity describes a marketplace of identities, and the patterns of variation are best considered in terms of the adolescent linguistic market. Its relation to the adult linguistic market is complex and transitional, but essential. In adolescence, the market takes on a new sense, as adult class begins to loom. But in elementary school, the relation between adult class, power, and the institution is obscured by relations between children and adults, as power is concentrated in age differences. In secondary school, the relation between the local marketplace of identities, the school, and one's future potential in the adult market becomes manifest. This is both because secondary school is the time when one makes curricular choices that have implications for the next stage beyond high school, and because the institutional structure of the high school provides for relations of institutional power to develop within the peer cohort. Thus aspects of relations between children and adults are transformed into peer relations. This is the point at which the transfer of power begins, from those who dominate in the adult world to the young people who will come to dominate. The linguistic market of childhood, then, begins to merge with the linguistic market of adulthood.

1.2   Class and the Linguistic Market

The jock–burnout opposition that dominates social discourse at Belten High foregrounds conflict models of social class. The continuous juxtaposition of jock and burnout in day-to-day life within a confined environment, and the consequent foregrounding of difference, competition, and conflict, can be seen as providing an early orientation to social class as oppositional. At the same time, there is a sense that the two categories represent the extremes of the school social order, and some students manifest impatience with and resistance to the discourse of opposition altogether. Yet the passionate and concerted work that goes into creating and maintaining mutual opposition in all symbolic realms presents a view of two poles as pulling apart, giving life to the kind of non-consensual view of variation outlined by Rickford (1986). And it brings to the fore a view of competing markets of identity, and the related (and opposed and competing) linguistic markets.

The view of class stratification of variation in terms of competing linguistic markets hangs somewhat in the limbo of disparate foci of variation studies. Both the standard and the vernacular are associated with maximally engaged populations – but populations engaged in opposing extremes of the social order. The vernacular, the language of locally based communities, is the source of regular sound change; the standard, the language of institutionally based networks, is a locus of resistance to change. The issue of the nature of the dynamics behind linguistic innovation and resistance is at the bottom of a good deal of discussion and disagreement within theories of variation.

Survey studies (e.g. Labov 1966, Trudgill 1974) focusing on the socioeconomic and stylistic stratification of variables over large populations imply (whether intentionally or not) a consensual view of language and class. In this view, the standard and vernacular poles, as well as the continuum between, result from a single set of linguistic dynamics. The most extreme version of this view was laid out by Kroch (1978), accounting for social differentiation of variation in terms of mutually opposed forces of innovation and resistance. Innovation, according to Kroch, is an imperative from within the linguistic system, and will proceed in the absence of conscious resistance. The socioeconomic continuum, according to Kroch, is also a continuum of linguistic practice, in which greater socioeconomic status brings greater resistance to change. The stratification of linguistic variables, therefore, simply reflects the stratification of resistance to change. Like the Neogrammarians, Kroch limits linguistic agency to resistence to "natural" linguistic processes. This view is consonant with Labov's interpretation of the stylistic continuum as a continuum of attention paid to speech. According to Labov, the individual's speech production is quite automatic at the vernacular end of his or her stylistic continuum, but requires increasing attention and care as production moves toward the standard end. Thus, change is likely to be accelerated when the speaker is distracted from standard norms.

The notion of the standard language market, as introduced into the study of variation by Sankoff and Laberge (1978), complements this view. Basing their work on Bourdieu's notion of symbolic capital (1977a, 1977b) and Bourdieu and Boltanski's work on the linguistic market (1975), the authors show that within a single socioeconomic stratum, speakers' use of standard variants in Montreal French correlates with their relative engagement in networks and institutions that require the use of standard varieties. The notion of the market provides an explanation of class stratification that specifically points to the actual situations and interactive needs that lead to the adoption of standard varieties. It also emphasizes the relation of language to the production of the self, and to the individual's own viability in the economic marketplace.

But the focus on the standard as the sole source of conscious norms for the entire speech community is, as many (e.g. Milroy 1980: 101ff) have pointed out, problematic. While Labov's own work in Martha's Vineyard and in New York City (e.g. 1972a, 1972b) is the origin of our understanding that the vernacular has positive value in local communities, his view of style creates mystery about the means by which this value is constructed. While formal style certainly involves greater attention to speech, and while speakers have to pay careful attention when they're speaking in the most extremely standard end of their stylistic repertoire, there is every reason to believe that a similar effort is required at the extremely non-standard end of their repertoire as well. One might consider that the two ends of the continuum require effort motivated by different – and even conflicting – orientations, and that people have to work to ensure their participation in either market. (Also, it is not clear that attention gets paid to speech only when a production effort is required; the intentional stylistic production of variants anywhere along a speaker's continuum could be the result of heightened attention.)

If survey studies of variation have appeared to elevate the standard language as the stylistic target of the entire socioeconomic hierarchy, ethnographic studies such as Labov's Martha's Vineyard study (1972b) and Milroy's study (1980) of working class networks in Belfast focus on the positive local symbolic value of the vernacular. A conflict view of class suggests (see Woolard 1985) that there are alternative linguistic markets, within which forms other than the global standard constitute the norm. The existence of alternative linguistic markets is not necessarily a reason to reject the supremacy of the standard market as constructed by Bourdieu and Boltanski (1975), for the creativity and the force of the vernacular can be seen as a response to relative powerlessness in the face of the standard. This does not nullify the vernacular's linguistic and cultural importance, but locates it in the political economy. The fact that the power of the legitimate market enables it to appropriate the creative products of the vernacular market, as, for instance, in the corporate marketing of hip-hop, underlines the basic relation between the two markets. While agents of the global market may come to the local market to find and exploit creative innovation, this does not enhance the status of local youth culture. In fact, one might say that the ability of the global market to stigmatize local innovation keeps the value of that very innovation sufficiently low to exploit, and even legitimizes only the genius of the global agents who have the "creativity" to recognize "quality" local innovations. Thus local change mediated by global agents can become legitimized as global change. One might even say that the power of the vernacular resides in the recognition of its powerlessness as the vernacular and the standard arise in mutual response and opposition to the potential threat that each poses to the other.

The linguistic market is part of a broader symbolic market, which includes patterns of consumption, demeanor, etc., and the power of the legitimized language in that market lies in the alignment of features of language with features of other symbolic resources. This integration involves a process of essentialization, whereby the properties of the standard language, along with dress, manners, etc., come to be seen as embodiments of cultural value: clarity, logic, elegance. (See Irvine (in press) for a particularly elegant discussion of this aspect of style.) It is the power to define such things as clarity, logic, and elegance that constitutes *hegemony*. The symbolic force of these resources, then, resides in their confounding with characteristics claimed as justification for participation in, and domination of, the legitimate market. Standard language gains its power by virtue of its association with the institutions of societal authority and power, and the nature of standard language is best described in terms of these institutions and their hierarchies. Although Bourdieu focuses on the "true" elites in his examinations of French society, it is perhaps more relevant to focus on the institutions in which access to economic power is constructed. Since it is the belief in the possibility of access that spurs adherence to legitimate norms throughout the population, and since in our society the corporate hierarchy is the legitimate path to mobility, corporate hierarchies are an instructive locus.

The pull of the standard language market is obviously quite heterogeneous. The importance of resembling those above in the hierarchy has been described in detail in the corporate setting (Kanter 1977). This emulation is not of random characteristics, but of an intricate co-construction of symbolic form and legitimation. The fact that those rising to the top of corporate hierarchies gain power over increasingly broad segments of the institution and ultimately of society, and participate in increasingly powerful and cosmopolitan networks, is translated into a belief that their interests represent in some ultimate way those of society at large. Corporate members' loyalty to the corporate institution requires that they set aside

local or personal interests and that they base their deliberations on the con-
scientious application of objective, dispassionate reasoning to information
from these global, "impersonal" sources. The importance of "rising above"
group and personal concerns dictates that corporate players relinquish close
local social networks for more scattered networks based on corporate
contact. In the corporate context, insofar as the individual's identity is based
on his or her institutional role, personal interests are considered to be inseparable from those of the institution. This ideological relinquishing of local
allegiances is of course related to a practical necessity: hierarchies are
increasingly dominated by geographically diffuse networks, and the requirements for servicing those networks outside of the workplace increasingly
militate against locally based personal networks.

Allegiance to corporate cosmopolitan norms emerges in the domination
of personal and symbolic behavior by conservative norms. The avoidance
of flamboyance and local "fads" conveys sobriety, solidity, responsibility,
immunity to casual influence, and the transcendence of personal and local
interest for the interests of the more global concerns of the corporation and,
by extension, of society as a whole. All of this is reflected in the choice of
classic styles of clothing, adornment, home furnishings, and automobiles,
all known for their slow, non-faddish rate of change; and involvement in
broad-based community organizations, sedate leisure activities, foreign
travel, a preference for "classical" forms of entertainment and the unsen-
sationalized press, and the adoption of a standard conservative speech
variety.

In keeping with its cosmopolitan status, standard language eschews
features identified with specific localities, which are taken as evidence
of flightiness and partiality. And in keeping with its educational base,
standard language eschews non-standard grammatical forms which are
taken as evidence of lack of clear, logical, and hence responsible thought.
The standard speech variety also extends far beyond phonology, vocabulary,
and grammar. Speech events associated with the accomplishment of institutional tasks reflect the nature of the community within which they
take place. Inasmuch as corporate ideology dictates that decisions be based
on information from "objective," external sources, and on institutional
rather than personal interests, it also dictates that discussions, deliberations, negotiations, and the presentation of their results be presented
in language that is relatively abstract, and free of emotional and personal
involvement.

Explicit study of the standard language market has focused on institutional engagement, correlating variables with occupations that require

varying amounts of standard language (Kroch and Small 1978, Zhang 1995, Sankoff and Laberge 1978, Sankoff et al. 1989). Indices of socioeconomic status used in survey studies, based primarily on occupation and education, essentially measure the degree of engagement in the standard language market. And the increasing tendency to substitute occupation for complex indices in studies of variation (Labov 1990) reflects the fact that current qualification for, and engagement in, a specific workplace is directly related to one's current use of standard language. Work on the local, vernacular market, on the other hand, has focused on non-institutional forms of engagement, by correlating the use of vernacular variants with indices of engagement in local networks and local cultural practices (Cheshire 1982, Edwards 1991, Knack 1991, Milroy 1980).

The local marketplace, in which local rights and privileges are controlled (local jobs, renting and buying homes, goods sold and exchanged locally, use of public space), is opposed to a non-local marketplace in which generalized resources are controlled (certain kinds of technical knowledge, goods sold on the open market). As generalized resources are controlled from outside, locally based networks excluded from the corporate marketplace must struggle to maintain control of local resources. Since maintenance of control of local resources is frequently essential to the survival of the local group in the face of corporate control, this struggle can involve a conscious opposition to the global marketplace. Just as the kinds of resources controlled in the corporate and the local marketplaces are mutually opposed, so are the qualifications for access to them. Membership in the local community can bring access to resources either through contact with those in direct control of purely local resources, or through local brokers who can bring contact with those in control of higher-level resources. Such resources, depending on the community, can range from personal protection to the satisfaction of material needs (housing, jobs, material support), to information (not only local information but information about public services and the broader marketplace), to services (protection, legal aid, practical help of various sorts). Unlike the corporate marketplace, in which membership is normatively controlled through impersonal and external qualifications, the local marketplace is highly personal, and membership can be consciously ascriptive. Having been born in the neighborhood is a more clearly acceptable boast or claim of membership in the local marketplace than is being the child of a professional in professional networks. (And while this may frequently not, in fact, be the case, it is a necessary public claim in a society built on the promise of universal meritocratic opportunity for mobility.)

And whereas the corporate marketplace is socially and geographically diffuse insofar as it is controlled by broad networks, the local marketplace is highly focused (Milroy 1980). Local networks are based directly in the area that they control, and their social power stems not so much from breadth of membership and contacts as from density and closeness of control. The symbolic capital of the local marketplace stands in clear opposition to that of the corporate marketplace, as the value of any symbolic behavior in the local context is enhanced by its clear local association. The term "local" does not simply apply to geography but to specific social groups and locally based categories. If the local marketplace in Detroit is dominated by auto workers, local symbols will include not simply geographic reference but reference to the auto industry, and if the local marketplace is dominated by a specific ethnic group, local forms will derive from the ethnic repertoire.

Local identity is the cornerstone of Labov's study of Martha's Vineyard (1972b), in which he established a relation between the centralization of the nucleus in (ay) and (aw) and speakers' orientation to the island. Specifically, he found that centralization was associated with the old autonomous island fishing economy, which was being threatened by the incursion of a mainland-dependent summer and tourist economy. There are several aspects of this local identity that are worth noting. Most simply, local identity can be defined in terms of loyalty to the local community, both in a concrete sense of orientation to local networks and in orientation to the local community in a more abstract sense. But in addition, Labov makes it clear that local identity is not simply defined spatially or even in a socially abstract sense, but in the interaction between place and the human life that unfolds there. The nucleus raisers of Martha's Vineyard had in common not simply co-presence, but co-participation in a community united by interest, activity, and point of view. They were identified by a combination of attitudinal and demographic features – a community oriented to shared and concrete everyday practice. One might expect that the centralization of the nucleus on the Vineyard gained its social significance in the myriad and varied interactions through which islanders engaged in locally based activity and sharing of interests, and in a mutual contrast and engagement with the culture and speech of people with conflicting interests. The local, then, is defined simultaneously in terms of shared location and a shared belief about what it means to be from that location. The Martha's Vineyard study above all illustrates most clearly and dramatically the relation between specific local meaning and place in the global society.

The competition for control of resources between localized and non-localized groups suffices in itself as motivation for the development and constant renewal of opposed linguistic norms, each set of which uniquely qualifies its users for participation in its own marketplace to the very extent to which it disqualifies them in the other. Milroy's study (1980) of local working class networks in Belfast emphasizes the relation between local solidarity and the use of the local vernacular. One of the most salient aspects of these networks is their local base, thus uniting local loyalty and loyalty to the friendship, family, and work network. This, according to Milroy, maximizes pressure for dialect conformity.

While the standard language market is relatively monolithic, the vernacular market is anything but. Invariability is the symbolic touchstone of the standard, while distinctiveness among local groups is essential to the workings of the vernacular. If the opposition between vernacular and standard is an important factor in the difference between the two, this is accomplished through a differentiation among vernaculars as well. It is only to the extent that the local vernacular is truly local that it will be valuable to the community – and localness is not generic, but stands in opposition to other locals. In urban areas, most particularly, local groups have to compete for rare resources. While people may gather in neighborhoods with people similar to them, these neighborhoods are not isolated from each other. If the life of the group depends on maintaining its own way of speaking, this way of speaking has to set them aside from the next group. This also is illustrated in the data from Labov's Martha's Vineyard study, in which it emerges that centralization is associated with a particular *kind* of local identity – one of several somewhat distinct and even competing local identities. While Labov focused on the opposition between the mainland and the long-standing community of English origin that had dominated the island economy for generations, he also raised the issue of two other ethnic groups on the island who might contest this local "Yankee" hegemony. These other groups were the original inhabitants of the island, a community of Native Americans, locally referred to as the "Gay Head Indians" on the one hand, and on the other, a community of Portuguese descent dating back several generations.

While the islanders of English descent lead in the centralization of (ay), the Native American islanders take quite an overwhelming lead in the centralization of (aw). The English and the Native Americans constitute distinct communities, both of which make strong claims to local authenticity, and both of which perceive a conflict between their claims. Indeed, Labov reports conflict between the communities around the very issue of the native status of the Gay Head community. Thus in this case, status – or perhaps power – involves relative rights to define what constitutes "island culture." One might speculate that the extreme values produced by the English and Native American populations – the English for (ay) and the Native Americans for (aw) – reflect distinct uses of nucleus centralization. While the centralization of the nuclei of these diphthongs may be a general local linguistic resource, its specific symbolic value can be differentiated through the balance between the two diphthongs. It is quite possible, then, that these diphthongs, both of which are clearly identified with Martha's Vineyard, are serving for the expression and construction not only of a specific kind of local identity but of competing local identities.

Labov's analysis shows two sets of norms pulling away from each other: mainland-oriented islanders moving in the direction of a lowered nucleus, and island-oriented islanders responding to this trend by reversing the change and moving in the other direction. This paints a very clear picture of the oppositional relation between vernacular and standard language as embedded in conflict between the local and the global. The social significance of (ay) and (aw) in Martha's Vineyard is not purely local – it is not something that arose in that specific context with no relation to larger social patterns beyond the Vineyard. On the contrary, the relation of the local economy to the global appears to be crucial to the local meanings on the Vineyard, and individuals and small groups align themselves in relation to the global issue through its local instantiation. In Martha's Vineyard it is the tourist trade that presents the global threat, and the locally run fishing trade that represents local power. It is various groups' relations to the tourist and the fishing trade that give local life to more global issues of power. Furthermore, and central to the argument in this book, every nuance of social relations and practices within, among, and beyond those groups is material for the construction of linguistic identities. The very personal is constructed within the communal, and the meanings associated with variation are inseparable not only from their relations to the political economy, but from the personalities of the local individuals who populate that economy. The sociolinguist trying to connect larger societal patterns of variation with the linguistic dynamics of Martha's Vineyard must connect the larger political economy with local dynamics and meanings, and ultimately with individuals.

All of this conflict is located quite squarely within what one would have to call the same speech community, for the social values of the two treatments of centralization lie precisely in their relation to local conflict. If the speech community construct is to have any explanatory power for variation, it will, as Rickford (1986) has pointed out, have to encompass this kind of conflict. Labov's observation of the dominance of Yankee identity on the island, and of the other groups' orientation to Yankee island culture, is clearly based on an important social and linguistic reality: that status and power involve symbolic domination. By virtue of their dominant status, the Yankees are in a position to define for others what constitutes "island culture." Thus the notion of the speech community will have to encompass a multitude of conflicting norms and kinds of power.

1.3 Liminality

By positing a vernacular market in opposition to the standard language market, sociolinguists have found a powerful explanation for the survival of vernaculars in the face of pressure from the standard, and for the initiation of change in the vernacular. However, the notion of conflicting markets, suggesting a pull in opposite linguistic directions, leaves a problem for the dominant view of variation, in which the socioeconomic stratification of variation is essentially seamless. If the standard language market resides in upper middle class networks, institutions, and communities, and the vernacular resides in the networks, institutions, and communities of the working class, then what of the people in between? The notion of conflicting markets could also be seen as justifying a view of variation as alternation between distinct dialects.

The evidence from community studies of variation (particularly Labov 1966, Trudgill 1974) points both to conflicting linguistic markets and to a class continuum of variation. There is evidence of a "seam" between the working and the upper middle class, suggesting that the two ends of the linguistic continuum exert powerful opposing pulls, aligned as they are with powerful resources and ideologies. People negotiating their way around the regions between the two ends are simultaneously where they are – somewhere in between – and differentially oriented to one market or the other. I hasten to qualify that the standard and vernacular markets do not reside at the extreme ends of the socioeconomic continuum – the upper and the lower class – but at the extremes of engagement in what one might call "popular culture." The lower class is excluded from engagement in popular culture, and the true upper class excludes itself. The standard language market is located in upper middle class institutions, while the vernacular market is located in vital and residence-based working class communities. The socioeconomic in-betweens are the people, by and large, who fall into the lower middle class, and the lower middle class emerges on the one hand as a middle place in a sociolinguistic continuum from working to upper middle class, and on the other hand as pulled between two linguistic markets. Trudgill's data (1974) show a considerable divide between the speech of the upper working class and the lower middle class. This is particularly evidenced in Labov's discovery (1966) of a lower middle class crossover in New York City sound changes in progress. This crossover is quite complete: the careful speech of the aggregated lower middle class is more standard than that of the next higher group, the upper middle class, and more vernacular than that of the next lower group, the working class. Stated more dramatically, for the three variables representing change in progress in New York City, (eh), (oh), and (r), the entire stylistic range of the lower middle class spans almost the entire local range of variability (Labov 1972b: 125–9).

There is an interpretation of this pattern that suggests that the lower middle class constitutes the buffer between the opposed linguistic markets, demonstrating a tension between participation in the standard and the vernacular markets. In one sense, the lower middle class is a residual category in schemes of socioeconomic stratification, which has led Milroy and Milroy (1992) to explore life modes as an alternative to the hierarchical and continuous model of social organization. At best, by stratificational schemes, the lower middle class is extremely heterogeneous in comparison with the working class on the one hand and the upper middle class on the other, certainly in relation to the linguistic market. Labov's description (1966: 142) of the occupational class strata is as follows:

Upper class	First rate professional, manager, official, or proprietor of a large business
Upper middle class	Careermen in professions, managerial, official, or large business positions
Lower middle class	Semi-professionals, petty businessmen, white collar, foremen, and craftsmen
Working class	Operatives: blue collar workers at the mercy of the labor market
Lower class	Laborers: last to be hired and first to be fired. Frequent job shifts

Professionals, managers, etc., are pretty uniformly engaged in the standard language market. Many of these are people whose job qualifications are not simply their knowledge and skills, but their demeanor – their persona – their ability to convey a sense of stability and status. Blue collar workers, on the other hand, are hired for their knowledge and skills (although their knowledge is frequently downplayed), and their general demeanor (within reasonable limits) is not part of their job qualification. On the contrary, a blue collar worker's ability to convey an image of physical engagement is more important, as well as an image of engagement in the local marketplace and an ability to command resources in that marketplace. But the employment categories listed as lower middle class are much more diverse. Petty businesspeople cater to a clientele – and that clientele may be a working class neighborhood, a lower middle class neighborhood, an upper middle class neighborhood, or a larger business. People in service businesses, such as plumbing, building, auto mechanics, can have very different relations to the linguistic market as well. Contractors are valued both for their ability to appear intelligent and trustworthy to their clients, and for their ability (as well as the client's perception of that ability) to work local resources. Clerical workers can do clerical work in a factory, a plumbing firm, a bank, or a law office (Sankoff et al. 1989). They can be in a back room processing claims, filing, or entering data – or in the front office serving as a crucial interface with the public. Another source of diversity is the relation between home and work. Traditionally, the ranks of the lower middle class are filled with upwardly mobile people with working class backgrounds. This means not only that many will be coming to their adult statuses from a vernacular childhood, but that they may well be coming to work each day from a working class home, whether with parents or with a working class spouse. This range of variation could, then, be a reflection of the linguistic versatility required for the range of communities that many lower middle class people participate in.

The linguistic behavior of the lower middle class no doubt reflects their pivotal position between the working class and the middle class – a position that goes back to the very origins of this class. The lower middle class arose with the growth of capitalism in the nineteenth century (Mayer 1975), when the separation of commerce from manufacturing gave rise to a rapidly expanding clerical class, many of whose members emerged from the working class with the help of free education. In commerce, a rapidly expanding class of clerks and sales representatives worked daily with the established middle class, and, more crucially, frequently represented them in the marketplace. Their literate and numerate skills, therefore, were useless without the appropriate dress, demeanor, and speech.

Since the office worker's contact with the upper middle class took place in the limited context of work, and since this undoubtedly did not involve much conversation off the topic of the business at hand, he (and I use the pronoun advisedly in reference to the nineteenth century) had a real need for information about upper middle class behavior and lifestyles. As early as the mid-nineteenth century, the self-help industry arose, and filling this need for information became a lucrative business. These purveyors packaged information about culture, dress, and language, and marketed it in a range of widely disseminated publications. Ultimately, this developed into a style of its own, much scorned in the nineteenth century for its hypercorrectness, and nowadays emerging in the recent "dress for success" movement that has gotten so many women into business suits and ties.

The lower middle class has always been characterized by insecurity in the marketplace – an insecurity that merges the social and the material. In times of scarcity, the members of the lower middle class have traditionally been the first to lose their jobs, and according to Mayer (1975: 432) their very existence was defined as liminal:

> In social terms, the lower middle class is valued for being the shock absorber that helps brake the eruptions of the underlying strata. A buffer between capital and labor, or between landlord and peasant, it also serves as a bridge and mediator between them. Moreover, the petite bourgeoisie is the preeminent channel for social mobility: skilled manual workers can and do move into it from below while from within its bulging ranks it raises its own spiralists to higher rungs on the income and status ladder. This lower middle class also serves as a net that cushions the fall of the skidders and superannuated of both the higher middle class and the *grande bourgeoisie*.

The tenuousness of their position and the importance of acquired symbolic capital to gaining and retaining that position make the clerk class supremely insecure. According to Lockwood (1989: 31), the linguistic hypercorrection of the middle class is as old as the clerical profession, and has been built into the job structure of this profession and others like it:

> Because of the actual conditions of their employment, the dress, speech and outward mannerisms of clerical gentlemanliness were often an exaggerated and perverted form of the real thing.

The lower middle class has an ambivalent relation to the working class. Arising from this class, and feeling most acutely the difference between manual labor and desk work, the lower middle class is put in the position of rejecting its roots. As history shows, this is an extremely precarious position, for the vagaries of the economy may at any time throw members of the lower middle class back where they came from. Sandwiched between denial and promise, the lower middle class is outward-directed, based on an ambivalent and tenuous relationship with those above and with those below. The two surrounding classes, on the other hand, experience no such ambivalence, as their relation to the economy is unambiguous.

The lower middle class shares its liminality with two other large societal groups: adolescents and females. The lower middle class, like the adolescent age group, has been ridiculed virtually since its inception – and in fact, the adolescent life stage and the lower middle class arose in about the same historical period. Women have been around longer. But all three groups are ridiculed at least in part because of their flamboyant symbolization. It is not insignificant that the early sociological work on class stratification, upon which Labov bases his 1966 analysis, viewed the labor force as male, and that their class descriptions are based on the kinds of jobs that men occupy. The workplace has carved a place for women, particularly in the lower middle class, that maintains their traditional marginalization in relation to the economy. Teller jobs nowadays, like secretarial jobs, are serving as entry-level jobs for women into banking and business; there are other paths for men. And in many of the jobs that women fill – particularly secretarial jobs – there is no set public description. This maintains secretaries in an undefined position, leaving room for women to be expected to perform the roles of general go-fer, or office wife. At the same time, it prevents their experience on the job from proving qualification for other jobs. This means that women's careers do not have the kinds of trajectories implied in male-based studies of work, and it also means that the individual woman's relation to linguistic marketplaces cannot be ascertained by her job title.

Comparisons have been drawn between the speech of the lower middle class and that of women (e.g. Labov, in press). Women, like the lower middle class, show a particularly wide stylistic range; and like the lower middle class, women are the common leaders in sound change. There is little question that at least part of the explanation is the fact that women share the liminality of the lower middle class. Trudgill (1972) has speculated that because women have not traditionally been able to achieve mobility on the basis of their work in the job market, they have had to rely on the development of symbolic capital. But in the job market as well, women overwhelmingly have had access primarily to jobs as "technicians of language" (Sankoff et al. 1989), or jobs that require the projection of a persona – usually an upper middle class persona, but in any case involving linguistic self-management. Teaching school has been a traditional means for upward mobility for women. And women's traditional entry-level white collar jobs have been as front people, whether as receptionists, hostesses, switchboard operators, or secretaries – all requiring standard language skills if they are in mainstream workplaces.

But gender dynamics in language do not lie simply in differential employment opportunity. They lie in the very broad-based differences in ranges of possibilities in everyday life. These differences are fundamental in society – at least as fundamental as class if not more. It is reasonable, therefore, to assume that gender is at least as important a social constraint on variation as class. But class and gender differences are quite essentially of different orders. Gender differences do not involve the same segregation in familiar situations that class differences do; on the contrary, male and female in our society not only grow up together in the same families, they go to school together, most of them work and/or play together, and they are expected to become selectively intimate with each other. At the same time, they are expected to be globally different from each other – sufficiently different that if men and women think to compare themselves with members of a different socioeconomic class, they will compare themselves with members of their own gender. If they compete with others, it is generally with members of their own gender. Males and females, above all, have radically different possibilities in the world, and when they do have similar possibilities, they are expected to pursue those possibilities differently. Thus if one can expect to find major gender differences in speech, one cannot expect them to be so much in global differences between male and female, as in differences in the qualities that differentiate *within* gender groups (see Eckert and McConnell-Ginet 1992).

1.4   The Speech Community

Sociolinguists use the concept of *speech community* to delimit the social locus of their account of language use. Because sociolinguists' treatment of language focuses on its heterogeneity, they seek a unit of analysis at a level of social aggregation at which it can be said that the heterogeneity is organized. Labov's treatment (1966) of all of New York City as a single speech community is based ultimately on a notion of shared social meaning. Labov (1966: 8) viewed the social stratification of variables in New York as constituting a set of class-based contrasts, whose meanings can only be understood within the context of the full set of contrasts (or at least a range of the full set):

> For a working class New Yorker, the social significance of the speech forms that he uses, in so far as they contain the variables in question, is that they are not the forms used by middle class speakers, and not the forms used by upper middle class speakers. The existence of these contrasting units within the system presupposes the acquaintance of the speaker with the habits of other speakers.

This system of contrastive social meaning is more commonly viewed in terms of shared norms (e.g. Labov 1972b: 120–1) as they are reflected in style shifting and subjective evaluation tests, and Labov's focus on norms has attracted criticism (e.g. Romaine 1982) on the grounds that speech communities can involve multiple and competing norms. The issue of norms is a delicate one, because there is a gray area between prescriptive norms and use norms. Strictly speaking, norms define normal behavior. Within the context of variationist sociolinguistics, we might take this to be the speaker's output in his or her most "usual" situations. Since every speaker's normal behavior is situationally determined, one might prefer to think in terms of a range of situated use norms (or what Hymes refers to in a broader sense as norms of interaction). Since use norms are socially stratified, and participation in the speech community involves the recognition of differential use norms and of the social groups they are associated with, one might consider that community norms include norms of "recognition." Finally, participation in a community also tends to involve norms of "interpretation" (Hymes 1972), which assign value to different ways of speaking. For example, a matched guise test that assigns job qualification (Labov 1966) to people on the basis of their speech reflects first and foremost norms of recognition of the relation between speech and social position. However, a matched guise that assigns personal characteristics (e.g. Lambert et al. 1960) to speakers (such as friendliness, trustworthiness, likeability) on the basis of their speech elicits norms of interpretation, focusing test subjects on their personal attitudes towards the people who occupy different social positions. This difference is central to Rickford's (1986) analysis of contrast in the Cane Walk speech community. While the members of the Estate Class and the Non Estate Class are united in their recognition of how people in different kinds of jobs are likely to speak, they are opposed both in their understanding of the causal relation between speech and job status, and in the ways of speaking that they evaluate positively. This picture is complicated by the fact that in a stratified society, the conflict of opposing loyalties does not rule out a common recognition of differential global status. In other words, the consensual and conflict models of social class are not entirely incompatible – upward (economic) mobility and class loyalty frequently go together as well – and the tension between the two may be an important source of complex social meaning.

If the speech community is to be the major explanatory social unit for the interpretation of the social meaning of variation, it must also be the major social unit for the construction of that meaning. The members of a speech community may agree on which particular demographic group or set of groups a speaker is likely to belong to – that is, the speaker's social address. But the meaning of variables lies in speakers' and hearers' relations to, and beliefs about, those groups. Thus norms of recognition point to, but do not constitute, social meaning. The speaker's day-to-day experience, particularly as a child or preadolescent, does not usually provide for the regular comparison of his or her own speech with that of a broad social spectrum. Rather, the speaker builds outward from local experience, gradually contextualizing family and neighborhood speech within a fitfully expanding sample that may include teachers, pediatricians, social workers, merchants, parents' friends, kids from other neighborhoods, etc. And those people may be friendly, cranky, bossy, fun, intellectual, tough, or snooty. Thus, although New York's upper middle class and working class will share the observation that richer and more educated people use more postvocalic /r/, the real associations with /r/ usage will be radically different, depending on their contact with those richer and more educated people, their feelings about being richer and more educated, about acting that way, and about those who are less rich and educated, etc. One might say that each individual has a hypothesis about the significance of r-fulness and r-lessness, and what brings together all the hypotheses in a community is the speakers' ability to coordinate their behavior – to make reliable sense of each other. This sense-making requires face-to-face interaction and a commitment to mutual interpretation. It is this emphasis on mutuality that distinguishes ethnographic approaches to the speech community (Gumperz 1962, Hymes 1972, Milroy 1980). Most particularly, studies of the ethnography of speaking focus on a level of language organization that is based in an intimate level of mutual understanding. Attending to how varieties are actually implemented on a day-to-day basis, these studies seek a unit that can encompass, and in terms of which one can explain, regular face-to-face interaction (Hymes 1974: 51, Blom and Gumperz 1972). Anthropological linguists focus more on the community aspect of speech community, not because people get together only to "do" language, but because language is a resource for doing other things.

1.5   An Issue of Boundaries

Since the study to be presented here is based in a school, defining the school as a speech community would yield an integrated background against which to make sense of the linguistic dynamics I have observed. The definition of the school as a speech community would seem to justify limiting my population to the school, and explaining the linguistic data in terms of that population. It would embody a claim that the school has a particular status in relation to the organization of language use among its population. On the other hand, I could define Belten's catchment area as a neighborhood-based speech community, and justify the school as the site of my research on the pure grounds that it offers an age-limited sample of the community at large. Or I could define Neartown as a speech community and justify Belten High as the site of the research on the grounds that Belten's student population is ethnically and socioeconomically representative of the town at large. But what of the larger suburban, or even urban-Suburban continuum in terms of which Neartown makes sense of itself? The issue of delimitation is as old as the study of dialectology. But meaning is constructed at many levels of social organization. Rickford (1986) has discussed the problem of boundaries and subsumption in the definition of the speech community, pointing out that there are important shared norms (at least of recognition) that link the speakers of Cane Walk to larger communities and ultimately to all of Guyana. The claim that the social unit that defines one's sociolinguistic sample constitutes a speech community, then, is above all a way of placing the study itself rather than the speakers. The designation *speech community* confers on an aggregate of people the judgment that they constitute a sufficiently mutual sense-making unit that important aspects of linguistic organization are embedded in their social practice. Whether New York City, Cane Walk, or Belten High constitute speech communities depends on whether the structure of those aggregates has explanatory power for the use of language. The definition of a particular speech community is, above all, a way of defining both the limitations and the broader implications of the study, for in carefully articulating what this unit accounts for in the lives of the speakers it delineates, one can also articulate what it does not account for. It is not enough to describe a speech community as an isolated unit, for no community is isolable; the description of a speech community is most importantly an account of that community's linguistic place in the wider society. An account of a speech community, then, will optimally acount for the articulation between the internal dynamics of the speech community and its relation to other localities, as exemplified by ethnographic studies such as Gal's (1979) study of language shift in Austria and Blom and Gumperz' (1972) study of code switching in Norway, which are based on accounts of opportunities and networks outside of the local community. Only in this way can we explain both why people within the community speak differently from each other, and how linguistic influence flows in and out of the community.

1.6   Communities of Practice

The term *speech community* tends to imply a coalescence of residence and daily activity, but speakers move around both inside and outside the community. Since if we focus on a community as a static unit, we ultimately preclude change, it is essential to view communities as social creations. As Milroy and Milroy have emphasized (1992: 2), quoting Mitchell (1986: 74), "a fundamental postulate of network analyses is that individuals create personal communities that provide them with a meaningful framework for solving the problems of their day-to-day existence." Day-to-day problems change, as do people, and few residential communities in the industrial world circumscribe their members' lives. Thus if dense and multiplex networks enforce conformity to the vernacular, as shown by Milroy (1980), they do so by consolidating symbolic resources, making the same resources appropriate in multiple settings. But networks are only more or less dense or multiplex, and "leakage" is no doubt crucial to the formation of the vernacular. For while people may concentrate their social and linguistic activity, they also get around, engaging in a variety of endeavors and in a variety of communities.

To the extent that linguistic influence is associated with the making of social meaning, it is to be found in groupings of people who are mutually engaged in the construction of new meaning. The co-construction of linguistic change and social meaning will take place in just those interactions in which social identity is at issue – in which speakers are constructing new nuances of meaning; not simply reconfirming the old. Meaning is made as people jointly construct relations through the development of a mutual view of, and relation to, the communities and people around them. This meaning-making takes place in myriad contacts and associations both within and beyond dense networks. To capture the process of meaning-making, we need to focus on a level of social organization at which individual and group identities are being co-constructed, and in which we can observe the emergence of symbolic processes that tie individuals to groups, and groups to the social context in which they gain meaning.

Lave and Wenger's construct *community of practice* (Lave and Wenger 1991 and Wenger 1998) is just such a level of social organization. A community of practice is an aggregate of people who come together around some enterprise. United by this common enterprise, people come to develop and share ways of doing things, ways of talking, beliefs, values – in short, practices – as a function of their joint engagement in activity. Simultaneously, social relations form around the activities and activities form around relationships. Particular kinds of knowledge, expertise, and forms of participation become part of individuals' identities and places in the community. It is not the assemblage or the purpose that defines the community of practice; rather, a community of practice is simultaneously defined by its membership and the shared practice in which that membership engages. The value of the construct *community of practice* is in the focus it affords on the mutually constitutive nature of individual, group, activity, and meaning.

In many cases it is easy to identify the common endeavor that assembles a community of practice: a garage band, a day care cooperative, a research group, a kindergarten class. That endeavor develops a life of its own as local practices develop around it, transforming the enterprise, the activity, and knowledge. The practices that emerge as a rock 'n roll band works together include such things as the choice of songs the band plays, the kind of music, a view of its place in the wider landscape of music, an attitude towards other kinds of music, the band's "sound" and the contribution of each instrument to that sound, ways of dressing, ways of getting and choosing gigs, ways of performing and behaving on gigs, ways of developing new songs and rehearsing, ways of behaving and talking in encounters with band members and when representing the band. This practice is one that develops – it grows out of the band's mutual engagement in being *that particular* band. The individual musicians, through their particular forms of participation, simultaneously construct identities of participation in that band. At the same time, that process of construction, engaged in jointly by the various members of the band, yields a band – or a community of practice – with a particular character. The character of that band in turn enters into the individual members' interactions with people outside the band, in the members' personae at work, at home, and at other bands' gigs.

The band itself will be part of other communities of practice, as will its members separately and severally. Each of the members of the band belongs to a variety of communities of practice that don't necessarily have anything to do with music: face-to-face communities such as families, churches, condo associations, crack houses, PTAs. These communities of practice may be more or less overlapping, more or less interacting, more or less consonant. In some cases, the practices may conflict seriously, leaving the individual with the problem of arriving at some resolution – whether it involves emphasizing conflict or minimizing it. The handling of this affects the individual's place in each community of practice, and thereby affects each community of practice. The forms that individuals' participation takes in various communities of practice may be quite different – in some cases they may participate quite marginally while they may be central to others; and while they may be disengaged in some, their participation in others may be a central part of their life. The individual's identity emerges in the process of articulation and resolution of participation in all of these communities of practice, and each community of practice's identity emerges through its participants' joint engagement in this process.

When describing social networks, analysts specify particular kinds of ties: ties that frequently represent co-participation in a community of practice. A multiplex network cluster is a cluster whose members' communities of practice overlap significantly. Linguistic homogeneity within these clusters, then, is a function of continual mutual engagement in practice. An important part of community practice, and particularly important to the study of variation, is meaning-making. An illustration of this process occurred during a group interview that Sue Uhland and I did in a northern California community in 1985 with seven high school students who constituted a self-conscious community of practice. They had defined themselves as a "subculture," based on a style, set of values, and a currently popular music genre called "dirge." They quite consciously distinguished themselves from the predominant social categories in the high school – preppies and stoners, the local equivalents of jocks and burnouts – and they particularly abhorred what they saw as the snobbishness and class-consciousness of many kids in their affluent high school. And although dirge music and style were related to punk and new wave, these kids distinguished themselves carefully from those two styles. As we sat around the table in a coffee house near the high school, they described their style, its origins, and the values that underlay it. Among these values were a commitment to egalitarianism, fighting racism and elitism, and openness to new ideas. At one point, a girl whom I shall call Jane showed me a picture of her sister that she kept in her wallet. Hanging from the wallet was a short chain with a skull, and another skull was drawn on the leather of the wallet. I commented on the skull, and it became clear that the skull was a key symbol as the entire group showed me their other skulls, worn on the person in the form of rings, pins, tattoos, etc. So I asked, "What does it mean?" Jane said, "Death." The others nodded their heads gravely in assent. After a pause, though, a boy whom I will call Charles looked confused and said, "But I thought it meant 'pirates.'"

There ensued a discussion of the relation between death and pirates in their symbolic practice. The group concluded that of course they weren't really embracing death, after all they were fairly happy kids. But talking about and focusing on death was a particular form of resistance for white middle class teenagers, not unlike the resistance that pirates represented for them. In other words, in focusing on death, they were setting themselves aside from the norms for white middle class adolescents in just the way pirates set themselves aside from the norms of law-abiding society. A pretty sophisticated discussion, and a sophisticated conclusion that on the one hand allowed Charles's belief to be included and on the other renegotiated the meaning of the skull. Symbols don't always get negotiated so overtly, but this was a rare opportunity to see the workings of the social construction of meaning.

The way in which the initial difference in belief was resolved was specific to the social practice of that particular small community – and was an explicit exercise of the norms of egalitarianism and mutual respect that inform that practice. Other things could have happened. Charles could have been declared wrong, or he could have been declared right and Jane wrong. And while one might claim that the outcome would be determined on the basis of the objective merits of each idea, such a claim would be naive at best, and naive not only in considering a group of kids negotiating something as fluid as a group symbol, but naive as well in considering scientific discourse (Traweek 1988). If the social relations in this community of practice had been hierarchical, it is likely that the resolution of the disagreement would have been otherwise – that the participants' relative "meaning-making" rights would have driven the process of negotiation. It is apparent that the effort to resolve the differing views was in the interests of maintaining the community – not just keeping the community together, but maintaining a particular set of relations and rights of participation in the community.

The quite abstract process of constructing meaning in variation may seem quite distinct from the negotiation of the meaning of a skull and cross-bones. However, the conscious, overt negotiation of meaning can be suggestive of the mechanisms at work in variation which is, arguably, constructed more on the fly and less subject to conscious manipulation. The fact that variables are tiny elements that occur over and over in the stream of speech, and that speakers do not have the time to monitor each occurrence of a variable, does not mean that there is no such control. Rather, there may be situations and events in which variation is foregrounded, and in which new elements of variable style take root. But furthermore, it is clear that certain people have greater rights for making meaning with variation: certain speakers appear to be trendsetters.

It is possible for an outsider to enter a community of practice and immediately assume significant meaning-making rights; and it is possible for an outsider to enter a community of practice with very lowly rights. This will depend on the community's assessment of that individual's potential, which to a great extent may derive from an assessment of the individual's participation in other communities of practice. Just such a dynamic was observed in Tway's study (1975) of lexical change in a porcelain factory, where individuals bringing their reputations to new units were in a position to bring new names for old things as well. A kid who hangs out with "cool" people is likely to be viewed as a reliable source of stylistic information. Kids will pick up new forms from others not simply on the basis of their status, but on the basis of their assessment of that person's meaningful connection to statusful communities of practice. Kids moving into secondary school who already know older kids there experience a rise in status among their peers, to the extent that these contacts provide valued knowledge and access in that setting. A newcomer from Detroit will have status among burnouts to a great extent in virtue of his or her connection to, and knowledge of, the urban center. As elements of style move across boundaries, it is within communities of practice that people make sense of them. It is within the community of practice that speakers are evaluated, that their differences are given meaning; it is from the perspective of the community of practice that the world takes form and that others are placed within it. Relatively close ties, therefore, can be an important source of meaning. Milroy and Milroy (1985) focus on weak ties as a source of linguistic innovation across community boundaries, and repeated casual contact in public settings are certainly an important point of contact among local groups. I would claim that the linguistic influence in such contacts, however, depends on the perceived identity of the speakers, hence of the social significance of their speech features – a perception which is in turn mediated by the hearer's closer contacts.

For the kids in the small Dirge community of practice, the mutual construction of identity, and the reification of aspects of mutual practice in symbols like the skull and crossbones, second-hand clothing, and spiked hair, was a centrally important enterprise at the time. They had to articulate their engagement in that peer community with their simultaneous engagement in other communities of practice such as their families and their classes in school. Dirge was no doubt not equally important to them all, nor were the friendships within the group. Closely connected to their face-to-face engagement in their local community of practice was their alignment with other fans of dirge music and with their complex relation to local fans of related punk and new wave music. Thus the construction of identity and the symbolic activity within this group tied them to each other in relation to larger structures and ideologies. The Dirge group came together no doubt through a complex set of circumstances, part of which involved a mutual response to the dominant values in the school. Ultimately, the formation of this group was a mutual response to the situation they found themselves in, a way of dealing with their lives at that time. And the extent to which they engaged in the construction of joint symbols was a function of the importance of participation to them at that time.

Viewing speakers in terms of the communities of practice that they participate in recognizes the fluidity and complexity of identity and social participation, pulling us away from a tendency to "pigeon-hole" speakers. At the same time, communities of practice don't form freely and randomly in social space. The kinds of situations that people find themselves in, their needs, the kinds of responses they tend to have to these situations and needs, and the kinds of people and resources available to engage in these responses with, will vary depending on where they live in society. And it is the collection of types of communities of practice at different places in society that ultimately constitutes the assemblage of practice that is viewed as class culture, ethnic culture, gender practice, etc.

Thus while every individual participates in multiple communities of practice, there is nothing random about this multiplicity. People's access and exposure to, need for, and interest in different communities of practice are related to where they find themselves in the world, as embodied in such things as class, age, ethnicity, and gender. In general, working class people are more likely than middle class people to be members of unions, bowling teams, and close-knit neighborhoods. Middle class people, in turn, are more likely to be members of tennis clubs, orchestras, professional organizations. Men are more likely than women to be members of the Lions Club, football teams, armies, and boards of directors, while women are more likely to be members of secretarial pools, aerobics classes, the League of Women Voters. And, as will become clear in chapter 6, it is not surprising that in the high school, middle class kids are more likely to be jocks, while working class kids are more likely to be burnouts.

The relation between participation in communities of practice and social categories is also manifest in differential forms of participation within the same communities of practice. In communities of practice that involve both women and men, both working class and middle class people, and people of different ethnicities, these groups may tend to have different forms of participation, different meaning-making rights, different degrees of centrality. There will also be differences in the way in which people articulate their multiple memberships. A male executive is more likely to find more opportunities to discuss his leisure activities at work than a female executive, and executives will gain greater professional points by displaying family pictures prominently in their work spaces than will secretaries or factory workers. Ultimately, categories such as age, class, ethnicity, and gender are produced and reproduced in their differential forms of participation in communities of practice. And these categories are not produced separately, but co-produced. A secretary's inability to be heard in the workplace is simultaneously related to her femaleness and her socioeconomic status. And the common practice of secretaries making and serving coffee in the workplace is a clear carry-over of forms of participation from another community of practice – the family, and perhaps a reminder that much of the world continues to consider the family to be her primary and legitimate community of practice.

Analysis in terms of communities of practice is closely related to network analyses. Labov's Cobras and Jets (1972a) constitute tight communities of practice, and Cheshire's kids in the park (1982) may constitute a loosely articulated community of practice. And in fact, both studies emphasize common practice in explaining linguistic behavior. The community of practice is also inherent in Milroy and Milroy's adaptation (1992) of Højrup's life-mode analysis in the construction of a model that encompasses class and social network. I introduce the concept *community of practice* not because I believe that it will replace current constructs so much as because it focuses on the day-to-day social membership and mobility of the individual, and on the co-construction of individual and community identity. In this way, it ties social meaning to the grounded social aggregate at the same time that it ties the grounded aggregate to abstract social structures.

1.7 Variation, Style and the Making of Social Meaning

As the following chapters will show, the jocks and the burnouts constitute communities of practice that have emerged within, and in response to, the school's institutional structure. The two communities of practice represent the extremes of orientation to the school, hence the extremes of local social possibility, and differences in foregrounded practices are rich with social meaning. Intensely engaged in affirming their places in the world, and in maintaining their mutual opposition, the jocks and the burnouts construct and continually refine styles that both distinguish them from each other and relate them to other communities of practice whether in school or out. In turn, these highlighted extreme styles serve as touchstones for the rest of the school population, which together constitutes a vast and diverse social and stylistic landscape.

Style is at the same time an individual and communal endeavor. It is a tangible means of negotiating one's meaning in the world. And it relies on, and contributes to, the styles and meanings of groups and categories in the world. The burned-out burnout style of Judy and her friends has meaning in relation to other major styles in the school: jock style, punk style, teacher style, etc.; and in relation to the common burnout style. At the same time, elements of their style, such as their fringed rawhide boots, point away from school altogether and towards a "country" milieu. Judy's own personal style is also her individual production, as she negotiates her own place in her group and in relation to others outside the group. This stylistic orientation is not simply to groups or categories, but to specific embodiments – whether in individuals, groups, or abstractions – of such things as Detroit, danger, trouble, friendship, family, school. Stylistic production is, in other words, the terrain for the negotiation of social meaning, and identity.

I view identity as one's "meaning in the world." A person's place in relation to other people, a person's perspective on the rest of the world, a person's understanding of his or her value to others – all of these are integral to the individual's experience of the self, and are constructed in collaboration with others as those others engage in the same construction for themselves. The individual's engagement in the world is a constant process of identity construction – one might most profitably think of identity as a process of engagement (and disengagement) – and the study of meaning in sociolinguistic variation is a study of the relation between variation and identity. While the ethnographer does not have access to identity, we do have access to some of the practices that people attend to in working out their meaning in the community. Individual identity is not constructed in a vacuum; it is co-constructed with group identities.

The process of making meaning in the world, then, can be seen in the meanings being constructed in and around communities of practice. In the course of joint engagement, activity is structured and made meaningful through the continual joint recognition of salience. As they facilitate community activity, abstractions, material artifacts, symbols, repeated actions, verbalizations, specialized lexical items, and so on become part of the joint way of doing things. They mark, or reify (Wenger, 1998), the special nature of community activity. Tied as they are to community practice, they can serve simultaneously as symbols of community membership and as a basis for the further building of joint meaning and activity. These reifications are constructed in the course of activity within a community, to serve the purposes of that community – to allow members to do the work of the community. Communities of all kinds (including scientific ones) develop, change, and perhaps even progress through the sharing, manipulation, working, and reworking of reifications. These reifications are not usually built of new material, but are an elevation of some aspect of the everyday. Styles, and components of styles, are just such reifications. And so are social categories.

The jock–burnout opposition elevates aspects of school orientation to hegemonic status, separating the world into school-oriented and school-alienated people. This opposition overwhelmingly overshadows differences in other realms – there are no school-wide categorizations that divide people on the basis of such things as artistic interest, food preferences, or religiosity. While a number of burnouts are interested in music and the visual arts, the relation forged in the school between artistic activity and school orientation precludes the development of an "artistic set" that would include burnouts. It is not an accident that those who are most active in the school's prestigious choir are commonly called "choir jocks."

Individual identity is constructed in relation to the meanings that are being constructed in the world – in relation to categorizations such as jocks and burnouts, whether it's in affinity to one or the other, in fighting association with either, or in turning away to incorporate artistic interest, food preferences, or religion. Social meaning and identity have to do with people's forms of engagement in communities of practice and in the world at large. It has to do with engagement in the day-to-day social practice that makes communities what they are and that articulates those communities with others and ultimately with what we call society. The individual's identity is carved through his or her forms of participation in the group, and the group's identity is carved through the interplay of the individual forms of participation that constitute its life. And both individual and group identities are in continual construction, continual change, continual refinement.

People call upon symbolic material of all kinds to mark their progress in this joint process of construction. The negotiation of the meaning of these symbols becomes overt only when aspects of meaning become reified – when they become touchstones, or landmarks, in the process of construction. At that point, speakers can point to social meaning – they can identify others as jocks or burnouts, as elite or working class, educated or not, prissy or tough. Our understanding of sociolinguistic variation is full of such touchstones – invariant be, negative concord, reduction of -*ing* all have quite well-defined significance within a widely defined speech community. Others, on the other hand, do not become overtly meaningful, but remain fluid – a resource for working out subtle aspects of human relations and identity. It is not always a matter of associating a linguistic form with an existing meaning, but to craft subtly new meaning through the innovative use of linguistic form. In this way, the construction of social meaning and the construction of language are one and the same. Variation does not simply reflect a ready-made social meaning; it is part of the means by which that meaning emerges. A study of social meaning in variation, then, cannot view speakers as incidental users of a linguistic system, but must view them as agents in the continual construction and reproduction of that system. Social meaning in variation is not a static set of associations between internal linguistic variables and external social variables; it is continually created through the joint linguistic and social engagement of speakers as they navigate their ways through life.

The view of variation that I present here is not new; rather, it hangs suspended in our intellectual practice. The first modern quantitative study of variation, Labov's study of Martha's Vineyard (first published in 1963), correlated linguistic variants with a variety of categorizations that quite explicitly represented different orientations and forms of engagement in the community. These orientations and forms of engagement were not static, but embodied an increasing concern for self-determination with respect to the mainland. Labov's analysis of the reversal of the lowering of the nucleus in (ay) clearly showed the inextricable link between local social change and local linguistic change. The many studies of variation that followed the Martha's Vineyard study have recognized social categories as stand-ins for social practice, and have appealed to practice to explain large-scale correlations. One could say that the study of variation is implicitly a study of social practice, but it is built on a theory of structure. Since structure and not practice has been the primary object of study, data on variation do not include robust accounts of practice. Thus when practice is frequently invoked as explanation, for instance to account for the lower middle class crossover (Labov 1966) or for gender differences (Trudgill 1974) found in survey studies, the explanation is not based on an examination of practice in that community, but on general accounts of class-related or gender-related practice. Furthermore, since the theory is based primarily on structure, there is no obvious place to put practice other than as an epiphenomenon on the structure. My aim in this discussion is to make explicit what has been implicit in much of the work on variation, in an attempt to resolve some problematic issues in the relation between social and linguistic theory. Above all, it is an attempt to incorporate a broader view of change into the account of variation, treating language as a process that is actually inseparable from social process. This requires a different view of the social locus of linguistic organization. Current treatments of variation stretch out time, emphasizing the continual minute process of change in everyday language use. But by not focusing simultaneously on the minute process of social change in everyday life, it essentially divorces language from society. To the extent that we study variation for an *in vivo* observation of the internal processes of linguistic change, the details of the social embedding of variation can be backgrounded. The moment we focus, however, on the social meaning of variation, and on the social organization of the spread of change, we need to take seriously the co-construction of language and society.

This leads to an essential change in the view of the speaker, following Milroy (1980), who has emphasized the importance of the individual speaker in the study of variation. The tradition in the study of variation has been to reject the individual as a unit of analysis, seeking significance in groups of speakers judged to be similar according to selected criteria. The individual is thus valued as a representative of a group or category. That group or category is at the same time elevated as the carrier of social meaning, reducing the speaker to a performer of group norms, what Giddens (1979) colorfully terms a "cultural dope." With a speaker whose primary motivation is appropriateness, social meaning in variation is purely indexical of, and derived from correlation with, social address. Speakers' agency is limited to making false or wishful claims about their address, or perhaps to expressing solidarity with or distance from their interlocutors' addresses (e.g. Bell 1984). What remains beyond the speaker's reach is the actual relation between social address and variable. Yet the meanings of variables do change, and meanings of the kind that Labov found in Martha's Vineyard are far more complex and more timely than indices of social address. And it is this timeliness that is at the center of the making of meaning – the view of speakers as moving through life, making a place for themselves, sometimes accommodating, sometimes struggling, changing things, keeping things the same.

The view of the speaker as cultural dope requires not only that the speaker not be an agent, and that the meaning of variables have a timeless quality, but also that the central dynamic of speech and communication be sameness. The emphasis on the social as exclusively communal in the study of variation has encouraged variationists to reject the individual as a unit of analysis, precluding any realistically situated subject. A theory of practice will focus on how the positioning of the subject in society produces – and is reproduced by – linguistic practice. The validity of the study of the individual subject will be in the rethinking of the relation between the individual and the community, and of the relation between structure and practice.

It is impossible for a social theory of language to view *langue* as a pre-existing convention, for a social theory of language must be about the process of conventionalization. By the same token, it is impossible for a social theory of language to view the individual speaker's competence as a simple internalization of convention. Convention and individual competences are mutually produced and reproduced in practice, thus linguistic practice is not simply the consensual use of a common system. Convention is not a thing but a process, and the possibility of convention resides in speakers' ability to hypothesize about others' behavior and to take interpretable action, along with a commitment to doing so within a particular social unit. Our speaker, or speaking subject, can not be a clone but must be an agent in a process of convention-making.

2

The Social Order of Belten High

Belten High stands on a street that runs all the way through the suburbs and into Detroit. Like most high schools of its era, it is a rectangular structure with large windows, surrounded by athletic fields and parking lots. The far ends of the building are given over to "noisy" spaces – vocational classrooms, music rooms, and auditoriums at one end, and the cafeteria, student store, and athletic and custodial facilities at the other. In the center is a courtyard, an attractive open area with grass, trees, flowers and benches, and paths that afford diagonal shortcuts among the four wings that make up its perimeter. The social world of Belten High is anchored in this locale, and becomes visible in the transformation of meaningless space into meaningful territory.

The physical and the institutional structure of the school – its spaces, schedules, routines, activities, rules – serve as constraint and resource for life within the school. Students come to the school with their own histories and their own sense of trajectory, responding variously to the school's affordances. Thrown together, they find ways to meet their goals, fulfill their dreams, satisfy their desires, do what they have to do, get through the day, or simply to survive. Collections of people come together around common endeavors: common goals, dreams, desires, jobs, necessities, and/or problems, finding joint responses and strategies for dealing with them in the context of the school. They develop joint practices, joint ways of functioning in the school – they constitute school-based communities of practice. Each individual, sharing different endeavors with different groups of people, is likely to enter into multiple communities of practice, some of which will be more essential to the individual than others. And some of them will work out better than others for a variety of reasons: compatibility with other members, the forms of participation available, and the connections to one's other communities of practice. It is in juggling the benefits of these various communities of practice that the individual finds a personal path.

2.1   Jocks, Burnouts, and
the High School Corporate Culture

While most concern about US high schools focuses on the curriculum, the extracurricular sphere permeates day-to-day life in school. It is primarily around extracurricular rather than academic activities that the adolescent social order revolves – and not around the activities themselves, but around conflict over whether the school's norms of participation in this sphere should define adolescent existence. The extracurricular sphere of the public high school is commonly seen as the primary site for civic education, and normative citizenship in the school involves at least some participation in this sphere. But extracurricular activities are more than a list of entertaining possibilities that any student might choose from; they constitute a tightly organized, highly competitive, hierarchical social system. In fact, they constitute a corporate setting very much like that of the business or the academic world, within which ambitious students cooperate and compete to develop individual corporate careers. These careers "count" more than (or to the exclusion of) students' curricular activities in a global status system within the school, and count as well towards admission to the next institutional level, college. Thus the hierarchical popularity cycle that adults tend to attribute to adolescents' social preoccupations is solidly based in adult-invented and adult-controlled institutional arrangements.

The school year is built around a relatively unchanging sequence of social and athletic activities designed to enhance the social atmosphere in the school and the school's competitiveness with other schools. School personnel control resources for the development of these activities, and students organize themselves to make use of the resources: to compete for management of the resources and to build careers through the strategic use and distribution of these resources among the student body, and through the organization of successful activities. The distribution of resources is facilitated by a student hierarchy in which the individual's place is a function above all of corporate roles (cheerleader, student council member or officer, varsity athlete, honor society president, etc.), relations with teachers, and the size and breadth of the individual's student constituency. And access to roles in the extracurricular sphere is limited by this hierarchy. The work and servicing of networks required to compete in this sphere is an all-consuming enterprise, and for the student building a career in the high school, identity, activity, and social relations come to be built on the institutional structure of the school. The term "jock" has been used for some time in many areas of the eastern and midwestern United States to refer to such corporate individuals. And while participation in athletics is highly desirable in this enterprise, sports themselves are not criterial for this designation. In fact, a student who participates exclusively in athletics is likely to be called a "sports jock," while one (particularly a boy) who participates exclusively in social activities may be called an "activities jock."

Students who do not care to participate in this sphere can move off to do other things, leaving school at the end of the required day and pursuing activities elsewhere. And students who want to pick and choose among the activities can do so as long as they limit their choices to activities that are not contested within the jock hierarchy – the "less statusful" activities. But nobody can ignore the extracurricular sphere, because of the particular ways in which it enters into other areas of practice in the school. In exchange for their cooperation and work, jocks are granted special freedoms, recognition, and visibility – they attain institutional status, and gain control of many aspects of the daily life of the school. They become public personae within the school, and frequently within the local community. Thus they do not simply dominate the activities themselves, but the school as a whole. It is not surprising, then, that jocks' institutional ascendance attracts resentment both from people who are unable to compete, and from people who do not wish to; and that there should be a fundamental opposition in the school based on the very practices that underlie this ascendance. One can view the burnouts as having emerged in opposition to the jocks – in opposition to their values, their practices, their privilege. But it is just as true that the jocks have emerged in opposition to the burnouts, who never embraced the school but strive to transcend the domination of adults and their institutions, and whom jocks see as simultaneously representing desired autonomy and dreaded failure.

If participation in the corporate activity of the school creates privilege, it is also an extension of privilege, for the students do not randomly filter into the extracurricular sphere. There is a class basis to students' attraction to, and distancing from, this sphere and from other aspects of the school institution. Thus the social categories of jocks and burnouts are not trivial configurations but the very means by which adult social class is embedded in the adolescent social order, hence reproduced. As will be shown in some detail in chapter 5, the jocks and the burnouts come by and large from the upper and the lower half of the local socioeconomic continuum. While parents' class is not a predictor of a student's category affiliation (or lack thereof), there is a highly significant relation between the two. The two categories represent class-based responses to the institutional arrangements of the school, embodying a trajectory from childhood to adult class. The differences between jocks and burnouts reify class polarization for the adolescent age group, bringing middle class institutional practice into stark contrast with working class personal and local practice. And both the jocks' engagement in institutional practices and the burnouts' objections to these practices clearly emerge from different childhood experiences, from different expectations and ambitions, and from a different sense of what school participation can offer.

Like most suburban schools, Belten High is designed above all to prepare its students for college, and eventually for participation in adult middle class and corporate (broadly defined) practice. As in most comprehensive high schools, the structure of curricular and extracurricular activities is carefully articulated with college requirements, providing a clear and effective trajectory beyond high school. The full range of college preparatory and advanced placement classes, college board examination preparation, and college admissions counseling guarantee the effectiveness of the academic program. The careful management of the extracurricular sphere by a professional student activities director ensures that the various student government and other social activities are competitive on a national level. The articulation of varsity sports with school leagues guarantees the attention of college scouts – in fact, more than one varsity athlete told me of foregoing participation in a better league outside of school both to show loyalty to the school and to gain access to college scouts. For the college-bound student, the school's legitimacy is unquestionable, and while participation in the school's corporate context involves submitting to the ultimate authority of adults and the school, the promise of enhanced future social and economic power may be seen as compensating for the denial of more immediate autonomy.

The burnouts, on the other hand, most of whom are bound directly for the local workforce, see less reason to submit to school authority. While the school boasts a considerable vocational program, between what it provides and the district-wide programs that students can bus to, it provides little support in seeking employment, and incomplete preparation for skilled jobs. And because vocational education is by definition quite skill-specific, students bound for the trades will often need additional education beyond the high school, and vocational students generally feel that many of the skills they gain in the high school are outmoded. The burnouts, therefore, question the school's legitimacy in the most basic terms. And whereas the extracurricular sphere serves the jocks' futures as well as entertaining them in the present, it holds no such promise for the workforce-bound.

Burnouts view the extracurricular sphere of school as an adult-dominated make-believe world with no purpose beyond its own survival. Resenting the school's view of itself as a social institution, and feeling that the school does not offer them the kind of support they need to prepare for the local job market, they feel little responsibility to it, and resent any role it plays in restricting their personal freedom. Rather, they focus on developing a direct relation with the world outside the school, locating their social world in the neighborhoods and the wider urban–suburban area, and seeking both connection to work, and entertainment and excitement, on their own terms.

In a very real sense, then, the jocks are an institutionally oriented community of practice, while the burnouts are a more locally and personally oriented one. While these orientations go a long way towards predicting differences in the use of language, there are other aspects of day-to-day practice that unfold from these different orientations that deepen the differences between jocks and burnouts and fill in the affective side of the jock–burnout split.

An important aspect of the corporate structure of the school is the expectation that students will concentrate their efforts on their own school, and in competition with other schools. While jocks may pride themselves on knowing important "players" from other schools, they stop short of developing time-consuming relationships with them. The one exception may be a cross-school romance. But while the mystery of a partner in another school may add to one's visibility, such romances are considered both inconvenient and limiting, since strategic heterosexual pairing within the school is an important way of extending one's networks and visibility.

Further defining the scope of one's social networks is the age-graded nature of the institution. From the earliest years in elementary school, there is a strong norm that children's friendships should be limited to students in their own school year. Throughout schooling, it is believed that kids who hang out with people in classes below them are socially insecure or "slow," and that those who hang out with people in classes above them are growing up too fast, and are "looking for trouble." Although the passage to secondary school interrupts the strict age-grouping in subject matter classrooms, the age cohort is maintained as an institutional unit in practice. Class cohorts are segregated in separate homerooms, and form constituencies for the governing structure of the student body. Each class has officers and a cabinet, and representatives on the school-wide student council. Many of the activities are structured by graduating class, with each class organizing activities for the entire school, and with regular competitions among the classes. And while it is expected that heterosexual couples will form across class boundaries (in fulfillment of the cultural norm that women should be not only smaller but younger than their male partners), there is a strong norm that close friendships will not.

By and large, school norms dictate that one's social networks should be restricted to the population of the school, and determined by and large by co-participation in school activities. This means that friendships can be subordinated to school responsibilities, and it is commonly felt that hanging onto friends who aren't engaged in activities is limiting, and reflects a fear to strike out on one's own. Changing friendships, then, is a key part of the social mobility that makes a jock career, and the entire cohort's friendship history shows a period of volatility during junior high school, as kids move towards or away from the extracurricular sphere, and as they begin to build the networks that will serve their particular trajectory.

Closely related to friendship mobility is the fact that participation in the extracurricular sphere involves participation in a consensual status hierarchy. Assessment curves in the academic arena and the small number of key roles available in the extracurricular arena make normative participation in the school fundamentally competitive. Furthermore, to the extent that one's status is based on one's roles in school, one's visibility, and one's associations, social life itself becomes competitive. Friendships can be fluid, as people compete for "the better friends" (a phrase I heard more than once), as well as for visibility and roles. And this fluidity and competitiveness affects the very nature of friendships. Many jocks report keeping their problems to themselves, frequently not sharing them even with their closest friends. There are several reasons for this. On the one hand, the middle class separation of the family and friendship makes confidential family business less shareable in the public arena. In addition, jocks emphasize the importance of maintaining an image of competence and control – an image that could be damaged by the admission of personal problems. And finally, inasmuch as jocks function in a competitive hierarchy, they cannot afford to allow negative information to get into the system. The jocks and the school work for each other. The jocks' careers are built on – and build – the school's extracurricular success. Thus there is a sharing of interests, a collegial relation, between jocks and school personnel. Jock friendships and even jock romances are legitimated by the school, for they are seen as based in school and ultimately functioning in the service of corporate activity. Jocks see their hierarchical and competitive relations as motivated by, and justified by, their corporate activity. While they adjust their social ties to suit corporate requirements, they do not see themselves as personally disloyal, but as acting on the necessity to set aside personal interests in the interests of responsible institutional participation.

The burnouts, on the other hand, see relations with their own peers as purely informal, and as unfolding around the school rather than in it or as part of it. Thus they do not recognize a corporate justification for jocks' social organization, and view their hierarchies and competition as purely a result of personal preference. Furthermore, they conceive of two kinds of possible relationship with teachers: institutional and personal, and the institutional relationship is fundamentally adversarial. Where burnouts develop friendly personal relationships with teachers, they expect them to transcend rather than reproduce the institution. Thus the notion of collegiality with a teacher has no pride of place.

Burnouts also steadfastly resist age grading, and the school's more general interest in regulating association. The school is for burnouts, as it is for others, a primary place for making friends if only by virtue of the amount of time spent there, but it is not the primary locus of their social activity. Burnout social networks reside in neighborhoods and in the larger urban–suburban continuum, transcending age, institutional, and municipal boundaries. Burnouts' friendships focus on activities outside of school, and joint time in school is spent making plans for after school, and ignoring, escaping, or getting around school. Burnouts are, thus, counter-cultural within the school institution, and they set a good deal of store by successful subversion in school. But while the school sees their behavior as overwhelmingly negative, burnouts embrace strong social values that they see as conflicting with school values.

So far, the discussion of jock and burnout practice has treated burnouts in opposition to jocks and to school practice. This is because the school is the locus of this study, and a neighborhood study would have a very different emphasis, for the burnout side of the story begins in the neighborhood. Some students describe certain of the lower income neighborhoods of the Belten catchment area as "burnout" neighborhoods, associating that social category both with rebelliousness and with low socioeconomic status. A significant number of burnouts do come from these neighborhoods, and to a considerable extent, burnout networks reach back into childhood networks in these neighborhoods. The product of suburban working class and lower middle class migration, Neartown's less affluent neighborhoods are transitional between traditional working class neighborhoods and the diffuse neighborhoods that result from middle class mobility (Bott 1957). Kids from these neighborhoods recall a closeknit neighborhood life in childhood which, for many burnouts, continues into adolescence. With a tradition of neighborhood, neighborliness, and mutual help, parents in these neighbor-hoods generally encouraged their children to form strong ties with their neighborhood peers and with their peers' families. Many of Belten's resi-dents of these neighborhoods recall being in and out of each other's homes as children, and many of them still are. Furthermore, with a tradition of sibling care, kids spent a good deal of time with older and younger siblings and their friends, making social networks age heterogeneous. With the intensity of peer activity outside the home in the neighborhood, a peer culture developed early, in which children shared information, guidance, emotional support, and material resources. This egalitarian and open flow of resources frequently compensated for a lack of parental resources, and led to strong peer alliances. Many burnouts point to the loyalty, solidarity, and supportiveness of their networks as the most important thing in their lives, and as what sets them apart from jocks. Where jocks are concerned with image management, burnouts are proud of sharing their worries, their concerns, and their problems. It brings them closer together, and it under-scores their engagement in the real world, and their experience with, and acceptance of, real problems.

With its emphasis on age grading, school prescribes a break in childhood networks, and from the beginning of elementary school, the school sepa-rates friends of different ages. This creates a tension between kids' and school norms, which does not decrease as the neighborhood-based net-works become increasingly heterogeneous as time goes by and the value of urban experience makes burnout networks particularly open to new people from the urban area. Urban mobility brings in more people from Detroit, who maintain friendships from their old neighborhoods and schools, and older members bring in friends from other communities through jobs and urban exploration. But where the school legitimates jock friendships and romances, it sees burnout relationships – particularly those that transcend the school boundaries – as illegitimate. The burnouts' emphasis on continuity and on transcending institutional boundaries of both age and place leads the school to view their relationships as subversive.

As the burnouts' relationships lead them into greater involvement in the local area, the corporate life focuses jocks away from the local community and onto more global networks and institutions. The burnouts' expanding networks will ultimately facilitate their move out of high school and into the workplace and young adult local life. By and large, the jocks plan to attend college away from home, and some of them already expect to leave the local area after college. Many of them lament that they will probably lose track of their high school friends but consider it inevitable; some of them look forward to starting over with more sophsticated friends from other places. Their connection to the local area is principally a family connection, to be loosened as they move off into their own futures. Graduation from Belten, therefore, represents a major life transition, and a departure from home and local community. Most of the burnouts, on the other hand, see the years after high school as an expansion, not an interruption, of their current local lives, replacing a job for school as their daytime commitment, maintaining their current friends and possibly marrying their current romantic partners. Although in the difficult economic climate of the early 1980s, particularly in the automotive industry, a few burnouts talk about leaving for the sun belt to find employment, most of them intend to spend their adulthoods in the Detroit area. Thus while the burnouts seek continuity in place of residence and social networks, the jocks seek continuity in institutional involvement.

With jocks in charge of legitimate resources in school, the burnouts must struggle to define and control opposing resources in the interests of their own autonomy. The jocks pursue autonomy through adult roles in an adult-dominated environment, and the burnouts pursue it in the transformation of this environment to suit their own needs. If the jocks control much of the legitimate space in the school, burnouts in schools across the country carve out their own territories whether they be in stairwells, breezeways, loading docks. Where the jocks enjoy special legitimate freedoms in school, the burnouts share strategies for getting away with illegitimate freedoms. While the jocks socialize at school functions, burnouts cultivate hangouts in the local area outside of school – in neighborhood parks, pool halls, bowling alleys, cruising strips. And while jocks expand their social networks as a function of their corporate roles in school, burnouts expand theirs along local lines independent of the school – through family, neighborhood, and work contacts and through encounters in public spaces. And where jocks cultivate school information resources, the burnouts cultivate their own resources in the outside community. Job information, drug sources, legal information, access to urban and young adult networks, sexual, birth control, and abortion information, knowledge of the urban area, all flow in burnout networks. Many jocks tailor their needs with care so as not to need much of this information, which is not easily available from adults.

It is a complex development of history, trajectory, and ways of coping that makes the jocks and the burnouts quite distinct and class-based communities of practice. While many of the practices that arise in each of these communities may be related to class, they are not necessarily tied directly to class for any given individual. Close, trusting friendships are not restricted to the working class, and competitive, hierarchical orientations are not restricted to the middle class. And to any individual, independent of their class origins or aspirations, close friendships or competition may make participation in one or the other community attractive on independent grounds. It is the practices that define the jock and burnout communities, but inasmuch as configurations of practices define class, a middle class kid who adopts burnout practices or a working class kid who adopts jock practices is moving toward class mobility.

2.2 Gender and Social Category

As in the rest of the world, gender is fundamental to any system of social categorization. While the entire discussion above applies equally to boys and to girls, gender and social category are not simply cross-cutting categories, but interact in complex ways. Many of the basic constraints and dynamics are the same, but being a jock or being a burnout is different for boys and girls and even the very necessity of being a jock or a burnout is related to gender. The representation of each yearbook mock election type (e.g. most popular, class clown, most likely to succeed) by one male and one female reflects the fact that there are distinct male and female ways to be popular, to clown, and to show promise for the future. And this is inextricably tied, in turn, to heterosociability, or the social arrangements that support a heterosexual social order. The jocks and the burnouts began as two competing heterosexual crowds in late elementary school, and then emerged in junior high school as alternative ways of being "adolescent," constituting alternative sites for the heterosexual market. Indeed, it was the heterosexual market that gave the two crowds their visibility. Thus heterosexual discourse is fundamental to these social categories, and participation in these categories constitutes also heterosexual gender practice.

Just as the high school provides the setting for the emergence of an opposition between jocks and burnouts, it also brings an institutionalization of traditional gender arrangements, heterosexuality, and romance. The female supportive role is formalized in high school in the pairing of such activities as girls' cheerleading and boys' varsity athletics; and in the feminization of organizational activities such as holding bake sales and organizing dances. There is a gender–based division of labor in activities such as the construction of floats, where girls organize the making of tissue flowers and the boys build the structures. The institutionalization of the heterosexual couple is embodied formally in the dance as the most popular school-based social activity, the election of a homecoming king and queen, and the yearbook's choice of "cutest couple."

If one considers each term of opposition between the jocks and the burnouts, one can see that the categories are entirely gendered. Violence, urban toughness and know-how, and the ability to "rumble" are prominent themes among burnout boys. While some burnout girls may fight other girls on occasion, they do not enjoy the same claim to physical prowess and autonomy, and they do not draw the same admiration for a good fight. Throwing their bodies into the urban arena has different implications and potential consequences than it does for boys. There is differentiation at the other end of the continuum as well – as part of their identity work, jocks consider it important to maintain a clean-cut image, to conform at least pub-licly to adult norms for their age group, and to maintain an image of control. The clean-cut image for a girl above all involves sexual conservatism, and in opposition, burnout girls are frequently viewed by non-burnouts as "sluts," a label that fuses gender and social category. (See Eckert and McConnell-Ginet (1995) for a detailed discussion of such labels.) While a jock girl may engage in sexual relations with a boyfriend, both are bound to keep it private, for anything that contributes to a "slutty" image, including styles of hair, dress, and makeup as well as demeanor, can seriously threaten a jock girl's status and by association, her boyfriend's as well. To be labeled a *slut* is to fail in the school's corporate culture. In general, jocks view the prototypical burnout girl as slutty, and burnouts view the prototypical jock girl as phony and uptight. The crucial difference is not so much in private sexual behavior as in the fact that burnouts, in opposition to jocks, are not concerned with sluttiness – either in image or in behavior. While being "pure" is important to a jock, neither being pure nor being slutty is impor-tant to a burnout. Thus while burnout girls do not necessarily flaunt het-erosexual engagement, they are not particularly concerned with hiding it. Indeed, to do so would amount to taking on jock airs. Closely related to this is the burnout girls' rejection of jocks girls' popularity orientation, and the jocks' view of burnouts as surly and rude. Because jock girls' success in school depends almost entirely on their networks, they are constrained to cultivate connections and popularity. Thus maintaining a smile and a pleas-ing demeanor, and extending oneself socially, is a major preoccupation for jock girls. Burnout girls see this networking activity as competitive and "fake," and they take pride in being honest about their feelings. Reserving their smiles and compliments for occasions that they feel merit them, the burnout girls appear unfriendly to the jocks.

Among boys, jock–burnout hostility centers around issues of masculinity. Burnouts' withdrawal from school sports in junior high school created considerable resentment among coaches and among jocks, since a number of good athletes were lost to school teams. The public association of athletic prowess with success in the school's athletic programs, meanwhile, excluded the burnouts from the possibility of athletic recognition and caused a certain amount of resentment on their part. Jock–burnout competition arises when jocks and burnouts are together in an athletic context – as one burnout boy pointed out:

> God, in gym, man, it's jocks against the burnouts whatever you're doing, man. That's where, you know, it gets let out a little bit.

Male athletic prowess is tied to a wider set of issues that are important to both jocks and burnouts – maturity, masculinity, toughness, power. If the burnouts suffer from a lack of public recognition for their athletic abilities, the jocks suffer from an image, in contrast to burnouts, of being under the control of adults. Cooperating in school, maintaining a clean-cut image, doing their homework, and going to practice – all of these things have a positive side of corporate status and a negative side of docility. Male jocks, therefore, walk a careful line between working with the school and demonstrating their independence from adults. This is facilitated by the fact that they are given more freedom, by teachers, by their parents, and by their peers, to show their independence – to rumble around, get in some trouble, voice their opinions, act "smart." There is also a distinction between tough and preppy jocks, which follows lines of choice of activity. Connell (1995) distinguishes two kinds of masculinity – "technical" and "physical," one associated with technical (e.g. scientific, political) power and the other with physical power. This distinction is recognized in the sports arena in traditional differences between men who play rough contact sports such as football and hockey on the one hand, and non-contact sports such as track and tennis on the other. In the high school, this distinction applies to boys who are jocks by virtue of their athletic engagement (commonly called "sports jocks" or "jock jocks") and those who are primarily engaged in the non-athletic extracurricular activities (sometimes referred to as "activities jocks"). This latter kind of masculinity is fragile, no doubt partially because at this life stage, technical power is confined to the school arena and access to it is dependent on adult cooperation and consent. While physical skill and power are personal attributes that the individual can exercise (or threaten to exercise) in the here and now, adolescent technical skill and power carry promise primarily for the future.

All of this points to the fact that there is an important component of competition between male jocks and burnouts. This contrasts quite starkly with the nature of the relations between female jocks and burnouts, which have an important element of avoidance – a threat of pollution. One might say that this sums up the different positions of male and female in a patriarchal society. It also points to the fact that the differentiation between male and female depends quite crucially on the terms of differentiation among males and among females. Thus as long as we view gender and social category simply as memberships, it is difficult to deal with their interactions in a study of variation beyond fragmenting the categories. If, on the other hand, we view both gender and social category as organizing possibilities, interests, activities, and forms of participation in communities of practice, we can focus on those aspects of social practice themselves.

2.3   Constructing Difference

The division into jocks and burnouts begins in junior high, and is part of becoming adolescent. The prospect excites some kids, and makes others nervous. Being part of a crowd guarantees protection and wards off anonymity as the cohort moves into the wide open environment of secondary school. It also shows that one is entering into adolescent status. The pressure to affiliate – to participate in jock or burnout practice – is strong, and for many, perhaps most, it constitutes a serious dilemma. The following account of this dilemma is not unusual:

Dave: OK, seventh grade, day one, jocks and the burnouts.
Penny: Boom. Right at the beginning of school.
Dave: That fast. That fast. And I was never a jock and I was never a burnout. I hung around with most, you know, or like there was the jocks and the burnouts who'd sit and give each other dirty looks in the halls, you know. For no reason, you know. And I just thought that was dumb as could be, you know. So I associated with everybody. So that kind of left me right in between everybody else, you know. And so I kind of felt, you know, I was kind of – little bit – I mostly hung around with, I guess you could say the jocks, because most of my buddies were in that group, you know, or classified there. And uh, but I had some friends that

like hung around with the burnouts too, you know. And kind of left me right in between, you know. People said that I was actually, you know, quote, that I was one of the in between persons, you know. I'd just, "yeah, kick ass," you know. And so that kind of made me feel like a slight outcast, you know. Somebody left in between the realms, you know.

The hegemony of the jock–burnout opposition is reflected in the fact that the majority of the school population, who are neither jocks nor burnouts, are commonly referred to as *in-betweens*. In-betweens frequently describe themselves in terms of characteristics that they share with jocks on the one hand, and with burnouts on the other. Thus while the jocks and burnouts do not constitute the majority of the school population, their symbolic importance is to be found in the ways in which they foreground issues that preoccupy the rest of the population. Thus while the opposition between the jocks and the burnouts may be an appropriate perspective for an analysis of social meaning in the school, the categories themselves are part of the process of the construction of social meaning – a process that is engaged in by everyone in the school.

It is important to emphasize that while the jocks and the burnouts each constitute a clear and relatively homogeneous category, the in-betweens do not. In a world that focuses on categories – indeed in the view of many kids in school – in-between-ness constitutes marginality. In that case, more than half the kids in the school will have to be viewed as marginal. The status of the jocks and the burnouts as defining the poles of social meaning in school is as much derivative of the range of behavior represented by the in-betweens, as it is defining for them. Unfettered by the demands for conformity that are part of life in any visible and clearly defined group, the in-betweens can, theoretically, choose among behaviors that are either required or forbidden for jocks or burnouts. On the other hand, exercising freedom requires social resources: connections, information, company, material. All of these are frequently more abundant in large crowds than in small groups, and while the jocks and the burnouts constitute crowds, many of the in-betweens are isolated in comparison. Thus the extent to which in-betweens exercise freedom depends on the nature of their social networks. The in-betweens, then, cannot be simply interpreted as representing some imaginary "middle," and certainly not as a marginal population. Rather, they represent a variety of ways of being "out there."

In innumerable ways, jocks and burnouts arrange themselves and their lives in mutual opposition, creating and maintaining difference with a broad array of resources. Jocks and burnouts listen to different music, stand differently, consume different substances, do different things, hang out in different places, take different courses, decorate themselves differently. A more detailed examination of jock–burnout symbolic oppositions can be found in Eckert (1989). The patterns of linguistic variation to be discussed in the following chapters, and the linguistic styles that they contribute to, are part of a more general stylistic opposition that both defines and separates the cultural extremes of the school. The opposition over local and institutional orientation, and over the legitimacy of adult monitoring of the personal sphere, all come together in a complex array of symbolic behaviors, which are highlighted in school by the radically different "looks" that appear in jock and burnout territories.

2.3.1   School territory

Those who plant themselves firmly within the institution (jocks) and those who always seem to be on the way out (burnouts) use space in the school in a way that both symbolizes and facilitates their opposing orientations. The burnouts and the jocks quite dramatically work the margins and the center of the school respectively, and as a result have very different views of the school institution and its preoccupations. The forms of participation that they develop in the institution give them different understandings of the institution and its practices, while their differing orientations to the local and adjacent urban community yield different understandings of the world outside the school. While the jocks and the burnouts both develop powerful kinds of knowledge, that of the jocks is the kind that brings success in (and to) the educational institution while that of the burnouts is the kind that serves in resisting that institution and gaining access to resources elsewhere.

An important aspect of students' use of school facilities is the relation between these facilities and the school's *in loco parentis* role. The school provides such amenities as bathrooms, lockers, homerooms, and cafeteria to enable students to live in the building during the day – to establish a kind of home away from home. Jocks' use of these facilities conforms to the school's intended use, and signals their legitimate participation in school. Their control of some other kinds of facilities, furthermore, signals their institutional status and ascendancy over the rest of the student body. Burnouts' transformation of these spaces, in turn, symbolizes their rejection of school authority, and their opposition to the jocks' terms of participation in the school.

The hallways are lined with lockers, each shared in principle by two students. While the lockers are randomly assigned at the beginning of each year, students swap in order to be "locker partners" with their closest friends. This frequently results in more than two people sharing a locker, and indeed a crowded locker is one way of displaying alliances. The locker is expected to be the student's "home away from home," and being locker partners is the closest that kids living at home can come to "rooming" with their friends. Students are expected to leave their outer clothing, paraphernalia, and school books and supplies in these lockers, visiting the lockers regularly between classes and taking only what they need for those classes. Visiting lockers also serves as a way to join one's friends between classes, and since people know the location of key people's lockers, it is a way of finding people between classes. Thus there is always a social scene around lockers before school, during class breaks, and after school.

Burnouts, by and large, do not use their lockers. Their claim that they are not safe – that things get stolen from them – contrasts with many jocks' claims that they rarely even lock their lockers (so safe is the neighborhood). But the locker represents not only a home in school, it is a transitional area between the outside and the inside. It is where students are expected to leave their coats as they begin a day that unfolds within the school. It is also the place where they organize their books and supplies so that they can carry what they need to class, leaving the rest behind. In other words, the locker is a school address, a storage place, a place for social gatherings, a transition point between in school and out, and a locus of academic organization. All of these are reasons for burnouts to avoid their lockers. Burnouts reject an address that is not only in the school but assigned by the school, and they do not publicly sort through their books in preparation for class. Indeed, losing books and papers, and coming to class unprepared and/or unequipped are common forms of resistance in school. And finally, they do not leave their outer clothing behind when they come into school. Wearing jackets in school is part of a powerful and complex symbolic system based on adornment. It allows burnouts to go outdoors at any time – whether they're sneaking out the back door to leave early or to cut a class, but more important, it allows students to slip into the courtyard between classes and during lunchtime. The jacket announces that the burnout is not in the building to stay.

The courtyard, an attractive outdoor area in the center of the school, is the school's designated smoking area. The association of the smoking area with burnout territory emphasizes the burnouts' claim to the adult prerogative of tobacco, and the jocks' avoidance of this territory and their strong opposition to smoking clearly set the two in opposition. As implied by their name, the burnouts are known for their relatively open use of marijuana and chemicals. The alternative name for the category, local to Belten High, is "jells," short for "jelly brains," and refers to the effects of drug use. However, it is cigarettes that stand out as the burnouts' key symbol. While there are a few burnouts who do not smoke, most of them do, and cigarettes serve as a key burnout symbol. Many burnouts display cigarettes on their person (sticking out of purses, pockets, or rolled-up tee-shirt sleeves, or behind ears), and offering and exchanging cigarettes is a favored way of making contact and signaling solidarity. Smoking is an important part of the burnout style, and gestures for both holding and moving the cigarette, and for inhaling and exhaling are studied and stylized. Buttons that say "smoking stinks" serve to announce jocks' attitude towards cigarettes, which is also embodied in one of the most prestigious extracurricular activities, the anti-smoking committee. A number of jocks and in-betweens claimed to avoid the courtyard not because they were "afraid of" burnouts, but because they didn't want to get cigarette smoke in their hair. A few people around the fringes of the jock network smoke, but never in school, never at school functions, and a number of jocks said that while they would never smoke in high school, they might well start smoking in college, where its symbolic value would be different (Eckert 1983). One girl who was deeply involved in school activities (including the anti-smoking committee), but did not consider herself a member of the jock elite, told me she smoked in secret as her own personal commentary on the jock enterprise. "The people who smoke" is yet another way that many people refer to burnouts.

Just as lockers serve a social function for jocks between classes, the courtyard is where burnouts go before school, at lunch, and between classes to meet their friends, have a smoke, maybe share a joint. One in-between girl, who spends most of her free time in the courtyard, gives her version of the locker scene:

> They [jocks] like to take room up in the hallways talking with 50 friends around them, and you can't get around them, and – If they just – I don't know, it's hard, it's hard to say, but they just don't come out here [the court-yard] really.

While use of the courtyard is not restricted to burnouts, those in-betweens who do use the courtyard tend to be smokers who are willing to risk being viewed as burnouts, and many of them are friendly with burnouts. One in-between gave me this explanation for why she and her best friend don't use the courtyard:

> Candy and I are – you might say we party. I mean, there's jocks and jells like that. But we don't smoke cigarettes. And I think – I don't know – I get the impression that if people who don't smoke cigarettes go out there, everybody automatically thinks, "Oh, they want to be a jell." So – I wouldn't want everybody saying, "Oh, what are you, um, trying to be a jell now, or something (laughter) like –"

The courtyard is also a visible alternative to eating in the cafeteria. Many burnouts refuse to eat cafeteria food for the same reason that they refuse to use their lockers – they claim that it is not safe. Denying the school's right and ability to feed them, the burnouts take their food – primarily chips – from the cafeteria's fast food line and eat in the courtyard. In this way, even eating habits take on symbolic value, with the jocks eating hot lunches or lunches prepared at home while the burnouts transform junk food into counter-cultural food statements.

The courtyard offers a diagonal shortcut between the four wings of the school that surround it, but despite the convenient access that the courtyard affords between wings of the school, jocks will literally not set foot there. Figure 2.1, which charts the percent of jock, burnout, and in-between boys and girls in the interview sample who use the courtyard, shows this extreme division. Indeed, for some, "the courtyard people" is an alternative way to refer to burnouts.

If the courtyard is burnout territory, jocks control a range of territories in the school, both by virtue of their collegial relations with the adults who ultimately control space, and by virtue of the activities that are associated with many spaces. Lunchtime, when the closed campus policy forces students to stay in the building, is prime time to see the social order unfold in the school, as people gravitate to their habitual lunchtime territories. Most students eat in the school cafeteria, and then move to a specific place outside the cafeteria to hang out with their friends. Most of the areas of the school are off limits during lunchtime. Some students can go to rooms that house student activities that they participate in, such as journalism or choir. Some athletes can go to athletic offices and rooms. The rest of the students place themselves in the area that is open at lunchtime – the long hallway that connects the cafeteria to the courtyard. Where this hallway runs in front of the

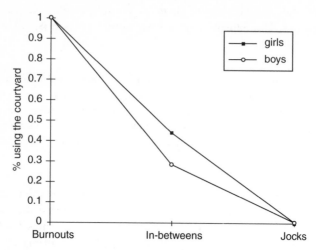

Figure 2.1   Percentage of jocks, burnouts, and in-betweens who use the courtyard

cafeteria is prime jock territory, as this is the area where tables are regularly set up for ticket sales and for bake sales to raise money for school activities. The courtyard and the hallway by its main entrance, on the other hand, is prime burnout territory.

2.3.2   Adornment

These territories combine with dress to yield a rich symbolic display, particularly during lunch hour, when this end of the school is the only free assembly area. Clothing is a particularly important symbolic resource because the wearer has only to be seen to display it, and it can be modified from day to day and over longer periods of time. Clothing style is also easy for the users to analyze and talk about (as opposed, for example, to language) so styles can be constructed in a conscious way. In Belten High, jock and burnout clothing style is differentiated in just about as many ways as possible. Burnouts wear dark colors, with girls wearing dark eye makeup as well; while jocks wear bright colors and pastels, with girls wearing pinkish candy-colored makeup. Burnouts wear rock concert tee shirts while jocks wear oxford cloth or polo shirts. Hair styles, nails, makeup, shoes, purses – almost everything carries category significance. But the most salient of all at the time of this fieldwork was the shape of blue jeans.

At the time of this fieldwork (early 1980s), the 1970s bell bottom jeans wave was coming to an end. A number of people were still wearing wide bells, and some were wearing the slightly more conservative flares, but straight leg jeans had made their way into the center of local fashion, and baggy jeans with pegged bottoms were the latest style. In other words, the ratio of the width of the bottom of the jean leg to the top of the leg was decreasing over time, and this decrease represented a continuum of global stylishness. The burnouts' faithfulness to bell bottoms was rich in symbolism. It associated them with the "freaks" of the seventies, whom they considered their predecessors. But equally important, wearing a style that was outmoded in the rest of the population symbolized lack of material resources – a fundamental term in the jock–burnout opposition. Burnouts pointed to the jocks' following of fashion trends as evidence of their affluence and their easy home lives. They saw their own lack of trendiness as directly related to their relative poverty and, in turn, to their personal problems. Wide bells were always cited as the way to "tell a burnout when you see one." One girl in Belten characterized a school in a poorer and more urban area of Neartown as a "burnout" school, pointing out that people in that school wore bells "this wide," extending her arms apart to their fullest width.

Formal observations showed that the continuum of fashion in jeans from wide bells to pegged baggies – from greatest to smallest ratio of leg bottom to leg top width – is closely related not simply to social category, but to finer gradations of social affiliation.[1] Assigning numerical values to jean styles on the basis of the ratio of bottom to top of the leg (4 = bells, 3 = flares, 2 = straight legs, 1 = baggies) yields a quantitative continuum that allowed me to quantify patterns of this aspect of clothing. Four hundred observations of people walking in the halls during classes (as opposed to between classes) show striking jeans patterns both with respect to location and to association. During class, when mobility in the halls officially requires teacher permission, the average width was 2.6, suggesting that those who have greater access to permission are likely to be wearing narrower jean legs. But in addition, jean width was not evenly distributed through the halls. In the front hall, which passes by not only the highly visible front entrance but the principal's office, the student activities office, and the auditorium, the average jean width was 2.3; while in the back hall, which is less supervised and close to the rear exits, the average jean width was 2.7, and in the middle hall that passes by the vocational classrooms, the average was 2.8. The symbolic significance of jeans leg width is not simply a matter of wide vs. narrow, but is actually continuous, with flares representing a true in-between style.

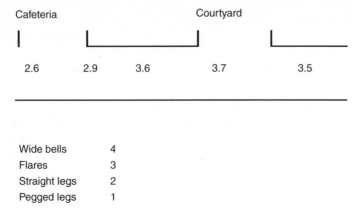

Wide bells   4
Flares   3
Straight legs   2
Pegged legs   1

Figure 2.2   Average jean width in lunchtime territories

If people wearing different jean widths were mixing freely, one would expect all kinds of jeans to co-occur in proportion to their overall frequency of occurrence. There were the same number of flares and big bells in the walking sample, but straight legs occurred twice as often with flares as with bells. And while there were 50 percent more straight legs than flares or bells, flares occurred about equally with other flares, with bells, and with straight legs.

At lunchtime, the choice of where to eat, and where to go afterwards, constitutes a highly visible act of identity. The available area is a social continuum, from the jock territory outside the cafeteria to the burnout territory around the entrance to the courtyard and in the courtyard. Figure 2.2 is a schematization of this area of the school, and shows the average jean width along this territorial continuum, based on 400 observations of jeans during the latter part of each lunch hour over several days. There is a clear and striking continuous correlation between the average jean leg value in the burnout territory of the courtyard (3.7) and the jock territory in the hallway in front of the cafeteria (2.6), and a transition in that value in the middle space inhabited by in-betweens.

Jeans, of course, are only one very important component of a style. Bell bottoms are worn with rock concert tee shirts, displaying musical preferences and memories of rock concerts attended. Cigarette packs are commonly rolled into the sleeves of these tee shirts or sticking out of small overstuffed purses (nothing big enough to hold a book), and wallets are often attached to the belt loops of these jeans by heavy chains, as a reminder of the urban need to protect one's belongings. Many burnout boys wear jeans jackets over sweatshirts with hoods, in the style of people who work outdoors; and some wear black jackets with "Detroit" written in big white letters on the back. Both boys and girls wear jackets from local automobile plants, carrying car insignias (such as Cobra) on the front. These outer garments signal not only that the wearers are not in school to stay, but suggests where they may go when they leave. Burnouts, both boys and girls, wear their hair longer than jocks, the girls keeping their hair straight in contrast to the feathered hair style popular among jocks and in-betweens. Burnouts also wear dark colors, except for their jeans, and girls also tend to wear dark eye makeup, sometimes with a contrasting light foundation. This urban look contrasts starkly with the jocks' straight-legged jeans, worn with preppy Izod shirts and crew-necked sweaters. These shirts tend to be in pastel colors, as does the makeup on jock girls' faces. School symbols appear in the form of honor society, cheerleading, pompon, color guard, and varsity team emblems worn on chains and letter sweaters, and on jackets hanging in lockers. This clothing style contrasts with the urban style of the burnouts both in the relative "innocence" of the colors and in the use of explicit institutional symbols. On some important game days, jocks wear letter sweaters and cheerleading uniforms to school as a simultaneous reminder of the upcoming sports event, and of the institutional status accorded to people who participate in this event. And during lunch hour, these clothing styles appear to match the general atmosphere in burnout and jock territories. The atmosphere in the courtyard is more sombre and confidential, as people stand or sit in groups, smoking cigarettes and talking quietly and occasionally fooling around. The jock hall has more of a cocktail party atmosphere, with people jostling and shouting, laughing and talking loud, circulating from group to group.

The purpose of this discussion is not simply to show how different and separate jocks and burnouts are; it is to emphasize that their linguistic styles are part of a much broader and deeply meaningful style. The burnouts' style locates them centrally in the urban area and the local, vernacular, linguistic market; while the jocks' style locates them centrally in the institution, and in the non-local, standard, linguistic market. The term *vernacular* is commonly used to refer to the speech variety associated with wallet chains, while the term *standard* refers to the speech variety associated with the honor society key. Each refers to a linguistic variety not in the abstract but in virtue of social practice.

Note

1 The issue of jeans is discussed in greater detail in Eckert (1980).

3

Sociolinguistic Research in the School

The pursuit of social meaning in variation calls for a hybrid research practice, for while we can get at local categories and their meanings only through close qualitative work, the study of variation is very essentially quantitative. Practice in the study of variation correlates aspects of variable linguistic usage with speakers' social characteristics that are believed to be related to linguistic choice. Crucial to this practice, then, is the collection of a speech sample from a population sample that represents the social characteristics under investigation. The survey methodology used in early studies of variation (Labov 1966, Trudgill 1974, Shuy, Wolfram, and Riley 1967) is eminently suited to this endeavor, allowing the collection of a sample according to speakers' membership in predetermined demographic categories such as age, sex, ethnicity, socioeconomic class. The essence of ethnography, however, is its exploratory methodology. Rather than testing hypotheses against predetermined categories, ethnography is, among other things, a search for local categories. Thus while survey fieldwork focuses on filling in a sample, ethnographic fieldwork focuses on finding out what is worth sampling.

A tension of scale is inherent in such work, since the larger the population we study the more superficial our understanding will be; on the other hand, as we shrink our linguistic sample, our quantitative results will decrease in significance, or will cover a minuscule piece of the sociolinguistic picture with no means of linking it to other pieces. The challenge in the study of the social meaning of variation is to find the relation between the local and the global – to find the link between speakers' linguistic ways of negotiating identity and relations in their day-to-day lives, and their place in the social stratification of linguistic variation that transcends local boundaries. Our ability to incorporate everyday local observations, then, depends on our ability to extract from them key elements of social structure, social practice, and social meaning that can be reliably correlated with the variable use of linguistic forms. This requires close familiarity with the communities we study, and an attention to community members' own view of the community's social structure, of their own place in that structure, and ultimately of the community's place in the wider world.

This study combined an ethnographic study in one school, Belten High, with shorter studies of about a month each in three other high schools in the Detroit suburban area, designed to both confirm the generalizability of what I had found in Belten, and to provide a socio-geographic context for the patterns of variation in Belten. The shorter studies were more like survey studies inasmuch as they involved the collection of a predetermined sample; they were ethnographic to the extent that data collection took place during an intensive period of participant-observation in the schools. And while I was looking for jocks and burnouts in those schools to constitute my speech sample, I also sought to learn more generally about the local social order in that school.

3.1   School, Power, and the Researcher

Conventional sociolinguistic wisdom tells us that schools and other normative institutions are problematic sites for the study of the vernacular. However, as a central site for social life among kids, the school is the locus of a good deal of vernacular speech. While certain settings and events that are specific to the school exert linguistic pressure against the use of vernacular, there are also certain settings and events in school that encourage the use of vernacular. Most particularly, the very fact that school is problematic for so many students makes the school a site for a good deal of resistance and rebellion. It is above all in school that kids are likely to have empassioned discussions of teachers they hate, unfairness they have suffered, boredom they can't tolerate. And the vernacular that they use for these discussions is itself an act of resistance and rebellion. Thus while the school poses powerful deterrents for the sociolinguist, it also poses unequalled opportunities for the sociolinguist who gains access to these impassioned discussions.

A second bit of conventional wisdom about fieldwork is that occupational status differences can impose serious constraints on relations between researcher and researched. Working with kids, age presents a status difference that is potentially far more powerful than differences in occupational status among adults, posing a potentially enormous barrier to the establishment of engagement and trust between a researcher and an adolescent population. It is impossible to over-emphasize how normative and power-laden kids' relationships are with adults. From the very earliest days, adults begin correcting kids, telling them how to behave and how not to behave. One could say that by and large, adults' role in kids' lives is to change them, that is, to help them grow up. A barrier under any circumstances, the effect of age is compounded in the school, where age stratification is foregrounded in the institutionally coercive arrangements between students and adults. The highly problematic setting of the classroom, in which 30 or so kids must interact with one teacher and not with each other, is a disciplinary setup. It means that school is *about* evaluation, discipline, and control. A good deal of a teacher's job in the traditional classroom, and a good deal of a teacher's skill, is related to keeping 30 kids quietly focused on one person. Unable to have a continuous one-on-one relationship with their students, teachers generally have to instruct and correct rather than guide. Teachers censor kids' movements, their demeanor, their activities, their opinions, their beliefs, their adornment, their language. Thus the teacher–student relation embodies all the asymmetries that go with age: asymmetries of power, freedom, knowledge, and resources. This enormous power imbalance that underlies all relations between adults and adolescents makes studying children in one's own culture a prime example of "studying down."

One way of overcoming the asymmetry of age difference is to minimize it, by being or appearing young, presenting oneself as in roughly the same life stage (see Cheshire 1982). The value of this is not in actually becoming an insider, but in eliminating obvious reminders of status differences. The most obvious reminder is there nonetheless, for the research enterprise itself is a clear sign of adult status, and an adolescent claiming to do this kind of work among strangers would no doubt be viewed with suspicion. Furthermore, since adolescents are the subject of massive clinical attention, which casts them as bundles of problems, the researcher has a ready-made role in the eyes of the age group. But if adult status can pose problems for the researcher, it can also provide an opportunity, because to the extent that kids are locked into power asymmetries with adults, many are starved for new kinds of relationships with adults. Most of kids' waking hours are spent in school, and since they are generally excluded from workplace and other adult spheres, they have few opportunities to develop more equal relationships with adults. An ethnographer has the opportunity to offer another kind of relationship, as someone who is interested in kids on their own terms, wants to listen to them, does not want to change them, and is not part of the local authority structure. The ethnographer also has the potential to present kids' point of view, to be a potential advocate to the world at large. This can be a valuable resource to the many adolescents who feel misunderstood and even mistreated by the adult world. In the end, while I try not to delude myself, I have been surprised by the relative unimportance of age differences in my work both in Belten High and in my current work with even elementary school kids. I have been both pleased (for myself) and dismayed (for the kids) by the swiftness with which even the most skeptical ones have told me things that could have been extremely damaging to them. Indeed, when one is working with kids there is always the risk that they will confuse the ethnographer's role with that of a psychologist or social worker, putting their trust in someone who does not have the resources to provide them with professional help. Knowledge of, and access to resources for such help, therefore, are essential to beginning ethnographic work.

It was clear to me early on in this work that I was going to write an ethnographic account of Belten High before I wrote a sociolinguistic account, because it was important to many of the kids I worked with, particularly burnouts, that I present their experiences and their perspectives to adult audiences. There were other reasons as well. Above all, I wanted my analysis of variation to be based on a previous and well-founded social analysis. Furthermore, in preparing for this work I had been stunned by the tiny amount of ethnographic work that had been done on adolescent social categories, and the small literature altogether on adolescent social structure and practice. Although something like the opposition between jocks and burnouts has been close to universal in high schools across the country for some time, there was very little written on it, and much of what had been written was based on fairly superficial observations. My ability to gain access to the detail of adolescent life in school was entirely thanks to the cooperation of the very open school district of Neartown. Because of their openness, I was able to function in the school as an anomalous character, with the adult privilege of mobility but the adolescent privilege of lack of responsibility for the behavior and safety of others.

Avoiding problems of association with authority and the normative aspects of the school institution is a complex balancing act, requiring careful arrangements in advance with school personnel. At the beginning of the work in Belten, I addressed a teachers' meeting, briefly explaining what my work would be. This did not, however, give the opportunity to work out conditions for this work in sufficient detail. As a result, there were a few awkward moments in the early stages of the fieldwork. For lack of staffing, teachers are frequently tempted to leave their classes in the charge of an available adult, and an ethnographer wandering around the halls is a prime target. On several occasions early on in the fieldwork, teachers called on me to help them in this way, putting me in a situation in which refusal was potentially face-threatening to them. Other kinds of participation in classrooms are dangerous to the ethnographic enterprise as well – a researcher may be a welcome resource to give presentations to classes. But because the classroom is a site of continual power struggles between adults and children, any adult who commands the attention of the entire class is in a position of potential authority over the kids. Furthermore, the sole person talking to a class makes a claim on the class's attention, and the presumption to tell kids about one's own interests – and on an adult's terms – contradicts the claim to be there to listen to them. An adult who sits quietly in a classroom, furthermore, may be a resource for the teacher – someone to address comments to, to solicit as an ally, if only a silent ally, in opposition to the students.

In order to avoid these situations, I stayed out of classrooms in Belten High altogether. While this relieved me of many problems, I did miss a good deal of what happens in the high school. In my current research in elementary and junior high schools, I am going to class with the kids that I'm following. This requires careful negotiation with teachers, it requires teachers who are confident of their own classroom performance, and it calls for humility in the face of the teaching enterprise. I do not know to what extent the lack of any of these three accounted for my decision to stay out of the classroom at Belten, but in fact I spent my time with kids in the hallways, cafeteria, courtyard – during free periods, at lunch, and after school. In these settings, it was easy to keep a low profile and to stay out of teachers' way. And because I was in the school on the teachers' and administrators' sufferance, and had to be careful not to annoy teachers, not to be in the wrong place at the wrong time, not to cause trouble, I was in much the same position as the kids. My own vulnerability put my search for trust on a level similar to that of the kids – since kids were in a position to get me into trouble, we put ourselves in each other's hands.

3.2 Doing the Ethnography

Anyone coming into the school and doing a number of good sociolinguistic interviews would learn about the jock and burnout categories. Finding the jocks and the burnouts and collecting a speech sample representative of the two categories would require closer contact, but could be done through school adults who are painfully aware of the two categories. What more does a sociolinguist need? As the following chapters will show, the significance of the jock and burnout categories lies not simply in their existence and membership, but in their day-to-day motion. The two categories are based in practices that unfold in daily and mundane activity, interaction, and movement. And membership is not an either–or matter, but composed of many forms of alliance, participation, comings and goings. Viewing jocks and burnouts as members or representatives of categories would not only gloss over the histories, uncertainties, and multiplicities that constitute social affiliation, but would also freeze the categories and mask the fact that they exist only in practice. It would preclude an understanding of how people go about being jocks or burnouts; and it would relegate the in-betweens, with little justification, to either residual or transitional status.

Because meaning is made in day-to-day practice, much of it tacitly, the study of social meaning requires access to this practice. Surveys, questionnaires, and experiments all have important places in the study of language in society. But they generally presuppose and test categories and meanings, rather than discovering them. Observations and interviews come closer to providing access to local meaning, but if used alone they have serious limitations for one must know what to watch for, and what questions to ask. Any or all of these methods, pursued within a context of ongoing ethnography, will bring the researcher close to day-to-day practice. But ethnography is not practical for everyone. It requires the qualities that are required for good interviewing: a willingness – preferably an eagerness – to be swept up in someone else's world, a suspension of judgment, and a swallowing of insecurity. But it also requires a considerable time investment, and frequently more of an investment than an academic is free to make. It requires a willingness to take on the concerns of another community on a daily basis, tolerance for sitting around a lot, waiting for something to happen, patience with empty spaces when one could be back in the office writing something. But in the end, it is unfathomably enriching in a very personal way, and yields sociolinguistic insights that cannot be obtained by other means.

The linguistic data to be analyzed in the following chapters were obtained in tape recorded interviews. But the knowledge of social practices in Belten High that informed this analysis and the selection of the sample population came from day-to-day participant-observation in and around the school, much of it with the tape recorder left behind. I went into Belten High with a background of one year's high school teaching experience, no research experience in schools or with adolescents, and relatively little ethnographic experience. I learned as I went, with the advice and support of my colleagues and students in the Anthropology Department at the University of Michigan. The following discussion of methods builds as much on my mistakes as on my successes. Some of this discussion builds, as well, on my current ethnographic work in elementary and junior high schools,[1] which has benefited tremendously from my earlier mistakes. And I trust that my next project will improve on what I am doing now.

3.3 Doing the Fieldwork in Belten High

My first day in Belten High, I must have walked a hundred miles. It was the first time I had been in a school in 15 years. During the preceding weeks, I had had nightmares that I had to repeat the last two years of high school or my PhD would be taken away from me. I had many demons to dispel as I walked around and around the halls of the school, telling myself that I was familiarizing myself with the locale. The fact is that I was scared silly, I didn't know how I was going to break in, and I felt stupid. After innumerable turns around the halls, duly noting unnotable things, saying "hi" to people I passed, trying to look cool as I glanced into classrooms, the bell rang and I fell into the class-change undertow. As people bustled out of rooms and down the hall, shouted and opened lockers, I felt overwhelmingly like an outsider. And when the rush subsided and everyone melted back into the classrooms, the halls became my lonely territory once again. But with the new class period came some activity in the auditorium – auditions for a play. I wandered in and watched from the back for a while, and struck up a conversation with a boy who was standing in the back as well. This boy was the front end of a string that I both followed and pulled in my efforts to get to know his graduating class.

My day-to-day life in the school was a combination of many things. I never gave up walking around and taking note of what was happening in different parts and corners of the school and who was where when class was in session, where people went and what they did between classes, who was doing what with whom and where. On regular occasions, I did controlled observations, sitting in one spot and recording information about what happened there, or moving around and noting what was happening where at a particular time. During lunch, I divided my time between cruising to see who was where, and sitting or hanging out with people while and after they ate lunch. Other times I hung out in fast food places with kids who were cutting class, or went for walks with people who were restless. I attended the alternative program for kids who were in danger of suspension, expulsion, or dropping out. After school, I went to extracurricular activities, to the park, to neighborhoods, to McDonald's. I interviewed people separately and in groups during study halls, lunch hours, and after school. And I networked endlessly, with the Belten High students consciously helping me in that endeavor.

Ethnography is a process of mutual sense-making among all participants in the ethnography. Any path the researcher takes into a community builds up a particular history, and a particular perspective on the community and the people who constitute it. We meet people, we talk to them, we watch them, they watch us – and all in a particular order, setting up our expectations for the next encounter. We are engaged in a process of sense-making, and we act on that sense as we go along. In the following chapters, I will present people as members of categories and friendship groups, nodes in a network, and doers of things. But this presentation is the neatened end result of a fairly messy process of discovery. Survey methodology is designed to avoid this mess; ethnographic methodology is designed to delve into it without losing one's way. The emphasis in the study of variation so far has been on interviewing techniques, and as survey sampling has fallen by the wayside in favor of smaller ethnographic studies, there has not been a corresponding shift of attention to the new perspectives and methods appropriate to the new context. It is not my intention here to discuss ethnographic method, but to point to issues that I believe are likely to be of particular importance to sociolinguists doing work of the kind that I have done.

A particular danger in the process of moving through a community is the temptation to funnel people into categories as one goes along, building an idealized neat picture that becomes increasingly resistant to new observations. From even before the first moment I entered Belten High, I began to paint a picture of the school and the people in it. I was looking for categories and patterns, anxious to know where my analysis would lead. The jocks and burnouts leaped out at me from the start – everyone talked about them, they were easy to spot. I was seduced by the analytic map that they offered. As the fieldwork progressed, and still in retrospect, it was apparent that this opposition was having the same effect on me as it was on the population of Belten High – it was focusing me on categorization, demoting to residual status people and choices that did not fit into the categories. At the same time, the process of getting to know people developed social desire, so that like the people I was there to study, my success depended on being accepted and liked. Unlike them, I could not afford to win acceptance within one group at the expense of another. While this was not difficult to balance, I did find myself viewing individuals and groups through a perspective created by my need for approval – a perspective that would not have been appreciably different had I been a new student in the school. This is always true in fieldwork, but it is particularly bothersome in the high school, since few of us ever quite overcome our own adolescent pasts. Therefore, we need to continually consult those pasts to monitor where and how we focus our attention, and to recognize our biases and blind spots.

Together, the drive to find categories and the desire for acceptance posed the greatest threats to my work in Belten High. In the kind of fast work that sociolinguists usually do, the category is the goal and prominent individuals are indicators of the locus of categories. But the sociolinguist who is looking for social meaning in variation must adopt a more careful ethnographic practice. In the end, the quality of my analysis of variation in Belten High depended on my ability to see everyone, and to see beyond the obvious categories. And while I believe that the analysis that follows tells us something of significance, I also know that it would have been far better if I had recognized this in its fullness from the start. I point this out simply to argue for sociolinguists to take both social theory and ethnographic methodology more seriously, and to find ways to take their time in the field.

Part of doing the ethnography is being aware of the process of discovery, and of the effects of building history in and with the community. Another part is making sure that the process of networking does not lead one to focus on a small subset of the population. The best way to meet people is through introductions by friends, or better yet through simple co-presence in relatively private situations. Given enough time, of course, the networking fieldworker may well work her way through the entire population in just such situations. But the timing of arrival at different places in the network can be as important as the arrival itself. In order to guard against the silo effect of networking, I constructed a random sample of the graduating class in advance, and consulted this sample on a regular basis in order to make sure that each person in that sample was – or became – a point of departure for my networking, and to ensure that there weren't groups that I neglected for a long time because they weren't "important enough" to have come onto my radar screen.

As we get to know a community and the people who jointly constitute it, we come to recognize groups and categories, and we become familiar with their character. Style serves as a guide in this discovery process, calling our attention to groupings of difference, and making us aware that certain differences have social significance. But how do we learn to attend to style? To what extent does what we hear in the groups we have access to point us in particular directions? In my early days in the school, as I was getting to know people, I spent a good deal of time making controlled observations. I recorded elements of adornment style (e.g. dress, hairstyle, makeup), people's whereabouts and activities in different parts of the school at different times (e.g. which halls were deserted, and which ones people were in during class and what they were doing there). I studied combinations – co-occurrences of different aspects of adornment both on individuals, and among grouped individuals (in other words, what kinds of clothes hung out together). At the time, I did not know what to record – what aspects of style were salient at Belten, what the spaces meant. I recorded some observations of elements of clothing that looked differentiated to me but that eventually turned out not to be salient to the students. But I recorded some that turned out to be salient as well. Ultimately, the physical segregation of the jocks and the burnouts became apparent in the geographic distribution of a variety of symbolic items and activities. And the independent observation of these items and activities provided a check on impressions and reports.

3.3.1   Interviews

If the community under study is sufficiently small, the ideal way to gather a linguistic sample is to record normally occurring interactions, as attested to by the richness of Arvilla Payne's corpus of Carol Myers' speech, reported on in Hindle (1979). Since it would have been impossible to get a systematic sample of naturally occurring speech for the number of people participating in the Belten High study, I relied on individual and group interviews to collect the speech sample. The linguistic corpus for this study consists entirely of individual interviews. While critics of this method have claimed that the interview is not a natural speech event (Wolfson 1976), it is not clear what constitutes a "natural" speech event, and what is natural about it. If we assume that speakers have a repertoire of speech events that they regularly engage in, and that other events are so strange as to elicit unnatural speech, we are working on a static view of linguistic practice. Conversations, perhaps particularly with strangers, are inventions. The parties to the interaction construct the interaction as they go along (Goodwin and Goodwin 1992): they construct their relative power and authority in the interaction as they co-construct what the interaction is about. The average person has watched any number of interviews on television, listened to them on the radio, many have engaged in them. The interview is a common gatekeeping event, but it is also an information-finding event. In the sociolinguistic interview, the explicit goal is to elicit information about the interviewee, and the interviewee can enter the event with something like a model from talk shows.

The speech in the quotation from Judy's interview that begins this book is anything but conservative, and this is not because she is not paying attention to her speech, but precisely because she is. While Belten High students are not particularly aware of their regional accents, they are aware of the broader styles that house their phonology, and Judy proudly presents herself to me in all of her wild, burnout splendor. Indeed, one can see every interview represented in this study as a performance of identity, for what the interview explicitly tries to accomplish is to discover who the interviewee is in the adolescent social order. To some extent, this is guaranteed not by the interview itself, but by the fact that the interviews take place in the context of ethnographic work in the school, and hence focus the interviewees on the social context within which they are to present themselves.

The sociolinguistic interview is designed as an interaction with a stranger, and to trigger the use of casual speech in what appears to be an information-gathering event. In the context of ethnography, the interview must play a different role. The interview is an opportunity to collect controlled information, but it is not the same event for each person since it is embedded in an ever-changing relationship with the community. The longer I was in the school, the greater the chance that new kids I met were already familiar with me and had an idea of what I was like and what I was doing. And the longer I was there, the more kids assumed I knew about their world in school. Interviews and interactions in the first weeks of my stay in the school had an exploratory quality, quite different from those in the last weeks, which built on a world of shared knowledge. It made a difference whether an individual was the first person I got to know in their friendship group or the last; or whether their entire group had been waiting for me to find them for some time before I did. People learned about me from their friends, learned what the interview was about, learned about my attitudes and my reactions. Those I met later already knew that I was sympathetic to adolescent concerns, and that I wasn't shocked by obscenities, sex, drugs, crime, or truancy.

For this reason, I made sure that interviews were never my first interaction with an individual, but took place after we knew each other – and frequently after the interviewee had participated in a group interview with other friends. But the individual interview did have important elements in common from one person to the next. It took place relatively soon after I got to know the person, and it was a way of getting "quality time" in the midst of the hectic school day. It was an opportunity for us to go off alone and talk privately, to get to know each other better, after having encountered each other, and having spent time in a variety of informal settings, usually in groups. The interview, therefore, was the interviewees' opportunity to present themselves to someone they already knew somewhat – to distinguish themselves from their friends. This notion of presentation, however, does not assume a fixed identity, a fixed persona that the interviewee then tries to get across and maintain throughout the interview. It grows out of the moment, and can change as the interaction proceeds.

Almost all of the interviews that I performed in Belten High began with "So, were you born in Neartown?" The interview then followed a general sequence through childhood friendships into junior high school and high school. "Have you always lived in the same house?" "Do you remember your first friend?" "Did you have a bunch of kids in your neighborhood that you played with?" "Did you make new friends when you went to elementary school?" etc. The flow of the conversation tended to grow out of explanations of the kinds of things they did with their friends as kids, how they started or stopped being friends with a particular person. By the time the interview moved up to junior high or high school, the interviewees came to determine what was talked about.

The friendship discussion in the interviews also provided the basis for the social network that structures the discussion in chapter 7. Any method of eliciting information to draw a sociogram has its problems. The problems in this case arise from the nature of the interaction within which the main body of network data was gathered. The sociogram is based, not on specific questions that would control the field of association, but on exploratory questions. Since the interviews began with a social network history, the end point of this history served as the starting point for exploring current association. This exploration included such questions as: "Who are the main people you hang out with?" "Do you have a best friend?" "Do you have friends who are [the other gender]?" etc. The latter question was necessitated by the fact that the overwhelming majority of kids gave members of their own gender exclusively as answers to network questions. As the interview progressed beyond direct questions of this sort, other associations came up, frequently much to the surprise of the interviewee, who was shocked at not having listed them earlier in response to my explicit network questions. Frequently a person would fail to mention someone who, it turned out later in the same conversation, was one of his or her closest friends. This is not surprising, since each social encounter, including an interview, is embedded in history – it occurs in the course of a particular day, a week, a season. Memories are retrieved and representations of one's life and associations are created within that temporal context. People tend to recall those they have interacted with most recently, or those that they have been with when they most recently encountered me. Thus if the question follows a group interaction that I have been privy to, the respondent is likely to begin by going over which members of that group they're friends with. Seasons, particularly for those engaged in the extracurricular sphere and most particularly in sports, determine a rhythm of association. Even the weekly cycle brings different people to mind, as weekend associations may be quite different from in-school ones. In addition, the individual's response is partially designed to serve the development of the relationship that the interview interaction is serving. Some people were clearly eager to impress me with the number of their connections, and particularly their important connections; others were eager to talk about their isolation or about the closeness of one particular friendship. For this reason, while the core of the sociogram was based on interview questions, the information was supplemented with ethnographic observations and subsequent conversations, which encompassed far more individuals than the interviews.

Identity is fluid, and particularly in telling the story of their lives, individuals may move through a broad range of identities – identifying with certain innocences of their youth, the kinds of games they used to play, their relations with their family, their fear the first day of school; they may feel anew their pride at a new sense of autonomy in junior high; they may feel wise and sophisticated as they talk about their early experiences with drugs or sex, or they may feel "mature" as they talk about their friends' misguided experiences with the same. As they present these stages of their lives to the interviewer, the interviewees may present a variety of sides of themselves. The interviewer and the interviewee, then, are developing a joint construction of the interviewee and of their relationship. And the end of the interview does not have a final product, but a collection of memories. When the interviewer thanks the interviewee, and says, "I really enjoyed talking to you," both may well recall what transpired in the light of that evaluation. And in the context of this ethnography, the interview was the beginning of the rest of our relationship as well. Frequently months after an interview, someone would refer back to something they'd said in their interview, to joke about it or correct it, or to comment on how much things had changed since then.

The fact that in the fieldwork I was simultaneously establishing the local speaker categories and collecting the speech sample made it difficult to guarantee a proper sample in the end, and obliged me to record speech from far more people than would eventually be included in the analytic sample. To add to this, I interviewed all comers, including many who had recently moved to Neartown, and hence did not qualify for the speech sample. The 69 speakers who make up the Belten High corpus were selected from a larger interview sample of 200, with a view to giving some spread across the social network and across the spectrum of identities and behavior. Some are people who identify themselves as jocks or as burnouts, some identify themselves as in-betweens but are involved in many school activities and are seen as jocks by others. Some are partiers who do not see themselves as burnouts, but who are not hostile to them. Some are loners, some are marginalized, and know that the other kids in their class consider them "weird." There are roughly equal numbers of male and female jocks, male and female burnouts, and male and female in-betweens in the sample represented in this study. If I had the study to do over again, I would include far more in-betweens, because these roughly equal numbers of each "category" render a less representative sample of the population as a whole. In the population of the school, there are more jocks than burnouts, and at least as many in-betweens as the two categories combined. In addition, a greater number of burnouts than other kids moved to Neartown from closer to Detroit and hence were not eligible for the speech sample.

The speaker sample was selected from a wider sample of interviews before linguistic analysis began. Thus no speakers have been excluded because of what appeared to be anomalous speech patterns (or included because of what appeared to be typical patterns). The social analysis also preceded the linguistic analysis, as did the categorization of speakers, which was based on speakers' own characterizations of themselves. Thus I count as burnouts or jocks those who told me they considered themselves burnouts or jocks, and as it turns out, their self-characterizations matched their place in the social network. The cutoff for arrival in Neartown for inclusion in this linguistic study is the age of eight, in keeping with current knowledge of the loss of the ability to develop a new local dialect (Chambers 1995, Payne 1980). It is not clear that this age limit holds for the kind of gradual phonetic variability that constitutes the differences in the Detroit suburban area, but to challenge this view in this study would have required a systematic comparison of natives and non-natives that was beyond my objectives.

3.3.2   The geographic sample

While Belten was the site of a relatively in-depth ethnography, I contextualize the data from Belten within a geographic array based on smaller samples gathered in relatively short periods of fieldwork in each of three other schools around the suburban area. I use pseudonyms for the high schools and the towns within which they are located, by agreement with the school districts and to protect those mentioned in the ethnographic discussions contained in this book and in my earlier ethnographic monograph (Eckert 1989). The total of four schools are along the north–south suburban axis on the one hand, and along the east–west axis on the other, with a relatively urban and a relatively suburban school along each axis.

The data were gathered in each of the geographic sample schools during a field visit of one to two months. I did the field work in Belten High alone, but I worked with a partner, Michael Jody, in the geographic sampling. These field visits were a blend of survey and ethnographic research. Rather than exploring each school's social order anew, we took the jock and burnout categories as given. The goal of the work was to gather a balanced sample of male and female jocks and burnouts for linguistic analysis – and at the same time to do enough ethnography to get a sense of the differences among schools. While we met many in-betweens in the course of this work, our main focus was on the extremes. In each school, we began with the jocks, asking the school staff to introduce us to the class and student body officers. While one might suspect that the best way to begin work would be with burnouts, so as to avoid appearing to be allied with the normative side of the school through association with the jocks, this turned out to be a poor strategy. Early experience in the first of these schools, Urban City, made it clear that the burnouts were not interested in participating in a study that they believed to be about "delinquents," and the first question they asked was whether we were talking to jocks or "normal people" as well. From then on, we began with the jocks, both because they were easier to identify cold, and because in doing so, we demonstrated that the study was about high school students in general. At the same time that we were beginning to interview the jocks, we found the burnout territory and began talking to kids there. As a control on networking, Mike and I worked separately. That is, each of us followed our own same-gender networks, finding the main groups of jocks and of burnouts separately among the boys and the girls. In every case, we ended up in the same network clusters – the male jocks and burnouts that Mike identified were part of the same clusters as the female jocks and burnouts that I identified. While the Belten High study involved longer-term work, each of these high school studies was brief and a much larger proportion of our time was spent interviewing than had been the case at Belten. Nonetheless, a month afforded a good deal of time to hang out, get to know a large number of kids, and to learn a good deal about general social practice in the school.

Note

1   This work, entitled "Gender Restructuring in Preadolescence," is funded by the Spencer Foundation and the Xerox Foundation, and is being pursued under the auspices of the Institute for Research on Learning.

4

The Vocalic Variables

The students of Belten High make social use of many linguistic resources. This study focuses on one syntactic variable, negative concord, and six vocalic variables. While these do not exhaust the local sociolinguistic repertoire, they do represent a diverse set of resources and provide a window onto the linguistic construction of social meaning in the Belten High community. Five of the vocalic variables participate in the Northern Cities Chain Shift. This shift, discussed extensively by Labov, Yaeger, and Steiner (1972) (hereafter LYS) and Labov (1991, 1994), is a rotation of the mid and low vowels as illustrated in figure 4.1. The Northern Cities Chain Shift (hereafter NCCS) affords an investigation of the relation between the age of a sound change and its social use, and as the following chapters will show, the vowels participating in this shift provide a kind of continuum of social meaning in the Detroit suburban area.

Labov (1994) describes the NCCS as a pull chain, set in motion by the raising of (aeh), followed by the fronting of (o) and the lowering and fronting of (oh).[1] Together these three changes constitute the earlier stages of the chain shift, and are abundantly apparent in the speech of all living age groups in Detroit (Labov 1994: 195ff). This forward rotation is currently being followed by the backing of the front and central mid vowels (ʌ) and (e), and the lowering of (i). The present study examines each variable in this shift with the exception of (i), whose variability is not prominent in the Belten data. While the general clockwise rotation of the chain shift accounts for a good deal of the variation in Belten High, the patterns of variation show a social use of a variety of variants resulting from the multidimensional mobility of some of these vowels. The study also examines variation in the diphthong (ay) which, while not part of the Northern Cities Chain Shift, is a versatile and highly meaningful sociolinguistic variable. Variation in (ay) involves two developments – nucleus raising (and backing) and monophthongization.

The Vocalic Variables

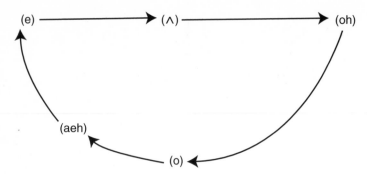

Figure 4.1 Northern cities chain shift

No two of these variables show the exact same social constraints, but they do fall into general categories of social significance which are related, in turn, to geographic patterns of variation in the urban–suburban Detroit area. The following discussion presents the internal constraints on the variables of this study, with the purpose of describing their socially significant variants and the internal factors that condition the occurrence of these variants. Some of these internal constraints will be included in the variable rule, or Varbrul,[2] analysis of social constraints. The internal constraints on variation have been established through an examination of the Neartown corpus alone, and are included only in the social analysis of that corpus.

4.1 The Data

Phonetic transcription of the variables was done impressionistically. There are inherent problems in the use of impressionistic transcription, perhaps particularly in sociolinguistics, where hearers' expectations can be an important factor in perception. However, there were commensurate problems with the use of the alternative, acoustic measures at the time when the transcription work was done. Acoustic measurement was still extremely slow. Also, normalization remained a problem in comparing the pronunciations of multiple male and female speakers, particularly at an age at which voices are still undergoing change, and several of the variables that are important in this study are distinguished primarily by lip rounding, which does not show up well on F1–F2 plots. Several measures were taken to maximize consistency in transcription, therefore. A period of calibration preceded transcription, in which the transcriber and I listened to the same tapes and established the variants that we could hear on a consistent basis. In the course of transcription, furthermore, in order to check on longitudinal consistency, each transcriber repeated transcription of a subset of previous tapes. Each variable for all speakers in both the Neartown sample (69 speakers) and the geographic sample (20 speakers per school, giving a total of 60 speakers in the geographic sample) was transcribed by the same person. The one exception was (e). Because of an unforeseen personnel change, one person transcribed the entire Neartown corpus and another transcribed the entire geographic corpus. There was no opportunity to calibrate the two systems, and the transcription system for the geographic sample shows only extreme backing. As a result, I cannot compare the Belten sample for (e) with those from other schools.

Each speaker is represented by a single sociolinguistic interview, as discussed in chapter 3, and the analysis of each variable is based on 50 tokens per speaker. This number was determined after transcription had been done for (aeh) for a number of speakers. In this early stage, 200 tokens were transcribed per speaker. Varbrul was then run on the full set of data to determine the major linguistic constraints. The set was then cut little by little, decreasing the number of tokens per speaker and rerunning Varbrul until the results began to change. This occurred as the sample approached 25 tokens per speaker. For the rest of the variables, 50 tokens were chosen systematically from the entire text of the interview. All interviews were orthographically transcribed into computer text files. For the purpose of selecting tokens, the interviews were printed out, and the total number of tokens was divided by the number of pages in the transcript. The resulting number of tokens was taken from the beginning of each page. As a result, the selection of tokens for transcription was automatic, and the values shown in this study represent a cross-section of the styles produced in the interview. In all cases, more than 50 tokens were transcribed for each variable, making it possible to make necessary lexical replacements as discussed below. For the final token file, tokens exceeding 50 for any speaker were discarded evenly through the file. As discussed in chapter 3, the interviews yielded a fairly relaxed interview style, and no attempt was made to distinguish between formal and casual styles.

All variables were coded for a range of possible internal constraints:

preceding and following segment
emphatic length and stress
preceding and following (where applicable) word boundary
occurrence in open vs. closed syllable
stress: primary, secondary, or monosyllable
common vs. proper noun
lexical item in which the token occurs

I use the term *advanced variant(s)* to refer to the variants for each variable
that are outside of the usual range of pronunciation for that variable,
and that show significant social correlations. The term *advanced* is meant
to refer to the speakers' movement away from common pronunciations
in search of salient social expression. This advance can be in the direction
of apparent change (for example, in the direction of the Northern Cities
Chain Shift) or it can be in an opposed direction if that direction moves
outside of the range of what can reasonably be called conservative variants.
The establishment of the advanced variants, or application values for
Varbrul analysis, was accomplished through an iterative process. Since
the social factor groups are predetermined by the social analysis, this
iterative process is not circular but seeks out the best fit between linguistic
variables and the internal constraints on their form on the one hand,
and the social phenomena under examination on the other. In each
case, repeated social runs determined which values of the variable had
particular social significance. In most cases, an identification was made
of what emerged as single advanced variants or sets of variants, defined
as those with clear social significance. In a few cases, more than one variant
emerged for a given variable as having different social significances. Each
of these variants will be discussed separately. For each variant, the most
powerful of these internal constraints were selected for inclusion in
all Varbrul runs for the examination of social constraints, eliminating
any that create small cells when combined with social constraints. In the
end, all social runs for a given variable have been performed with an
identical set of internal constraints, allowing for a systematic control
of effects resulting from accidents of distribution in the corpus. The
internal constraints are more powerful than the social constraints in
almost all cases. In the interests of space and clarity, tables showing
social factors will not include the factor weights for the internal
constraints.

4.2   The Older Variables

The movements of the older variables, (aeh), (o), and (oh), all involve fronting. In all cases, fronting is favored when the variable is preceded by velar and palatal consonants, and disfavored when preceded by labials. The glides /w/ and /y/, and instances where the preceding word ends in a high vowel /u/ or /i/, are included in the labial and velar/palatal groups respectively. This grouping is based on the similarity of effect of these vowels and glides when run separately. Fronting is inhibited in all of these variables by emphasis. The other major constraint for all these variables is the following segment, which affects each vowel somewhat differently.

4.2.1   (aeh)

The nucleus of (aeh) shows a raising trajectory along the front peripheral track. The lowest variant is [æ^], and the highest is a very high and front [e]. The percentage of each nucleus variant in the corpus is shown in table 4.1. For the purpose of this analysis, I combine [e] and [ε^] into a high advanced variant, opposing it to all others. The table shows the mean percentage of occurrence of the advanced variants across the Belten High speaker sample.

The conditioning for the raising of (aeh) is generally similar to that reported for Detroit in LYS, but strikingly different in some particulars. The following segment is the primary constraining factor group, and, as found by LYS, following nasals favor raising the most strongly. However, following obstruents show a pattern similar to the one that LYS found for Chicago, in opposition to Detroit. That is, where LYS found that raising before /k/ lagged behind /t/ and /p/ in Detroit, but led in Chicago, the Belten data show /k/ with a strong lead. And while LYS did not find much differentiation of effect among the following voiced stops, the Belten data

Table 4.1 Distribution of variants of (aeh)

Variant	[æ^]	[ε˅]	[ε]	[ε̌^]	[e]
% in corpus	22.9	16.8	21.9	32.6	5.8

▨ Advanced variants

Table 4.2   Constraints on (aeh) raising

	First rank constraint: following segment		
	Palatal/velar	Apical	Labial
Nasal	.927	.661	.597
Voiced obstruent	.805	.476	.370
Voiceless obstruent	.542	.409	.251
/l/	.172		

Second rank constraint: emphasis	
Emphatic	Non-emphatic
.224	.567

Third rank constraint: preceding segment						
Palatal/velar	Apical	Labial	/h/	/l/	/r/	Pause
.656	.561	.397	.597	.433	.354	.248

input = .369	sig = .000

do. More generally, as table 4.2 shows, the effect of the following segment is based on two hierarchies: point of articulation from back to front, and a rough sonority hierarchy, with greater sonority favoring raising. The only exception to this pattern is the inhibitory effect of following /l/. This table groups obstruents, and it groups velars and palatals, because neither distinction shows a significantly different effect on (aeh) raising.

As in the case of all but one of the variables (the lowering of (e)), emphatic stress disfavors the extreme variant. The point of articulation of the preceding segment has a similar, but weaker, effect to the following segment.

In the following chapters, the following segment will be included in the analysis of social factors for the raising of (aeh), distinguishing the most strongly favoring – [ŋ], [n], [g], and [ğ] – from all others. Because it is represented by only a total of 26 tokens, the disfavoring environment, a following /l/ or labial obstruent, will not be included.

4.2.2 (o) and (oh)

There is a good deal of phonetic overlap between the variants of (o) and (oh), as shown in tables 4.3 and 4.4.

Tables 4.5 and 4.6 show the internal constraints on the fronting of (o) and (oh) respectively.

As with (aeh) raising, emphatic stress weakly disfavors fronting in both (o) and (oh). The segmental constraints, both preceding and following, affect the two vowels differently, and in such a way as to reflect the distributional complementarity of the two phonemes. For both variables, the effect of the preceding segment maintains the pattern shown in the raising of (aeh), favoring fronting decreasingly as the point of articulation moves frontward from the palatal/velar position. However, this effect is stronger for (oh) than for (o). In the case of (o), preceding velars and palatals favor fronting, but all other consonants except /h/ have little effect. In the case of (oh), the point of articulation continuum of the preceding consonant shows a more detailed effect.

The following segment also affects the two vowels somewhat differently, particularly reflecting the two phonemes' distributional complementarity. Each variable fronts most in the environment in which the other does not occur. Fronting of (oh) is most strongly favored when word final, particularly when followed by a pause or by a vowel. The only word in the corpus in which (o) occurs word finally is *ma*, the word for mother favored by some burnouts, and occurring a total of 17 times (with no instances of fronting). Fronting is favored in both variables by a following nasal. However, the

Table 4.3 Variants of (o)

Variant	[æ],[ˤa]	[a]	[ɑ]	[ɑ^], [ʌ]
% in corpus	29	10	46	15

 Advanced variants

Table 4.4 Variants of (oh)

Variant	<a	a	<ɔ	ɔ
% in corpus	1	18	77	4

 Advanced variants

Table 4.5   Constraints on fronting of (o)

Constraint rank 1: following segment				
/m/	*/l/*	*Voiceless obstruents*	*/r/*	*Other*
.665	.605	.554	.197	.382

Constraint rank 2: preceding segment		
Velar/Palatal	*/h/*	*Other*
.622	.572	.453

Constraint rank 3: emphatic stress

Emphatic: .241	Non-Emphatic: .525

Input = .274 Sig. = .000

Table 4.6   Constraints on fronting of (oh)

Constraint rank 1: preceding segment			
Velar/palatal	*Apical*	*Labial*	*/r/,/l/,/h/*
.633	.550	.439	.387

Constraint rank 2: following segment			
Pause	*/ŋ/*	*Other*	*/l/*
.785	.637	.520	.450

Constraint rank 3: emphatic stress

Emphatic: .371	Non-emphatic: .516

Input = .176 Sig. = .004

particular nasal that most strongly favors fronting for each variable is the one that does not occur after the other: /ŋ/ in the case of (oh) and /m/ in the case of (o). /n/, the only nasal that occurs after both (o) and (oh), disfavors fronting in (o) and has little effect on either vowel.

It may be worth noting that while preceding /l/ inhibits the fronting of (oh), it has no effect on (o). This study does not examine /l/ as a variable, but in many American speech communities, light /l/ seems to have social significance. It is prominent in African American Vernacular English and in Latino Vernacular Englishes and to some extent in the English of Belten High. Since light /l/ occurs primarily before front vowels, it is difficult to assess the effect of /l/ on the following vowel without a separate transcription and analysis of /l/. In other words, the preceding environment in this case is itself variable. This may explain the relatively small effect of preceding /l/ on (aeh) raising, and the greater inhibiting effect of /l/ on (oh) than on (o). Since I did not study /l/ separately, I can only speculate, but all of the fronted variants of (aeh) and some of (o) may be sufficiently front to cause the palatalization of a preceding /l/, while none of the variants of (oh) are.

The preceding segment (palatals and velars vs. all others) will be the only internal variable included in the social analysis of both (o) and (oh).

4.3 The Newer Variables

4.3.1 (ʌ)

The variable (ʌ) is particularly rich in its social-symbolic use. It has two sets of socially significant variants: backing (with or without raising), and fronting, as shown in table 4.7.

Central raised variants of (ʌ) – [ɨ] and [ə] – appear primarily in closed class words (*was, something, what, but, does*). In some cases, these are somewhat reduced, but in most cases, they are full vowels, their raising conditioned by preceding labials. Because (ʌ) categorically reduces in *just*, all occurrences of *just* have been replaced in the corpus by open class words.

Socially meaningful variants are backing (and raising) along the trajectory [ʌ] > [ʌˀ] > [ɔ]/[ʊ] and fronting to [ɛ] and [ɪ]. The social use of fronting contrasts strongly with the use of backing, and can be seen as a reaction to the meanings expressed in backing. The use of the fronted variants do not constitute simple conservatism, since the most conservative speakers with

Table 4.7   Variants of (ʌ)

Variant	[ɛ],[ɪ]	[ɨ],[ə]	[ʌ]	[ʌˇ],[a]	[ʌˀ]	[ɔ]	[ʊ]
% in corpus	4	11	31	11	10	15	19

■ Advanced variants – fronting
▫ Advanced variants – backing

respect to the backing of (ʌ) do not front either. Lying outside of the envelope of the clear conservative variant, these fronted occurrences are clearly socially marked in opposition to the conservative variant as well as the backed variants.

4.3.1.1   Backing   As shown in table 4.8, backing is favored by both preceding and following labials, by preceding /l/, and by following /ð/ and /θ/. These latter follow (ʌ) in a limited set of words: /θ/ in nothing, and /ð/ in other, brother, and mother.

Table 4.8   Constraints on backing of (ʌ)

First ranked constraint: preceding segment		
/w/,/ŋ/	*Labials and /l/*	*Other*
.723	.640	.354
Second ranked constraint: following segment		
labials	/th/,/dh/	*Other*
.525	.612	.468
Input = .434	Sig. = .000	

In the social analysis, the three backed variants, [ʌˀ], [ɔ], and [ʊ], will be combined as the backed variant of (ʌ), with the difference between preceding labials (including /w/) and all other segments, as the internal constraint.

Table 4.9   Constraints on fronting of (ʌ)

First rank constraint: word stress		
Primary: .607	Monosyllable: .396	Secondary: .875

Second rank constraint: preceding Segment				
/tr/	Palatal obstruents	/y/	Labials	Other
.916	.840	.765	.350	.577

Input .028	Significance = .000

4.3.1.2 Fronting   Despite the small amount of fronting of (ʌ), the occurrence of the fronted variants ([ɛ] and [ɪ]) is socially significant, constituting opposition to the primary change of backing. Fronting is favored in secondary stressed position in polysyllables, and disfavored in monosyllables. Fronting also occurs primarily after palatals, as shown in table 4.9. There is a high rate of fronting following /r/, but only when it is the palatalized /r/ following /t/ (but not /d/) – as in *truck*.

4.3.2 (e)

Labov (1991) has shown backing to [ʌ] and lowering to [æ] as alternative trajectories for (e) within the internal dynamics of the Northern Cities Chain Shift. While backing has become the predominant direction in Detroit, lowering has predominated in Chicago. Both backing and lowering occur in Belten (table 4.10), and while backing predominates, lowering appears in a kind of symbolic opposition to backing, in a fashion analogous to the fronting of (ʌ).

4.3.2.1 Backing   The backing of (e) is favored by following /l/ and bilabials (table 4.11). Following labiodentals have little effect, and all other following segments have a fairly strong disfavoring effect. The preceding segment also has an important effect. Preceding liquids, particularly /l/, favor backing. Preceding /w/ also favors backing, but no other labials do. As in the case of the backing of (ʌ), the backing of (e) is disfavored in mono-

Table 4.10   Variants of (e)

Variant	αɛ	ɪ	ɛ	a/ă̌ˆ	ʌ
% in corpus	4	5	55	9	27

■ Advanced variants – fronting
  Advanced variants – backing

Table 4.11   Constraints on (e) backing

Constraint rank 1: following segment

/l/	/p/,/b/,/m/	/f/	Other
.871	.684	.519	.346

Constraint rank 2: preceding segment

/l/	/r/	/w/	Other
.862	.627	.602	.428

Constraint rank 3: word type

Polysyllable	Monosyllable
.588	.421

Constraint rank 4: emphasis

Normal	Emphatic
.526	.336

Input = .225	Sig. = .000

syllables, but with little difference between primary and secondary stress. Finally, backing is disfavored in emphatic occurrences. In all social analyses, following bilabials and /l/, and preceding /w/ and liquids, will be included as internal constraints.

4.3.2.2 Lowering   The internal constraints for the lowering of (e) are shown in table 4.12. As with the fronting of (ʌ), the reverse of the backing change of (e) shows relatively complementary conditioning to backing. The strong inhibitory effect of labials is evident in the fact that there is no low-

Table 4.12 Constraints on (e) lowering

Constraint rank 1: emphasis	
Normal	Emphatic
.446	.804

Constraint rank 2: following segment		
Velars/palatals	Apicals	Labials, /1/
.752	.569	.351

Constraint rank 3: preceding segment					
Bilabial, /1/	/f/,/v/	Apical	Pause	Velar/palatal	/y/
.305	.493	.508	.578	.666	.730

Input = .025	Sig. = .000

ering at all after /w/ or before bilabials. There is also no lowering before /l/. /w/ and bilabials (and /l/ in the case of the following segment) have been combined with labials in the regression that yields the figures in table 4.12. It is even clearer in this case than in the case of (ʌ) fronting that lowering is a response to backing. The movement of (e) in this case is not simply an extreme lack of backing, but lowering – a change in direction from the general trajectory. The most notable thing about the lowering of (e) is that it is the only variant in the entire corpus of six vocalic variables that is strongly favored by emphasis, which is the primary constraint. This clearly indicates that the use of this variant is a somewhat intentional reversal of the change in progress. Because of the small rate of occurrence of lowering, the internal constraints included in the social analysis will be limited to the following segment (velars and palatals vs. other environments). Emphasis has been excluded from these analyses because the small number of emphatic occurrences yields knockouts when emphasis is combined as a constraint with social factors.

4.3.3 (ay)

Not part of the NCCS, the developments of (ay) in the Detroit suburban area constitute strong sociolinguistic variants, as in the American South

Table 4.13   Percent of occurrence of nucleus variants of (ay) with three degrees of glide strength

	$^<a$	a	$a^\wedge$	Λ	$[\Lambda^>]$, $[\partial]$, $[\mathfrak{I}]$, $[\upsilon]$
Without glide	.47	.07	.33	.13	.00
With weak glide	.33	.05	.29	.33	.00
With full glide	.13	.07	.24	.52	.04

Advanced variants

(Schilling Estes 1996). There are two socially distinct developments in (ay): monophthongization and nucleus raising (sometimes with backing). The two can be seen as pulls in opposite directions from [ɑy]. The nucleus of (ay) ranges all the way from a fronted variant, [$^<$a], through [ɑ], to raised ([ʌ], [ə]) and raised and backed ([ʌ$^>$], [ɔ], [ʊ]). The relation between the quality of the nucleus and the presence of the glide is apparent in the covariation of the continua of nucleus value and glide strength, as fronting correlates with glide loss, shown in table 4.13.

4.3.3.1 Monophthongization   Monophthongized tokens can be identified either as tokens with no glide, or as tokens with nucleus–glide assimilation, in other words with both a front nucleus and no glide. The latter guarantees that monophthongization that is simply a result of fast speech will not be included in the analysis. The results with both identification measures are similar, but what differences there are indicate that a number of the tokens included by the first measure are neutralizations rather than full monophthongs. For this reason, the following discussion is based on an analysis of tokens with no glide and with a nucleus value of [$^<$a] or [a]. As shown in table 4.14, the primary constraint on monophthongization is the following segment. The strong negative constraint of following /r/ distinguishes monophthongization in Belten High from the monophthongization characteristic of southern dialects. The following segment shows a sonority hierarchy similar to, but more detailed than, that favoring the raising of (aeh). In addition, there is a stark effect from syllable type, as the favoring or disfavoring effect of the following consonant is enhanced in closed syllables. Tautosyllabic resonants and voiced obstruents strongly favor monophthongization, while tautosyllabic voiceless obstruents, which favor nucleus raising (see below), strongly disfavor monophthongization.

Table 4.14 Constraints on (ay) monophthongization

	/l/	Nasal	Glide/ vowel	Voiced fricative	Voiced stop	Voiceless obstruent	/r/*
Constraint rank 1: following segment							
Closed syllable	.916	.887	.898	.842	.729	.039	0%
Open Syllable	.807	.718	.726	.744	.567	.560	7%

Second rank constraint: lexical membership			
I don't	I'	I	Other
.965	.780	.605	.393

Input = .043	Sig. = .000

* Knockout constraint, not included in Varbrul run

The original token file for (ay), analyzed in this discussion, was constituted by tokens more or less as they occur in the interviews: that is, regardless of the lexical item containing the variable. The result was a file in which roughly a third of the tokens occurred in the pronoun *I*, with 1,063 tokens (926 full forms and 137 contracted forms). This file included 185 other distinct lexical items, whose frequencies of occurrence ranged from 1 to 495. *I* has a high rate of monophthongization, and the constraints on these occurrences of monophthongization indicate clearly that many of them result from the unstresed, phrasal clitic, position of *I*. Table 4.14 shows the secondary constraint on monophthongization – the lexical status of the variable, distinguishing three classes of occurrence of *I*:

(1) contractions
(2) the phrase *I don't* (Many of these are in the phrase *I don't know*, which occurs frequently, not as an answer to a question, but as something resembling a discourse marker.)
(3) all other occurrences of *I*.

The high probability of monophthongization in the phrase *I don't* (and slightly higher in *I don't know*) suggests that the discourse use of this phrase is giving these occurrences of (ay) a special status. At first glance, it would seem that the order of monophthongization from I to contracted I to phrasal I reflects an increase in reduction. However, this is ruled out by the inclusion of only full front nuclei in this analysis. In addition, I did a separate examination of the two components of monophthongization, nucleus fronting and glide loss. The contracted and other occurrences of *I* frequently involve only glide loss, suggesting that in these cases, the nucleus is reduced as a result of the phrasal clitic status of *I*. However, *I* occurring in the phrase *I don't*, and slightly more in *I don't know*, shows a completely different pattern, with extremely high values for both glide weakening and nucleus fronting. In order to maximize the analysis of potentially socially meaningful occurrences of monophthongization, I constructed a new file for the analysis of (ay), replacing all occurrences of *I* (including *I don't*) with other lexical items. The effect of the following segment remains the same in this file.

The internal constraints included in the social analysis will be the following segment: /l/, nasal, glide/vowel, and voiced fricative, regardless of syllable type since all of these have high rates of monophthongization in both closed and open syllables.

4.3.3.2   Raising and backing of the nucleus   As table 4.13 showed, the most common realization of the nucleus of diphthongal (ay) is [ʌ]. Because of its high incidence and because it shows no significant social differentiation in Belten High, I refer to raising to this variant as "common raising." Raising to [ʌˀ], [ə], [ɔ], and [ʊ], or what I will refer to as "extreme raising," occurs in a small subset of the environments that favor overall raising. Table 4.15 shows the constraints on extreme raising.

Table 4.15   Constraints on extreme nucleus raising in (ay)

Constraint rank 1: following segment		
Other	r	Voiceless obstruents
.118	.744	.896

Constraint rank 2: preceding segment						
Velar, palatal, /h/	Apical	Bilabial	/r/	/l/	/v/, /f/	kw
261	.674	.422	.503	.384	.908	.849

| Input = .007 | | | Sig. = .000 | | | |

The environments that favor nucleus raising are essentially the reverse of the environments for monophthongization. Raising is favored by following voiceless obstruents, particularly in closed syllables. The preceding segmental constraint is roughly the reverse of the point of articulation pattern that constrains fronting. The only departure from this pattern of constraint of the preceding segment is the difference betwen /kw/ (as in *quite*, *quiet*), which strongly favors raising, and other labials (notably including /w/) which only weakly favor raising.

Although the strength of an existing glide has no effect on nucleus raising, there is only a single occurrence of extreme raising in a monophthong. Tokens with zero glides, therefore, have been excluded from the regression represented in this table, and will also be excluded in the social runs. Extreme nucleus raising is particularly favored by following voiceless obstruents and /r/. The effect of labials is limited to [kw], and to the labiodentals /f/ and /v/. Because extreme raising occurs with low frequency, internal factors need to be maximized by controlling the potential for fragmenting the cells. Because of the relatively small incidence of extreme raising, only the following segment will be included in the social runs to control for internal constraints.

Notes

1 I adopt the notations used in Labov, Yaeger, and Steiner (1972) and Labov (1994) for the variables in the Northern Cities Chain Shift.
2 For a discussion of variable rule analysis, see Sankoff (1987). The particular version of the variable rule program used in this research is Goldvarb Version 2.

5

Outline of Variation in Belten High

Michigan spreads over the back of a large left-handed mitten reaching out from the northern US into the waters of the Great Lakes. Detroit is at the base of the thumb, its downtown facing east across the Detroit River to Canada. The land that surrounds Detroit to the north, the west, and the south is perfectly flat, and etched with a regular grid of evenly spaced major streets running north–south and east–west. Here and there around the west and the south of this grid, expansive automotive plants and the occasional park or mall interrupt the neatly laid out squares. Class and ethnicity are mapped onto this grid. For the most part, as one moves out of Detroit in any direction, the socioeconomic level rises gradually; and the African American population drops and, to the north and west, all but disappears.

Neartown lies in the midst of this urban–suburban sprawl. During the time I was in Belten High, there were two African Americans in a student population of 2,000. Although a variety of European and a scattering of Middle Eastern ethnic groups are represented in its population, Neartown plays down its diversity. There are no ethnic neighborhoods or businesses, there is little ethnic pride or posturing in the schools. But Neartown does not play down its socioeconomic diversity. Its internal geography reproduces locally the socioeconomic continuum within which the town is embedded, and the neighborhoods run from solid working class at the Detroit end of town to relatively affluent upper middle class at the other. The neighborhood, the town, and the wider urban–suburban area provide a socio-geographic landscape that touches on, and extends outward from, the school. From their particular vantage point in Belten High, students can look outward to orient and identify themselves in relation to that landscape.

The schools of Neartown have somewhat distinct socioeconomic makeups, which figure in students' socioeconomic placement of themselves and their surroundings. Wherever possible, kids orient to other kids, and high schools are a crucial part of kids' understanding of the local area, as student populations locate themselves in relation to generalizations about the student populations of surrounding schools. Belten's catchment area embraces the full socioeconomic spectrum of Neartown, but with a somewhat smaller population at the ends of the spectrum than the comparably poorer and wealthier schools in town. Kids at Belten also come from three junior high schools, each of which has a different socioeconomic character; and each of these junior high schools is fed by several neighborhood-based, hence quite economically homogeneous, elementary schools. Moving through the Neartown school system, then, brings increasing socioeconomic diversity and an increasing awareness of one's own place in the local socioeconomic spectrum.

Kids at Belten are sensitive to class differences. Many of them have an accurate socioeconomic map of the suburban area, and of the neighborhoods served by the school, and they are aware of many of the socioeconomic distinctions within the school population. However, students' awareness of parents' class is strongly tempered by relations among students themselves. Wealth becomes salient primarily to the extent that people do not assimilate socially to the dominant socioeconomic level of their school. If kids of greater means dress ostentatiously, or drive fancy cars, they will be stigmatized by the general student body not so much for being "rich," but for not conforming to local style. Ostentation is seen as a kind of social incompetence. A person who is visibly poor will be likewise stigmatized on the grounds of incompetence – on the apparent inability to keep up appearances. One jock girl, for instance, told me that she often wore painter's pants because she couldn't afford the appropriate jeans, and chose to strike out in a new but inexpensive fashion direction. She pointed out that a little creativity could overcome a lack of money, arguing that poverty is never an excuse to dress badly. Of course, she was not particularly poor, and it is not obvious whether her clever choice of painter's pants was saving her, or whether she already had sufficient status to set a style.

As school represents the transition from childhood to adulthood, it is also a major locus for the transition from parents' socioeconomic status to one's own. Social category affiliation is an institutionalization, within the school, of this transition. The two life stage elements are manifest in high school: kids still live at home, and in neighborhoods shared with some classmates and far from others. Their parents' socioeconomic status determines, to some extent, what they can buy, where they can go, and what they can do. It also influences their outlook on the world, and on school; their expectations and their desires. And to the extent that they hang out with other kids from their neighborhood, their friends' backgrounds are likely to have had a similar effect on them, intensifying class-based orientations. What they do in school – what curriculum they follow, what activities they participate in, and what kinds of grades they get – will determine to some extent what they do after they leave school. Thus all high school students are simultaneously coming from and going towards. What they do in high school is a pivot point, and for some it is a continuation of a style of life from home while for others it is a transition to a new style of life.

The first place to look in a study of the salience of class among adolescents is the socioeconomic status of their parents. In order to establish the baseline of the influence of parents' socioeconomic status on the Belten students' patterns of variation, and to ensure comparability with currently existing correlations between variation and adult class, I adopt the general measures of socioeconomic status introduced to the study of variation by Labov (1966). Any correlation between adolescents' patterns of variation and their parents' socioeconomic status could result from one of several possible mechanisms. On the one hand, it is possible that the adolescent speaker acquires class-based linguistic patterns directly from one or both parents. Alternatively, the main influence could be one's early peers. Inasmuch as parents' material possibilities determine the child's neighborhood, they determine the child's earliest and most accessible peers. Finally, it is possible that aspects of parents' socioeconomic status influence adolescents' own orientation to the world which, in turn, affects their speech patterns.

5.1   Measures of Parents' Status

The neighborhoods that serve Belten High cover all or parts of 14 quarter sections on the census map. According to the 1980 Census, the closest to the time of this study, the median household income in Belten's catchment area ranged from $24,000 in the poorer of the sections closest to Detroit to $40,000 in the section farthest from Detroit. Table 5.1 groups quarter sections by median income, based on natural divisions into three fairly homogeneous levels. The gap between levels 2 and 3 is particularly stark. Only two quarter sections at the extreme suburban end of the Belten catchment area fall under index level 3, and are generally recognized as "rich" neighborhoods. Correlations between linguistic variables and these levels, constituting a Neighborhood Income Index, could be

Table 5.1 Neighborhood income index

Neighborhood income index	Median income range	Number in speaker sample
1	$25,806–$26,750	28
2	$29,706–$33,688	33
3	$39,790–$40,017	8

Table 5.2 Housing index

Housing index	House value	Number in speaker sample
1	Under $20,000	5
2	$20,000–$24,999	7
3	$25,000–$29,000	8
4	$30,000–$34,999	23
5	$35,000–$39,999	13
6	Over $40,000	13

taken to suggest a relation between patterns of variation and general neighborhood.

While parents' income was not available for the individuals in the Belten High sample, available information relevant to parents' socioeconomic status includes the assessed value of the family residence, and the occupations and educational attainment of both parents. A housing index, based on the assessed values of the homes of Belten High students, is shown in table 5.2.

The parents of the members of the Belten speaker sample range in education from second grade to the PhD. This study uses an index of education level, based on that used in Labov (1966), but with the addition of a sixth level for parents who have had at least some postgraduate education. This index and the distribution of educational levels of speakers' mothers and fathers are shown in table 5.3.

Figure 5.1, displaying the education indices of the mother and the father of each student in the speaker sample, shows a rough relation between mothers' and fathers' educational levels.[1] The range of fathers' education, however, is greater than the range of mothers' – there are no mothers in the

Table 5.3   Education index

Education index	Education level	Fathers in speaker sample	Mothers in speaker sample
1	Grade school or less	2	0
2	Some high school	4	3
3	Finished high school	23	39
4	Some college or trade school	12	13
5	Finished college	23	13
6	Some graduate school	5	1

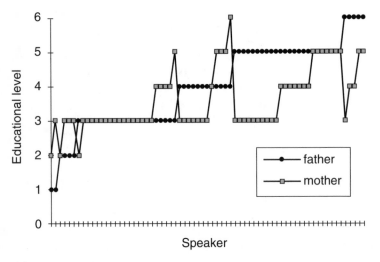

Figure 5.1   Parents' education by speaker

sample who did not finish elementary school, and there is only one who did graduate work. In correlations with education, therefore, fathers are considered both on a six-point scale and on a four-point scale, merging the levels at each of the extremes: levels 1 and 2 on the one hand, and 5 and 6 on the other.

As with education, occupational categories are assigned values according to the system employed in Labov (1966). These categorizations are difficult to apply to men's occupations, and they are even more difficult to apply to

Table 5.4 Parents' occupational index

Occupation index	Description	Fathers in speaker sample	Mothers in speaker sample
0	No employment outside the home	0	41
1	Laborers	3	1
2	Service workers	2	4
3	Craftsmen, foremen and kindred workers	15	3
4	Clerical, sales and kindred workers	14	13
5	Proprietors, managers, officials	13	0
6	Professional, semiprofessional	22	7

women's. I will not dwell on these difficulties here, however, since fewer than half the mothers in this sample work outside of the home, making it impossible to use mother's occupation as an indication of socioeconomic status. Table 5.4 shows the distribution of parents' occupational levels in the speaker sample.

Finally, a socioeconomic index was constructed for fathers, based on a combination of home value and father's education and occupation. The addition of these three indices gives a range from a total of 6 to a total of 18. These were combined to yield six levels with as even a distribution of speakers as possible, as shown in table 5.5.

Table 5.5 Father's socioeconomic index

Socioeconomic index	Fathers in speaker sample
1 (6–8)	8
2 (9,10)	12
3 (11,12)	11
4 (13,14)	17
5 (15,16)	11
6 (17,18)	10

Jock and burnout affiliation correlate with all measures of parents' socioeconomic status: with father's education ($p < .05$), mother's education

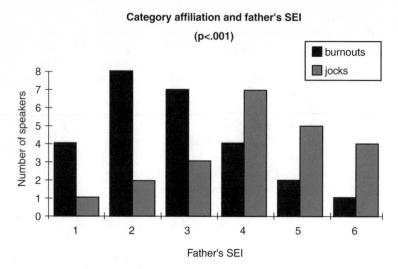

Figure 5.2 Category affiliation as a function of father's socioeconomic class, based on interview sample of jocks and burnouts

(p < .01), but most particularly with father's occupation and father's socioeconomic index (both p < .001). Figure 5.2 shows the clearest of these relations – that between jock and burnout affiliation and fathers' socioeconomic index. It is clear from this figure that there is a certain amount of mobility – a mobility that potentially bleeds the effects of parents' socioeconomic status on adolescents' language. On the other hand, it is clear that there is a trajectory from family origins to adolescent social category. It is notable in this figure that the categories peak to either side of the center of the local socioeconomic range, and not at either extreme. They are based squarely in the significant mass of the population, reflecting the general makeup of the school population.

5.1.1   Variation and parents' socioeconomic status

Perhaps the most important finding of this study is the small extent to which the speech of Belten High students reflects their parents' socioeconomic characteristics. Negation, the one grammatical variable in this study, is the only one that is clearly influenced by parents. This is, in fact, a powerful influence, as there are significant correlations between negation and all

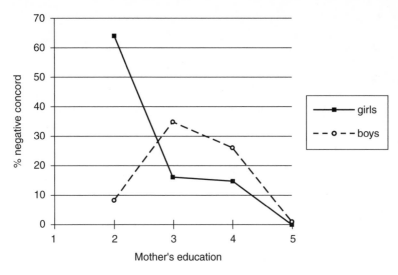

Figure 5.3 Negative concord and mother's education

measures of parents' socioeconomic status. The best correlation overall is with mother's education, and this holds within both gender groups (figure 5.3). If this relation holds up under greater scrutiny, it remains to be established whether it indicates that mothers are more likely than fathers to monitor their children's grammar, or that children are more likely to emulate their mother's grammar. There are some interesting gender differences in this relation. Girls' use of negative concord (mean = 15.057%) is more conservative overall than boys', it is more homogeneous than boys' (mean = 25.500%), and while the girls show a wider range of levels of use overall, their levels are more homogeneous overall (standard deviation = 22.460) than boys' (standard deviation = 32.426). In addition, as shown in figure 5.4, girls' use of negative concord conforms better to mothers' education (and to fathers' education) than boys'.

It should not be surprising that this particular variable reflects speakers' family origins, since of all the sociolinguistic variables in English, negative concord is arguably the most conscious and the most stigmatized non-standard variable, hence the one most likely to be monitored by parents. The fact that the boys' patterns of negation correlate less well with parents' education is undoubtedly related to the fact that boys are less constrained to conform to parents' norms in general. Eisikovits, in her study of working class adolescents' use of non-standard grammar (1987), shows a gender

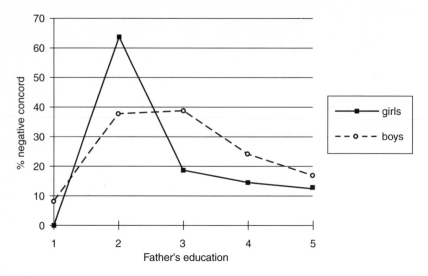

Figure 5.4   Negative concord and father's education

divergence as speakers move through adolescence, with girls' speech becoming increasingly standard and boys' speech becoming increasingly non-standard. She notes that the two gender groups have different senses of maturity, with the girls focusing on "settling down" and the boys focusing on autonomy. The association of non-standard grammar with autonomy makes perfect sense if one considers that children may not distinguish among different kinds of language use that are subject to sanction. This is illustrated in the cartoon "Family Circus" by Bil Keane, in which a girl tattles on her brother, saying, "Jeffy used a bad word! He said *'ain't'*!" And just as boys' profanity is tolerated in a way that girls' is not, and indeed is associated with masculinity (through fearless autonomy from authority), so their use of non-standard grammar may have similar associations. The gender patterns of negation to be shown in the following chapters will confirm this.

Among all the vocalic variables, only the raising of the nucleus of (ay) correlates with any of the parents' indices, and only in the speech of girls. Like negation, it is parents' education that shows an effect – both the father's and the mother's. As shown in table 5.6, the correlation with mother's education is stark, with a break between those whose mothers have been to college and those who have not. There is no extreme nucleus raising among those whose mothers have been to college; and among those whose mothers have not been to college, there is an inverse relation between

Table 5.6   (ay) raising and parents' educational levels. Girls only

Educational level	1	2	3	4	5	6	Input	Sig.
Mother	na	.801	.459	(0)*	(0)	na	.016	.000
Father	460	870	627	476	352	357	.010	.000

* Values in parentheses are knockouts, not included in the calculation

nucleus raising and mother's educational level. There are only two girls whose mother's educational level is 2, making the apparent cline less convincing, and producing something more like a dichotomous correlation. There is a fairly smooth inverse correlation between (ay) raising and father's education, with the exception of the lowest educational group. There is, however, only one girl whose father falls in this group – the same girl who shows no negative concord in figure 5.4.

The general lack of correlation between the vocalic variables and parents' socioeconomic indices could be partially due to the sample selection. The speaker sample in the study of Belten High is not a random sampling based on parents' socioeconomic factors. Rather, choice of speakers was based on place in social networks and particularly in relation to social categories, foregrounding the speakers' own socioeconomically related choices. A sampling that did not take social categories into account may well downplay individual social mobility and show a greater correlation between linguistic variables and parents' status. However, the clear correlation of parents' social characteristics with negation suggests that this is not the case, and that the vocalic variables are imbued with peer-based meaning. It is just this difference that forms the heart of this research, which focuses on the transitional nature of adolescence, and particularly on the relation between the speaker's construction of identity and linguistic variation. Indeed, the one girl in table 5.6 whose father falls in educational level 1, but whose nucleus raising value for (ay) is relatively low (and who shows no negative concord in figure 5.3), is a jock, and as we will see below, (ay) raising is typical of burnouts.

5.2   Peer Categories

The depth of the social differences that constitute the opposition between jocks and burnouts is witnessed by the fact that, along with gender, the

Table 5.7   Variables by gender and social category. Jocks and burnouts only

Variable	Girls	Boys	Burnouts	Jocks	Input	Sig.
(aeh) raising	.574	.435	ni	ni	.372	.000
(o) fronting	.589	.410	ni	ni	.277	.000
(oh) fronting	.669	.373	.599	.421	.171	.009
(ʌ) backing	ni	ni	.571	.437	.494	.000
(e) backing	ni	ni	.540	.467	.262	.016
(ay) raising	.586	.434	.707	.257	.009	.045
(ay) monophthongiz.	.426	.555	ni	ni	.072	.006
(ʌ) fronting	ni	ni	.364	.622	.076	.000
(e) lowering	.583	.437	.405	.580	.035	.024
Negative concord	.412	.567	.709	.306	.238	.000

▪ Secondary social constraint

major determiners of the use of sociolinguistic variables in Belten High are jock or burnout affiliation, and engagement in the practices that constitute those categories. The following analysis of variation will focus on the two polarized categories – the jocks and the burnouts – in order to outline the structure of variation in Belten High. Subsequent chapters will expand the view to incorporate in-betweens as well.

When gender and social category are treated as independent variables, the variables described in chapter 4 fall roughly into two categories of social correlation: those that correlate primarily with gender and those that correlate primarily with social category. I will show below that this typology is oversimplified, and that the key to social meaning in variation lies in the interactions between the two. Table 5.7 shows the overall correlations for the main variants for each of the vocalic variables, among the jocks and burnouts only.

The variables fall into three rough groups: those constrained solely by gender (and these are divided into female and male leads), those constrained solely by social category (and these are divided into jock and burnout leads), and those constrained by a combination of the two. The older changes in the Northern Cities Chain Shift (raising of (aeh) and fronting of (o)) correlate only with gender,[2] with the girls leading in both cases in the use of advanced variants. The monophthongization of (ay) is also constrained only by gender, and is the only vocalic variable in which boys lead across the board in the use of advanced variants. The newer changes in the Northern

Table 5.8 Negative concord: mother's education, gender, and social category

Primary constraint					Secondary constraint		Tertiary constraint		
Mother's education					Category		Gender		
2	3	4	5	6	Jocks	Burnouts	Girls	Boys	Input = .170
.729	.680	.589	.034	.418	.321	.693	.383	.590	Sig. = .000

Table 5.9 Negative concord: mother's education and social category

	Mother's education					*Category*			
	2	*3*	*4*	*5*	*6*	*Jocks*	*Burnouts*	*Input*	*Sig.*
Girls	.850	.415	.570	(0)	na	.110	.746	.184	.000
Boys	.134	.741	.531	.041	.421	.355	.703	.199	.000

▨ Secondary social constraint

Cities Shift (backing of (ʌ) and (e)) correlate only with social category, with the burnouts leading all groups in the use of advanced variants. (oh) fronting, lying at the intersection of the two series, correlates with both, but with gender a stronger social constraint than social category affiliation. (ay) raising correlates with both gender and social category as well, with girls and burnouts leading. Finally, the reversals of (ʌ) and (e) backing show a reversal of the category constraint, with jocks leading. In the case of (e), the category constraint is secondary to gender, with girls leading.

In the discussion of parents' class characteristics above, negative concord and (ay) raising were the only variables to correlate with any aspect of parents' socioeconomic status, particularly mother's education. In the face of social category, this correlation breaks down completely for (ay) raising, and begins to break down for negative concord. When boys and girls are combined (table 5.8), mother's education is the primary constraint, and shows a relatively fine-grained correlation with negative concord except for the higher value at educational level 6. However, there is only one person represented in this cell. When boys and girls are examined separately (table 5.9), mother's education retains its effect for girls, but is demoted to secondary constraint. Among the boys, while mother's education emerges as the primary constraint, this status is due to differences among education levels, and the hierarchical relations are interrupted. Thus social category takes over in both cases.

Although most of the variables are constrained primarily by gender or social category, it would be a mistake to view them as "markers" of one or the other. As Brown and Levinson (1979) have discussed in some detail, the notion of sociolinguistic variables as social markers implies a one-to-one correlation between variables and social characteristics. In particular, they note that if most variables, such as (oh) in this corpus, correlate simultaneously with several social factors, there is no way to determine which is being marked when a speaker uses extreme variants of (oh). If we are to take interactions among social factors seriously, we have to think of variables as performing their symbolic function in more subtle ways than as markers of individual factors or factor groups. An additional problem with the markers view, as we will see below, is that a factor group such as gender or social category may have an important effect on variation and not show up in across-the-board correlations. The search for social meaning in variation, therefore, only begins with figures such as those shown in table 5.7. The cross-cutting variables point to areas to explore, but do not in themselves provide explanation.

As discussed in chapter 2, social category and gender are closely intertwined in the social order of Belten High, as throughout society. The interaction between gender and social category is clear when gender is opened up with social category, yielding four groups – male jocks, female jocks, male burnouts, and female burnouts. While the differences among the four new speaker categories are not all significant, some suggestive patterns emerge. Of all the variables, (oh) fronting and negation are the only ones in which gender and social category appear to actually function independently. I do not take this statistical independence to be an indication that the two are actually independent markers in practice, however, since I cannot conceive of speakers as separating the two – as, for example, "doing jock" and "doing male" separately rather than "doing male jock." Each person's gender is deeply intertwined with the particular style of male or female that he or she is pursuing. The variables show a range of interactions between the two factor groups, with a consistent change in gender/category patterns as we move through the Northern Cities Chain Shift and into (ay) and negation, with a gradual transition from variables in which girls lead in the use of advanced variants, through variables in which burnouts lead and boys gradually begin to lead as well. Overall, the variables fall into three patterns, described by the factor weights for each combination of gender and social category.

5.2.1 Pattern 1

The oldest participants in the Northern Cities Chain Shift, the fronting of (aeh), (o), and (oh), show a pattern primarily of gender differentiation, in which girls lead boys overall in the use of advanced variants. In the case of the oldest variables, (aeh) and (o), gender is the only robust correlation. Figure 5.5 charts the factor weights for the four gender/category groups for these two variables. For both of these variables, the gender difference is not equally robust across the population, but is greater among burnouts than among jocks. Indeed the statistical significance of the gender difference for (aeh) for the entire jock–burnout population shown in table 5.7 is actually a result of the polarization between burnout girls and burnout boys, whose use of advanced variants constitutes the two extremes for the entire jock–burnout population. The difference between jock girls and boys, falling between the two, has a low statistical significance (p < .078). The pattern in figure 5.5, which I will call Pattern 1, shows an overall female lead in the use of advanced variants, with the burnouts defining the envelope of variation.

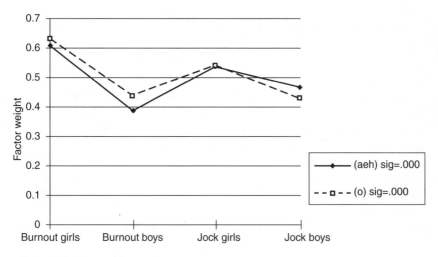

Figure 5.5 Pattern 1

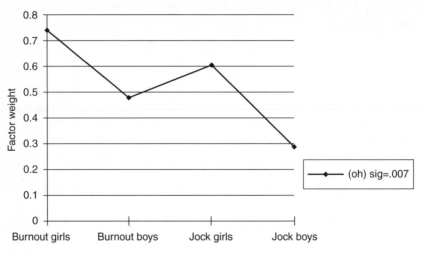

Figure 5.6   Pattern 1a

There is no robust social category pattern in the use of either (aeh) or (o). However, viewed in relation to patterns to follow, the pattern that does exist is worth pointing out. Specifically, the jock–burnout relation is reversed in the two gender groups. The burnout girls lead the jock girls slightly in the use of both of these variables ((aeh): $p < .071$, (o): $p < .045$), while the jock boys lead the burnout boys slightly in (aeh) raising ($p < .049$) and there is only a negligible difference in the boys' use of (o).

As one progresses through the early stages of the Northern Cities Chain Shift, from (aeh) to (o), and then to (oh), the jock boys' values gradually lower in relation to the other groups, until the burnouts lead the jocks in (oh) fronting among both boys and girls. This development also yields a gender difference for jocks that exceeds that among burnouts. Thus this decrease in jock boys' values for (oh) simultaneously increases overall gender differences, and increases a difference between jock and burnout boys, introducing the overall category difference for (oh) that makes gender and social category appear to be independent variables. I will refer to this pattern, in which both girls and burnouts lead in the use of advanced variants, as Pattern 1a (figure 5.6).

The reversals of (ʌ) and (e) backing (figure 5.7) show a pattern similar to that of (aeh) and (o), but diverging from Pattern 1 with a change in the status of categories, as jocks lead burnouts across the board. The lowering of (e) shows a gender pattern similar to (aeh) and (o), with girls leading boys

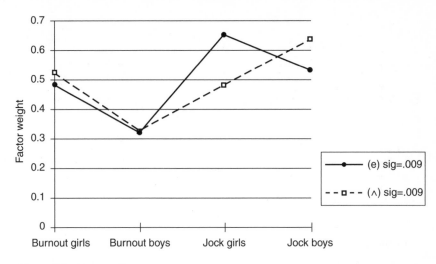

Figure 5.7 Pattern 1b

in both categories. (ʌ) fronting shows a similar pattern, with the exception that the jock boys take a strong lead over the jock girls. This pattern, in which jocks lead burnouts, is Pattern 1b.

5.2.2 *Pattern 2*

In Pattern 2, it is social category that dominates, with the burnouts leading. The backing of (e) and (ʌ), and nucleus raising in (ay) (figure 5.8) show a pattern primarily of social category differentiation, with burnout boys and girls leading jock boys and girls in the use of advanced variants. All of the gender differences are statistically insignificant except the burnout girls' lead over the burnout boys (p < .018) in (ay) raising. However, there is a noticeable pattern by which the gender relation is reversed between the burnouts and the jocks. While the burnout girls lead the burnout boys in two of the three variables, the jock boys lead the jock girls in all.

5.2.3 *Pattern 3*

The monophthongization of (ay) (figure 5.9) shows a complete reversal of Pattern 1, with gender once again the primary term of differentiation, but

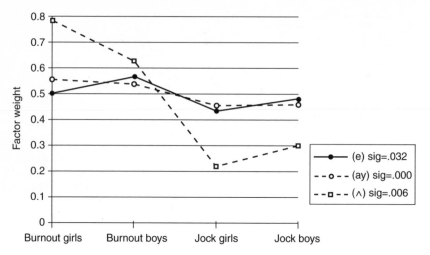

Figure 5.8   Pattern 2

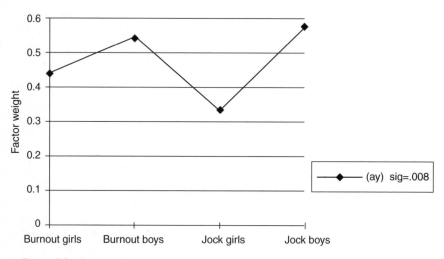

Figure 5.9   Pattern 3

now with the boys leading the girls. The difference between jock girls and boys, furthermore, has increased, and the category difference among boys has disappeared. The burnout girls' lead over the jocks girls in monophthongization has a low statistical significance (p < .069). I will call this pattern, in which boys lead girls, Pattern 3.

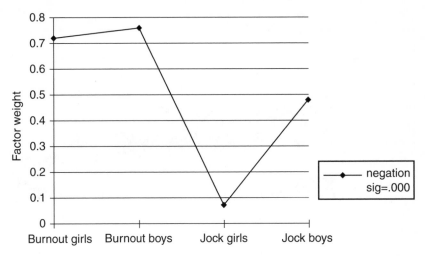

Figure 5.10 Pattern 3a

Negative concord (figure 5.10) displays Pattern 3a, conforming to Pattern 3, but with the addition of a category difference with burnouts leading in both gender groups. The relation between negation (Pattern 3a) and monophthongization (Pattern 3) is similar to the relation between the fronting of (oh) (Pattern 1a) and Pattern 1, inasmuch as it shows a clear pattern of both gender and social category difference. In this case, however, the gender difference among burnouts is small, while it is extreme among the jocks.

Taking all of the variables together, the speaker groups differ considerably in their use of linguistic resources. Table 5.10 shows the order in which each speaker group uses each of these variables. This table shows the gradual shift in social constraint as the variables move from the jock-dominated reversals of Pattern 1b through the female-dominated Pattern 1, through the burnout dominated Pattern 2 and into the male dominated Pattern 3.

Table 5.10 shows that the burnout girls lead everyone else in the use of advanced variants for half of the variables: Pattern 1, Pattern 1a, and two of the Pattern 2 variables. Furthermore, they do not lag in the use of any variables, making them the most comprehensive users of advanced variants. At the opposite extreme, the jock girls are the most conservative users of advanced variants, leading only in the use of the reversal of (e) backing, and lagging behind all other groups in the use of all Pattern 2 and 3 variables.

Table 5.10 Use of extreme variants for each variable

Patterns:	1b		1	1a		2		3a	3
	(Λ) front	(e) lower	(aeh)	(o)	(oh)	(Λ)	(ay) raise	(e)	neg	(ay) mono
Jock girls										
Burnout girls										
Burnout boys										
Jock boys										

Darkness of shading represents degree of use of advanced variants (black = highest, white = lowest)

Jock and burnout boys each lead in the use of advanced variants in two of the ten variables: the burnouts lead in the use of the remaining Pattern 2 variable and Pattern 3a, and lag in the use of Pattern 1 variables. This gives them a pattern that contrasts maximally with girls and with jocks. Jock boys, finally, split their lead between the one variable that is clearly a male variable, monophthongization, and the reversal of (Λ) backing.

5.3 Variation, Gender, and Social Category

The common observation that female speakers tend to lead in the use of "prestige" variants (e.g. Trudgill 1974) would lead one to expect an inverse correlation between an overall female lead in the use of extreme variants on the one hand, and a burnout lead on the other. In these data, negative concord and (e) lowering are the only variables that conform unequivocally to this pattern. This is not accidental, however, for these two variables have a particularly iconic status within the inventory of variables studied here. (e) lowering is the clearest case of a change "from above" in these data, not simply reversing a current sound change but changing its direction altogether. There is plenty of evidence that this is a somewhat intentional reaction to the predominant direction of change. Lowered (e) is the only advanced variant in the entire corpus whose occurrence is favored by emphatic stress and length (see table 4.11). It is also the only variable

Table 5.11 Combinations of gender and category constraints in Belten High

	Jocks > burnouts	*Mixed*	*Burnouts > jocks*
Female > male	(e) lowering	(aeh)	(o), (oh)
Mixed		(ʌ) fronting	(e) backing (ay) raising (ʌ) backing
Male > female			(ay) monoph. negation

for which the social constraints outweigh the internal constraints in the regression. Thus this links the female lead to the clearest case of what one might call a "prestige" (or more aptly, "anti-vernacular") variant. Negative concord, on the other hand, is unquestionably the most consciously stigmatized of the variables in this study. While I would argue that most claims of women's general conservatism are exaggerated, there is overwhelming evidence that women are more conservative than men in general in their use of grammatical variables (Eckert 1997a). These two variables, then, represent the extremes of social meaning in this study: the most consciously vernacular variant (negative concord) and the most consciously anti-vernacular variant ((e) lowering) can serve as benchmarks for consideration of the relation between gender and social category. However, it should be kept in mind that they represent the extremes and while they can frame the discussion of gender they do not tell the whole story.

Another way of viewing the pattern shown in table 5.10 is shown in table 5.11. In gender correlations and social category correlations, there are variables in which each dichotomous group (male–female, jock–burnout) leads across the board and there are variables in which the relation is mixed (e.g. girls lead among burnouts but boys lead among jocks). Table 5.11 plots these categorizations, with the nature of the correlation with social category across the horizontal axis and the nature of the correlation with gender across the vertical axis. Thus a variable in the upper left hand cell (in this case (e) lowering) is a variable for which girls lead in the use of extreme variants among both jocks and burnouts, and in which jocks lead in the use of extreme variants among both girls and boys. The criterion for placing a variable in a corner cell is that at least one of the correlations in each case be statistically significant. In other words, in order for a variable to appear in the column defined by jocks > burnouts, the jocks must lead the burnouts in the use of the extreme variant of that variable both among the boys and among the girls, and the correlation must have a significance level better than .050 in at least one of the two cases. If the category relation is not the same in both gender groups, or if it is the same but not statistically significant in at least one case, the variable will be listed as "mixed." This table differs from the patterns shown in figures 5.5–10 because they take into consideration the consistency of gender and social category relations rather than their overall statistical significance.

The social use of all the variables in table 5.11 falls along the upper right diagonal of the table, so that three cells are never filled: the intersections of a male lead and a jock lead. While all cells that include a female lead are filled, the only male lead cell that is filled is the one that intersects with a burnout lead. The female lead shows no such specialization, and certainly does not show a tendency to bundle in the cells diagonally opposite the male lead cell. That is, boys favor variables in which burnouts lead, but girls do not favor variables in which jocks lead; on the contrary, the one female lead cell that contains two variables is at the burnout lead end. Thus while there is evidence that boys avoid non-vernacular variants, there is no evidence that girls seek non-vernacular variants or avoid vernacular variants. While girls may be more conservative in the use of the most stigmatized variable (negative concord) and the most frequent users of the clearest "prestige" variable (e lowering), the rest of the variables do not support an overall view of girls as conservative or "prestige oriented". While a few variables may show an overall conservative female pattern, most variables show tremendous diversity among girls. It is this diversity above all that characterizes the girls' speech, contrasting with boys' relatively smaller intra-gender differentiation. With the exception of (e) lowering, monophthongization, and negative concord, girls show greater dispersion for all variables, as shown in the standard deviations for each gender group (table 5.12).

The most consistent gender-related pattern across variables is the relation between the social categories within gender groups – between jock and burnout girls on the one hand, and jock and burnout boys on the other. With the sole exception of (aeh), whenever female burnouts lead female jocks, male burnouts lead male jocks; and whenever female jocks lead female burnouts, male jocks lead male burnouts. The degree of gender differentiation within either category, however, may vary sufficiently to prevent an across-the-board social category corrrelation. I have argued elsewhere (Eckert 1990b, 1997a) that the primary importance of gender lies not in dif-

Table 5.12 Mean values and standard deviations for each variable by gender group

	Girls		Boys	
	Mean	*Standard deviation*	*Mean*	*Standard deviation*
(aeh)	.474	.126	.313	.110
(o)	.389	.161	.217	.115
(oh)	.329	.216	.107	.120
(ʌ) backing	.426	.122	.451	.111
(e) backing	.383	.157	.365	.098
(ay) raising	.015	.054	.020	.043
monoph.	.059	.064	.117	.081
negation	.151	.225	.255	.324
(ʌ) fronting	.047	.050	.037	.045
(e) lowering	.053	.037	.029	.040

ferences between male and female across the board, but in differences within gender groups. In developing patterns of behavior, in assessing their own place in the world, and in evaluating their progress, people orient above all to their own gender group. Gender creates such a profound identity divide that while people may be able to compare individual skills and, rarely, characteristics across gender lines, such an assessment of the whole self is difficult. Furthermore, a general constraint against competition across gender lines leads people to compete, hence evaluate themselves, within their gender group. A teenage jock girl does not measure her social success in relation to male jocks; a burnout girl does not measure her coolness in relation to male burnouts; a male jock does not measure his athletic ability in relation to female jocks. And while there is no question that people contrast themselves to the other gender, I would argue that they do it with reference to their own gender group.

The relation between gender and social category in relation to language use lies in differences in how boys and girls go about being jocks and burnouts. The constraint on jock girls to be squeaky clean seems to be reflected in their across-the-board lag in the use of Pattern 2 and 3 variables, all of which are associated entirely with burnouts (Pattern 2) or partially with burnouts (Patterns 3, 3a). By the same logic, the burnout boys' lag in the use of Pattern 1 variables suggests that they, in turn, are constrained to avoid variables associated with girls. Many have speculated that certain men's low rate of use of "women's" variables is a function of their eagerness to differentiate their speech from that of women. Haeri's (1997) discussion of palatalization in Cairene Arabic offers a very strong argument against this view of gender difference, supported by data on a very clearly "female" and potentially "feminine" variable which is used by very non-stereotypical women and very "masculine" men. I would follow Haeri in arguing that if some boys are avoiding female-identified Pattern 1 and 1a variants, what they're avoiding is some characteristic associated with girls rather than simply femininity. This is supported by the fact, similar to Haeri's case, that while girls may dominate in the use of Pattern 1 variables, there is no evidence that these variables are avoided by boys who wish to foster a "masculine" image. If Pattern 1 variables were simply associated with femininity, then one might expect jock and burnout boys to avoid their use equally. This is true in the case of (o), but the jocks have a noticeably higher level of use for (aeh) than burnout boys. It is still possible that boys are avoiding variants that will detract from a "masculine" image, but only if one keeps in mind that there are many kinds and aspects of masculinity. By the same token, if the Pattern 1 variables simply connote feminity, it remains to be explained why the burnout girls make greater use of them across the board than jock girls. Certainly traditional femininity involves the kind of obedience and squeaky cleanness embraced by the jock girls, so if femininity is what is driving girls in the use of Pattern 1 variables, the burnouts are embracing a kind of femininity that has so far not been identified – and that I will discuss in following chapters. What will become clear is that "feminine" and "masculine" are constituted of characteristics and behaviors that have meaning independent of gender (Ochs, 1991).

5.4   The Geographic Context

The patterns that emerge in Neartown are not isolated, but fall into a wider social and geographic pattern within the urban–suburban continuum. The original intention in collecting the geographic sample was to plot the distribution of variables, and trace the spread of change, in the urban–suburban area of Detroit. For this reason, I selected communities to the north and the west of Detroit, and close in to and farther out from the city. The relation between urban and social geography, however, complicates the purely spatial interpretation, because each school has a distinct social makeup, resulting in a distinct social category situation. These social differences also have an interesting relation to the data of variation.

Along the western axis is Neartown at some remove from Detroit, and Urban City, which lies near the western boundary of Detroit. Urban City is a solid working class community, but with enough of a middle class presence to create noticeable socioeconomic differences between jocks and burnouts. There were distinct territories in school, and the opposition was similar to that in Neartown. However, because of its overall higher socio-economic level, Neartown was a well-known destination for the upwardly mobile segments of border cities like Urban City. As a result, there were a number of kids in Belten High who had been born in Urban City. Those who moved to Neartown after elementary school sometimes found it difficult to fit in – one burnout who moved from Urban City in junior high told me that he had been a jock in Urban City, but since a jock there acted and looked more like a burnout at Belten, he had been unable to fit in with the Belten jocks.

Crane City is a relatively small suburb, located directly to the north of Detroit. At the time of this research, the population of Crane City was suf-fering considerable financial stress because of automobile plant closures, and there was a fairly high unemployment rate. This was reflected in a high level of stress among the students themselves and the considerable care that the school was taking to deal with it. A number of kids were living with friends, because their parents' financial stress was creating unbearable family difficulties, both financial and emotional. Others were striking out on their own. The school had been gradually reworking its practice in order to provide a safe place for kids, and a number of kids who were on their own were coming to school and possibly finding their only square meal there. The nurturing attitude of school adults was reflected as well in the student population, where there was less conflict between social categories than I'd seen in any of the other schools. The Crane City population is more homo-geneous, and the socioeconomic differences between jocks and burnouts are not as extreme as in any of the other schools, and in keeping with this rel-ative homogeneity, the split between jocks and burnouts at Crane City High had a different quality from the other schools. The social distance between the two categories was smaller, the jocks and the burnouts knew each other, and rather than manifesting much hostility to each other, they considered each other to have different interests, perhaps to be somewhat misled. The closer relation between jocks and burnouts was also aided by the relatively small size of the school. Some of the jocks, however, felt that the low socioeconomic level of their school was depriving them of an optimal institutional experience. Attendance at regional events had brought home to them the fact that more affluent schools provide opportunities for jocks to engage in more, and more sophisticated, activities than their school, and they feared that they would not be able to compete with people from such schools in college.

Athens, unlike Neartown, Urban City, and Crane City, is a new suburb. It is near the extreme northern rural edge of the suburban area, where rapid building and expansion of the suburban area has juxtaposed an affluent yuppy population to the community's fairly depressed working class rural population. The jock–burnout opposition in Athens High School involved a far more extreme socioeconomic opposition than in any of the other schools. The economic differences were stark, and underlined a conscious oppposition between old and new, and urban and rural, residents. And while many of the jocks spent their summers in Europe and were headed to elite colleges, many of the burnouts had friends and relatives in prison and were preoccupied with very different concerns than travel and college. The distance between the two was emphasized in the school by the physical isolation of many of the burnouts in the separate building that housed the support program for at-risk students.

With a few exceptions, the variables examined for Neartown show statistically significant social correlations across the suburban sample. Figures 5.11–19 show the percentage use of advanced variants by town and social category for each of the phonological variables. In these figures, the solid lines and symbols represent the towns that are at the suburban end of the geographic array (referred to hereafter as suburban schools), and the dotted lines and empty symbols represent the towns at the urban end (which I will refer to as urban schools). Circles represent the northern suburbs and squares represent the southern suburbs.

Two of the Pattern 2 variables in Belten are sufficiently more advanced in the urban area to be unequivocally considered "urban variables." Overall (ay) raising, shown in figure 5.11, is more advanced in the urban schools than the suburban ones, and common raising is socially salient in the other schools, while only extreme raising is salient in Belten. Nonetheless, it is clear that overall raising is higher in the urban schools, where it is male-led across the board, but with no consistent social category pattern. It is notable that although burnout girls lag behind burnout boys in overall raising to a tiny extent in Crane City, and although they lag behind jock girls as well in Urban City, the use of extreme raising (figure 5.12) tells a different story. Burnout girls in Crane City lead the rest of their cohort overwhelmingly in the use of extreme raising, and in Urban City, the burnout girls remain behind the burnout boys but lead the jocks in the use of extreme raising. This suggests a pattern more similar to that in Neartown, where extreme raising has special status. Extreme raising involves more backing and

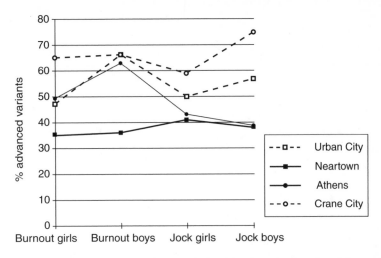

Figure 5.11   Percent common + extreme (ay) raising by suburb and social category

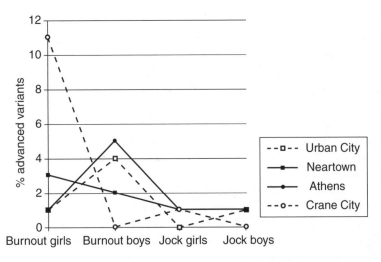

Figure 5.12   Percent (ay) extreme raising by suburb and social category

lip rounding, and stands out from common raising. Thus a relatively infrequent use of extreme variants may well be more noticeable than the more frequent use of common raising. This raises a question about the relation between quantity and quality in variation, which will be discussed further in chapter 8.

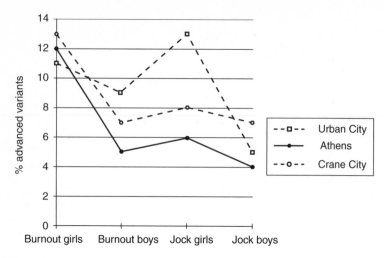

Figure 5.13 Percent advanced variants of (e) backing by suburb and social category

While Belten (e) backing cannot be included in the geographic sample (as discussed in chapter 4), the figures for the urban communities (figure 5.13) show a lead over Athens in the use of advanced variants for this variable. (e) backing shows Pattern 2 in Crane City, and something approaching Pattern 1a (due to the high usage of jock girls) in Urban City. If one considers the northern and western suburbs separately, the remaining Pattern 2 variable, (ʌ) backing, shows an urban lead, particularly in the western suburbs (figure 5.14). Belten's burnouts' lead in (ʌ) backing is magnified in the urban schools. In Urban City, this is expanded with an additional male lead, creating a Pattern 3a variable, with boys and burnouts leading across the board. The boys in all three schools far exceed the Belten boys in their use of advanced variants. On the other hand, the Urban City jock girls dip way below the rest of the Urban City speakers, and are even more conservative in their use of extreme variants than the Belten jock girls. Athens shows Pattern 3, while Crane City shows Pattern 2, with the urban–suburban difference occurring only among the burnout girls. The Crane City burnout girls are the most extreme speakers in their cohort by far for all these urban variables except common raising.

The status of Belten High's Pattern 2 variables as urban variables establishes the link between burnout speech and urban speech. The mixture of male and burnout leads among these communities further confirms a link

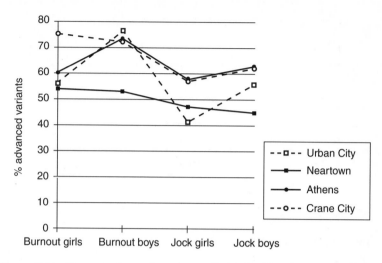

Figure 5.14 Percent advanced variants of (ʌ) backing by suburb and social category

Table 5.13 Combinations of gender and category constraints for urban variables across the suburbs: (e) backing, (ʌ) backing, (ay) raising

	Jocks > burnouts	*Mixed*	*Burnouts > jocks*
Female > male		**(e) Urban City**	**(ay) Athens** **(e) Athens** **(ʌ) Crane City** (e) Crane city
Mixed			**(ay) Urban City** **(ay) Neartown** **(e) Neartown** **(ʌ) Neartown**
Male > female		**(ay) Crane City**	**(ʌ) Urban City** (ʌ) Athens

between male speech and urban speech. Table 5.13 is similar to table 5.11 above, showing the gender and category patterns for each of the urban variables, all of which show Pattern 2 in Belten. The bolded variables are those that show statistical significance for at least some social variable. What is

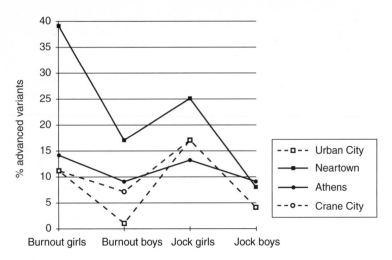

Figure 5.15   Percent advanced variants of (oh) by suburb and social category

most striking about this table is that there are no urban variables in which jocks lead burnouts in the use of advanced variants. And while the male lead, as in table 5.11, corresponds with a burnout lead, most of the variables show either a female or a mixed gender lead. Both the figures and table 5.13 show clearly that burnout girls are quite commonly in the lead in the use of urban variables.

Across the schools, burnouts lead in the use of advanced variants of urban variables in all but two cases. The exceptions are Urban City (e) backing, in which girls lead but the category is mixed, and Crane City (ay) in which boys lead but the category is mixed. The mixed status of the category difference is due to a low statistical significance for a burnout lead among both boys and girls. In the case of Crane City (ay) raising, the jock boys are the clear leaders in the cohort in the use of advanced variables, and the burnout lead among the girls is negligible. It comes close, therefore, to filling the lower left hand cell.

While the Belten High Pattern 2 variables are more advanced in the urban communities, most of the Pattern 1 variables are either more advanced in the suburbs or spread evenly throughout the area. Three variables, (oh), (o), and (ʌ) fronting, show a suburban lead. (oh) shows the same female lead as Neartown across the board (figure 5.15). However, the two urban communities show a reversal of the jock–burnout pattern, with the jock girls leading the other groups. (oh) is clearly a suburban variable, and it is notable

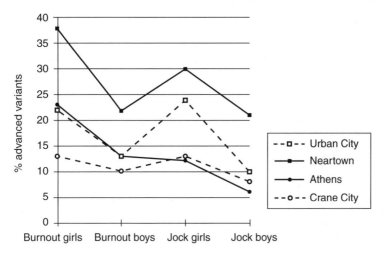

Figure 5.16 Percent advanced variants of (o) by suburb and social category

that the jock girls in the urban schools take a clear lead in the use of advanced variants in their schools and that these urban jock girls are the only group to use these variants at the same level as any group of suburban speakers. It is possible that speakers in the urban schools are sensitive to the suburban lead in this variable, and that the jock girls, feeling their jock status threatened by their involvement in less affluent, hence less "active" schools, are using suburban variants as a way of enhancing their jock identification.

(o) (figure 5.16) also shows a suburban lead, if one takes the northern and western suburbs separately. As in the case of (oh), the jock girls in the urban schools lead their cohorts, once again suggesting that speakers in these urban communities are sensitive to the suburban lead.

If we continue to consider the northern and western suburbs separately, (e) lowering and (ʌ) fronting are also suburban variables (figures 5.17–18). It is important to point out, however, that the very small rates of occurrence of these variables, particularly of (e) lowering, make any interpretation of these patterns extremely tentative. The jock lead in both of these variables that was found in Belten High is continued for the most part in the other schools.

Table 5.14 shows an array similar to tables 5.11 and 5.13 for the suburban variables. Unlike the previous two, this one shows some variables in the lower left diagonal half. However, it is notable that every cell below the top

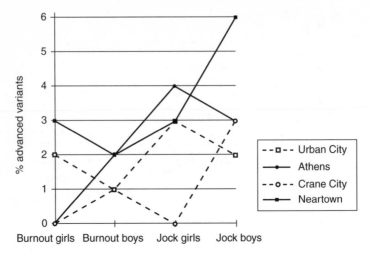

Figure 5.17 Percent (ʌ) fronting by suburb and social category

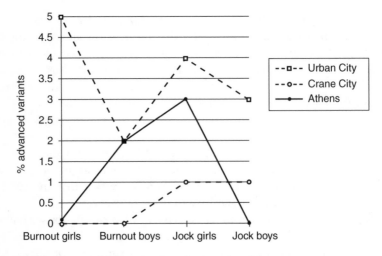

Figure 5.18 Percent (e) lowering by suburb and social category

row contains exclusively the reversals of the urban changes (e) and (ʌ) backing. Of these, only half show statistical significance, and given the relatively low rates in all cases, it is possible that this distribution reflects an unsettled pattern. Also, these figures are not controlled for internal constraints. However, I will not dismiss these cells, but simply point to the fact

Table 5.14 Combinations of gender and category constraints for suburban variables across the suburbs: (o), (oh), and (ʌ) fronting

	Jocks > burnouts	*Mixed*	*Burnouts > jocks*
Female > male	(e) Neartown (oh) Urban City (ʌ) Urban City	(o) Crane City (oh) Crane City (oh) Athens (o) Neartown (e) Urban City	(o) Athens (oh) Neartown
Mixed	(ʌ) Athens	(ʌ) Neartown (e) Crane City (e) Athens	
Male > female		(ʌ) Crane City	

that while the overwhelming pattern continues to exclude the combination of male and jock leads, these new reactions to urban changes, or "prestige" variants, do not appear to be necessarily female property.

(e) lowering (figure 5.18) shows a clear suburban lead in the north, but since we cannot compare the western suburbs, and since Urban City leads Athens in lowering, I recognize that its assignment to the suburban category is somewhat problematic. (aeh) shows a completely mixed pattern, with an urban lead in the northern suburbs, and a mixed lead in the west (figure 5.19). Urban City and Athens's pattern 2 contrasts with Neartown and Crane City's pattern 1 and 1a.

Monophthongization (figure 5.20) is not a clear urban or suburban variable in either the western or the northern suburbs. Within the communities, boys, burnouts, or both lead in the use of extreme variants. In Crane City, monophthongization shows Pattern 2, with burnouts leading, and with girls leading within each of the social categories. In all the other communities, the boys lead the girls across the board in the use of monophthongization, and in Athens and Urban City, the burnouts lead the jocks as well, yielding Pattern 3.

Table 5.15 displays these two variables, which continue to favor the upper right half, with the exception of the one case in the entire corpus that falls in the lower left cell, the monophthongization of (ay) in Athens.

Table 5.16 is another representation of the geographic relations among the patterns in the four suburbs, this time focusing on the patterns across

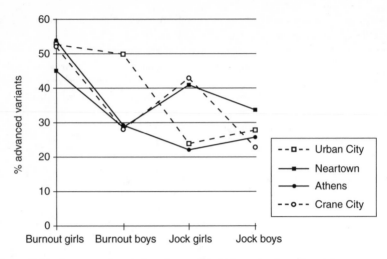

Figure 5.19   Percent advanced variants of (aeh) by suburb and social category

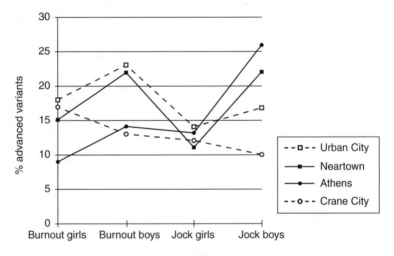

Figure 5.20   Percent (ay) monophthongization by suburb and social category

suburbs. The table shows that while the pattern of a given variable may differ across suburbs, there are constraints on that differentiation. No variable shows all patterns. Furthermore, while a given variable may show a female lead (Pattern 1) in one community and a burnout lead (Pattern 2) in another, or a male lead in one community and a burnout lead in another, no

Table 5.15 Combinations of gender and category constraints for generalized variables across the suburbs: (aeh), (ay) monophthongization, (e) lowering

	Jocks > burnouts	*Mixed*	*Burnouts > jocks*
Female > male		**(aeh) Neartown** **(aeh) Crane City**	(ay) Crane City
Mixed		**(ay) Urban City**	**(aeh) Athens** **(aeh) Urban City**
Male > female	(ay) Athens	**(ay) Neartown**	

Table 5.16 Variable patterns across the suburban schools

	Urban City	*Crane City*	*Athens*	*Neartown*	
(e) lowering					Suburban
(ʌ) fronting					Suburban
(o) fronting					Suburban
(oh) fronting					Suburban
(aeh) raising					Mixed
(e) backing					Urban
(ʌ) backing					Urban
(ay) raising					Urban
(ay) monoph					Mixed

☐ Pattern 1b: Jocks lead
▨ Pattern 1: Girls lead
▩ Pattern 2: Burnouts lead
■ Pattern 3: Boys lead

variable shows a female lead in one community and a male lead in another. Finally, except in the highly insignificant case of (e) backing in Crane City, a jock lead combines only with a female lead across suburbs.

As we move down from suburban to urban variables in table 5.16, the pattern combinations shift from 1a, 1, and 2, to 2 and 3. The association between urban, burnout, and male status in the social meanings of variation, therefore, is clear, as is the association between suburban, jock, and female status. However, while the male, urban, and burnout association is quite stark, the female-led variables run the gamut from jock to burnout, and from suburban to urban to mixed.

5.5   Jock, Burnout, Urban, Suburban, Male, Female

The findings of this chapter indicate a relation between the use of variables in a given community and their distribution in the urban–suburban continuum, integrating gender and social category in the process.

Two main geographic patterns have emerged in this examination of patterns of variation in the wider suburban area. The newer sound changes, (e) and (ʌ) backing and (ay) raising, are more advanced closer to the urban center. If one takes these geographic patterns to be evidence of geographic spread, then these new changes appear to be spreading outward into the suburbs from the urban center. And in schools across the suburban area, burnouts are leading locally in these changes. This could be taken as an indication of greater access to these changes stemming from the burnouts' urban-oriented life style. It can also be taken as an indication that these urban-led changes have urban-related social meaning that gives them positive symbolic value for burnouts, and possibly negative symbolic value for jocks. At the opposite extreme, the reversals of (e) and (ʌ) backing are more advanced in the suburban than the urban schools, suggesting that they are suburban in origin. And in each suburb, jocks lead in the use of advanced variants, suggesting that the suburban, or non-urban, association has positive symbolic value for jocks and negative value for burnouts. While social category is the major factor in the use of the new changes and their reversals, gender comes into play as well. Jock girls lead in the use of the suburban variables, while depending on the suburb, burnout boys or burnout girls may lead in the use of the urban variables. Thus one could claim an association between female and suburban, and male and urban, but this is only true to the extent that it is mediated by social category.

The association of burnouts and urban variables, and jocks and suburban variables, sets up an opposition of social meaning that appears to be at work in the older changes as well. These changes show a more variable geographic pattern. The intermediate change in the NCCS, (oh) fronting, shows a suburban lead, while the older (o) and (aeh) fronting show no overall urban lead. With no strong urban symbolic value, older changes may be eligible for some negotiation in social value. These older changes show greater variability in social use across the suburbs than the newer changes, but one pattern that stands out is that girls lead across the board in the use of all of them. The non-urban significance of these variables shows up in the fact that in the urban schools it is the jock girls who lead their entire cohort in the use of (oh) and (o), while the burnout girls lead in the suburban schools. This suggests that these variables have lost their urban symbolic value in the urban center. (aeh) raising, on the other hand, is led by girls, but by burnout girls. In the northern suburbs, this is clearly a burnout variable, while in the western suburbs it is not. There is sufficient variability in the patterns across the suburbs to prevent delicate conclusions about the relation between the age of a change and its geographic and social distribution in the older changes. The newer changes have a very clear urban–suburban significance, which is no doubt related to the urban spread of the changes and probably to age differences within communities as well. The greater variability of the older changes suggests that as changes lose stark geographic and age differences, and hence their value as an urban adolescent symbol, they become more fluid in their symbolic potential, showing greater local variability in use.

We can conclude from these data that gender in variation is not about being "male" or "female" so much as about being a male or female jock or burnout in a particular place in the urban–suburban continuum. And when we look at it from this perspective, one of the most striking findings of this chapter is the fact, and the nature, of boys' conservatism. Boys lead in the use of very few variables across the suburbs, and girls lead their cohorts overall more than boys in the use of advanced variants in urban, suburban, and mixed variables. In those cases where boys do lead, it is almost exclusively in the case of urban variables, and girls are the exclusive leaders in the use of suburban variables. This draws a picture of male speech as both conservative and vernacular. Female gender, on the other hand, corresponds to greater use of advanced variants of all kinds, and in two ways. In the case of suburban variables, all girls tend to make high use of advanced variants. In the case of urban variables, girls make greater use of the variables by displaying a greater category difference, with burnout girls taking a large lead over jock girls. Gender, then, has to do not only with differences in rates of use between male and female, but with the kind of differences within groups.

In the next chapter, we return to Belten High, in order to explore further the use of variables, this time across the broader student population. The purpose is to transcend the category view of variation and prod at the possibility that at least some of these variables are related to the aspects of social practice that permeate the school and that contribute to, as well as derive from, the significance of the social categories.

Notes

1   It is interesting to note, as an aside, that when the father's educational level is lower (4 and below), the mother's educational level can be higher; but men with an educational level of 5 or over all have wives with the same educational level or lower. This middle class pattern, admittedly based on a small and unrepresentative sample, appears to illustrate the kind of pairing that Goffman (1976, 1977) discusses as part of the reproduction of the gender order. The systematic pairing of larger men with smaller women masks the actual size range of the sexes, confirming the belief that women are indeed the "weaker sex" and maximizing the physical power differential between men and women as well. A similar pairing of women with men who are older, earn more, and are more educated, foregrounds other aspects of the gender order.

2   *ni* marked in a cell indicates that the factor group in question is not included in the analysis represented in the table.

6

We Are What We Do

If linguistic variables are simply indices of category membership, one could expect category members to stand out in the population by their conformity to category-related linguistic patterns. On the other hand, if the variables are more generally related to the practices and orientations associated with the polar categories, then one might expect similarities of speech among people engaging in similar practices regardless of their category affiliation. Expanding the corpus to include a diverse set of in-betweens provides a more textured analysis of the use of the variables in relation to speakers' engagement in the practices that constitute the Belten High adolescent social order.

Table 6.1 shows the results of the analysis of the variables, with the in-betweens included as a residual category. The in-betweens pattern differently in relation to the jocks and burnouts from one variable to another, in some cases falling in between, but usually lagging behind the jocks. This should not be surprising because in-betweens in this linguistic sample were not selected according to particular characteristics they shared with jocks or burnouts, but according to their place in the overall social network. It is only when we break open the categories and examine the kinds of behavior that constitute the categories that we can compare the in-betweens with the jocks and the burnouts. At this point, then, we turn from a focus on what people are to what they do – from their affiliation with categories to their participation in practices.

6.1 Forms of Engagement

Students spend about six of the best hours of each weekday in school. Some of them remain for several hours after school, engaged in extracurricular activities, and some of them spend several hours on homework. The school's

Table 6.1 All variables by gender and social category. Jocks, burnouts, and in-betweens

Variable	Girls	Boys	Burnouts	In-betweens	Jocks	Input	Sig.
(ae)	.571	.420				.376	.000
(o)	.583	.410				.277	.000
(oh)	.646	.355	.631	.441	.456	.163	.002
(ʌ) backing			.564	.467	.476	.434	.000
(ʌ) fronting			.338	.552	.596	.080	.000
(e) backing			.602	.409	.506	.400	.000
(e) lowering	.585	.424	.473	.461	.563	.082	.035
(ay) raising			.706	.503	.256	.010	.000
monoph.	.419	.587	.561	.421	.530	.058	.008
negation	.431	.587	.786	.344	.399	.160	.000

▓ Secondary social constraint

"ideal" participant can easily spend 11 or 12 hours a day on school-related activities, making school an intensive full-time enterprise. It is not unknown for particularly zealous students to suffer extreme stress and even breakdowns. These are the prototypical institutional beings of the adolescent age group. The school's least enthusiastic participant, on the other hand, can get away with spending as few as four or five hours a day in school, and with the absolute minimum required number of days of attendance. And many of these people limit their time in school in anticipation of pursuing friendships and interests outside of the school. Most of the student body falls between these two extremes, but wherever they fall, they are participants in the school community, and their choices constitute a negotiation of a place within that community.

It is not surprising, then, that the most important differences within the school reside in the extent to which students involve themselves in the institution, and the ways in which they appropriate school resources to their own ends. It is around these issues that the fundamental opposition arises between the jocks and the burnouts in school, as they define the two extremes of school engagement. The jock–burnout opposition emerges in every moment spent in and out of school. Jocks and burnouts on the whole spend their time differently, use the school building differently, use the local area outside of school differently, and have different kinds of relations with school personnel and each other. Jocks and burnouts utilize just about every resource in and out of the school to construct their mutual opposition: space, movement, demeanor, adornment, participation, consumption, human relations. Ultimately, these differences construct an opposition between the global and the local, the institutional and the personal, the corporate and the non-corporate, the middle and the working class. The jocks' and burnouts' engagement in opposing linguistic markets is most clearly illustrated in their differential use of institutional and local resources.

The school insulates students from the surrounding area, first of all by providing an encompassing array of social, artistic, and athletic activities that eliminates the necessity of looking to the local (and adult) sphere for opportunities to participate in such activities. The school also brokers many relations to the local environment, organizing charitable activities (such as canned food drives) in such a way that students do not come into contact with the beneficiaries of the charity; and serving as gatekeepers to outside constituencies wanting to gain contact with high school students (such as local businesses or the local police wanting to organize programs for youth). The school brokers students' mobility as well. The choir, the band, and sports teams travel for performances and competitions; cheerleaders and teams go to training camps; student government representatives go to conferences. In this way, relations beyond Neartown are mediated by the school, and students travel not as individuals but as representatives of Belten High, encountering other students as representatives of their schools, and under adult supervision. When jocks go to Detroit on their own, it is to the city's institutions – Tiger Stadium, Cobo Hall, the Renaissance Center – and not to dally on the city's streets or in its parks. Thus the jocks' engagement in the local and urban area is first and foremost an institutional engagement, rather than a personal exploration. It is just this adult-organized and supervised existence that burnouts seek to avoid.

6.2   Urban Engagement

While the jocks stay in school at the end of the day, participating in activities and athletic practice, the burnouts exit to public areas far from school. By hanging out at local street corners, bowling alleys, fast food restaurants, and roller rinks, kids in the suburbs can take possession of the local area, transforming public spaces into meaningful adolescent resources. Within Neartown, the local parks and elementary school yards that dot the residential areas provide places where kids can gather outside of school and away from adult supervision. The neighborhoods and main streets of

Neartown merge into adjacent suburbs, and ultimately into Detroit City, and each park has its own character, which in turn is related to its proximity to the urban center. Hines Park, meandering through several western suburbs from Northville to Detroit, is a conduit linking the western suburbs and Detroit. Edward Hines Drive, which stretches through the park, creates a good cruising route, passing through various spots frequented by high school kids throughout the area, where kids can meet people from other places or simply hang out together with a more open atmosphere. Hines is a major resource for suburban kids, whether they go there to find their local friends or to meet kids from other schools and towns; and whether they go there just to hang out and party, or to cruise the Drive. Smaller parks within the suburban area, each with its own reputation, also contribute to the cruising and hangout landscape. A park at the border of Detroit is a favorite with some, known for frequent police visits, and for the wild crowd it attracts:

> *Lucy*: That's a place to go.
> *Judy*: A lot of guys. Wooo.
> *Lucy*: Not a place – not a place to pick up guys, though.
> *Penny*: Why not?
> *Judy*: There's too many. God, now, I was with this guy, and uh they're crawling in my car. They're animals. (laughter)
> *Lucy*: (laughing) They are, they are.
> *Judy*: They're crawling in my windows, going, "Buy some quaaludes?" I'm going, "God!"

As kids move into adolescence, there is increasing pressure to get to know people, to gain access to people, activities, places, information. The kid in school who has positive access to large numbers of desirable contacts will be the most desirable for others to know, and the production of an outgoing personality is an important process for those who intend to gain status in junior high. While jocks report an emphasis on getting to know as many people as possible in school, and particularly getting to know the people who were important in their own elementary and junior high schools, burnouts report an emphasis on getting to know the people who were the cool partiers in their previous schools, who have contact with people in the upper grades and beyond the school as well, and who know how to get around outside of school. The burnouts' local orientation is not an orientation solely to the neighborhood, and certainly not to Neartown itself. Growing out of an eagerness for local access, it involves access to the resources of the greater Detroit urban–suburban area. For the adolescent, these resources may include automotive and auto body expertise and supplies, after-school jobs, bars that serve minors, pool halls, skating rinks, parks, concerts, parties, excitement, and people who in turn have access to these and to other kinds of urban knowledge and resources.

Urban orientation in the Detroit suburban area is an extension of neighborhood orientation. Neartown has no downtown and few attractions, and neighborhoods of close-to-identical houses are interspersed with strip malls and parks. Kids complain that there is no place to go, and nothing to do – that there is no town center to attract people and to lend local character. When I drive kids home, they often joke about not being able to find their houses, or about the elusive details that distinguish their house from those that surround it: "You can't miss my house – it's the one with the yellow door." Part of the Neartown culture, it seems, is to joke about Neartown's inadequacies as a community. Some students speak nostalgically about the small towns their grandparents live in – communities with real downtowns – as if they were, like their grandparents, part of the gentle past. And however the kids may complain, many of their parents apparently like the homogeneity, and Neartown has affordable housing, it is safe, and it is known for its good school system.

The homogeneity of Neartown is in keeping with the lack of visible borders throughout the area, and the adolescent residents of Neartown must either live with the homogeneity or imbue the area with their own meaning. The transformation of the local area into adolescent social geography does not have the blessing of area adults and officials, and the constant police presence and watchfulness in parks has both annoyance and excitement value for those who hang out there. Because there are no legitimate places for kids to hang out in the local area, the general adolescent appropriation of public space is, broadly speaking, illegitimate, and this illegitimacy is closely tied with other aspects of adolescent social and linguistic practice.

To a great extent, this urban–suburban continuum was created during the boom of the automobile industry by a southern migration into Detroit, and a white migration outwards from it. It puts the Detroit area among the racially most volatile and segregated places in the country. The racialization of space in the Detroit area is fundamental to life in Neartown, ever-present in the fact that many of the residents of Neartown migrated from Detroit in flight from the growing African American population. Racism is a constant presence at Belten High, as kids variously indulge in it, accuse others of it, try to overcome it, worry about it. For many, the city of Detroit is synonymous with African American ghetto, frightening, dangerous, and almost foreign. And for many, it is also a place where white people survive by virtue of sheer toughness and urban smarts. Orientation towards Detroit, which ranges from complete avoidance to regular familiarity, constitutes an important difference among kids in Belten High. In the population of any suburban area, important differences are created around attitudes towards the urban center: the use of its cultural resources and other public attractions, its economic resources, and integration into its day-to-day personal life. For all kids at Belten, Detroit is a frightening and dangerous place, but for some the various attractions of the urban center are worth the risk. And the danger itself can attract as well as repel.

Detroit is ever-present, perhaps above all in family discourses and in the continual immigration of Detroiters to Neartown and into the schools. Each new Detroiter who comes to the school brings encounters between urban and suburban. Considered a move up, the higher socioeconomic status of Neartown emerges in new kids' adjustments. While a number of jocks have moved from Detroit since elementary school, many kids say that it is difficult for those who arrive after junior high to "make it" in the jock crowd. One reason is that the jock hierarchy is relatively tight by high school. But also, the newcomer may not fit in because of the socioeconomic/stylistic difference within the urban–suburban area. Inasmuch as the students in each school assimilate towards the socioeconomic style of the significant mass, a jock in a school closer to Detroit will, in some ways, resemble a burnout in a school deeper in the suburbs. While jocks in the wealthier areas simply say that the jocks in the more urban schools are really burnouts, jocks in those more urban schools are aware that they don't have the style or some of the skills that would allow them to fit in in a wealthier school. One boy who moved to Neartown in junior high from Urban City describes his first impression of Belten High students:

> All these short haired kids. My hair was long, it was really long, you know, and these people were, "well get your hair cut," you know. And they all had these Nike tennis shoes on. And that's what I remember. Nike tennis shoes. So, I went home and said, "Mom, screw these Trax tennis shoes, I got to get some Nikes," you know, "We're moving up in the world." (laughter) So I had to get Nike tennis shoes like the rest of them. You know, that's about the thing – they all dressed like way nicer than in Urban City. Urban City was strictly jeans and tee shirts, you know. That's what I remember.

If those coming from Detroit are at a socioeconomic disadvantage, they come with greater "street smarts." The city is known as a tougher, faster environment, and city kids are assumed to be more experienced with such things as violence, danger, drugs, and sex. This kind of knowledge may be advantageous among burnouts, but can be suspect among jocks – particularly for girls. One girl who moved from Detroit to Neartown in junior high found Neartown tame:

Rita: Yeah, they were – they seemed like, I mean, they were playing on – with dolls, you know, and everything, and I'm going, "oh, my God, what did I move into?" That's – that's why my parents wanted to move there, because things were starting to move like a little bit too fast, you know, because they were – if you, if you experience all that too young, what is there to experience when you're older? You know, and then when people get bored –

Penny: You mean, like sex?

Rita: Yeah, and they get bored, and then, what do they do? . . . some people just try and like amass information and all – all these experiences, like that kind of stuff. And they um, that – they – it's like they were in a race, you know, and they took every – all the good points out of everything.

Penny: Mm hm. Yeah. But ah, so, but basically, I guess you found the people here kind of innocent then.

Rita: Mm hm.

Penny: Do you still consider them innocent?

Rita: No. Where we are now is where we were in Detroit at about seventh, no well sixth grade, you know. That's like about the equivalent. And I don't know. Like those people, I never even talk to them any more, because I really don't think I'd get along with them anymore . . . Because I've heard that they've gotten, like my friend Joanie, she um, she dropped out of school, you know, and I talked to her mom on the phone, I just called them up, because I had nothing else to do . . . and I talked to her mom. And I don't think her mom really wanted to reveal too much. Like she wasn't very happy with Joanie. But she goes, "well, at least she's working," you know, and I thought, "hm, you're having trouble with your kid."

This girl's sense that kids grow up too fast in Detroit is amplified in the general sense of Detroit as a place where trouble is a way of life. Another boy, discussing the history of his troubles with his parents and the school, talks about some kids he used to hang out with. For this boy, as for most kids at Belten, the Detroiter, like Detroit, spells trouble:

Dan: What I used to hang around with was a crowd from Detroit, you know. And they were, they were nasty. All of them are dropped out of school now. But I kept my –

Penny: You mean these were guys who lived in Detroit, or who –
Dan: They lived in Detroit and they came – and they moved out here. You
           know, but they always went back down to Detroit, and they did – but I
           always kept, you know, far enough away from that, you know. I was with
           them, but I only went to a certain limit, you know.

He goes on to describe going to Detroit with them on a regular basis to see
their old friends, and he describes their old neighborhood, which he
describes as "nasty":

Dan: Well, you know – busted windows all over the place, boards, you know,
           you know – Detroit. You know the way Detroit is. But uh, you know, it's
           a lot different in Neartown. And I'm glad I grew up in Neartown instead
           of Detroit, you know, because I see the way they were and those guys
           are crazy.
Penny: Really.
Dan: Yeah. They're crazy. They're stop for nothing.
Penny: Really? Why do you suppose that is?
Dan: Because it was harder to cope with in Detroit, you know. It was a lot
           harder. It was more of a chance to get involved in crime, too. And parents
           were more worried about their making it than they were trying to help
           their kids out, too.

Some kids have relatives, friends, old neighborhoods in Detroit that they
visit on a regular basis. A few have part-time jobs in Detroit, or suburban
friends who work in the city. Some go to Detroit for sporting events, some
for the museums, some for parties, some to cruise, and some to rumble.
Going to Detroit to frequent public resources such as museums, Tiger
Stadium, Cobo Hall, the Renaissance Center is considered risky, and some
kids take pride in doing so. Going to Detroit on one's own (as opposed to
with one's parents) to interact with its residents is very different – it signals
a willingness or eagerness to court danger.

In some sense, Detroit is less a precise location than a state of mind,
or a general direction. The urban–suburban continuum defines towns as
more or less "Detroit," and to many, the closer suburbs count as Detroit.
Indeed, the nasty neighborhood that the above speaker describes is not in
Detroit at all, but in a suburb adjacent to Detroit. But ultimately, for the
kids in Neartown as in many other suburbs, Telegraph Road running
north and south through a number of suburbs and crossing the protruding
western reaches of Detroit, is the major urban boundary. Telegraph Road
has particular significance for suburban adolescents, because it is not only

an urban boundary, but also a cruising hub. Many kids negotiate the urban–suburban continuum through a grid of cruising routes, which are well-worn routes among suburbs and into the city. Kids in each high school have a favored Detroitward cruising route, and the routes from all the high schools overlap, providing continuous contact among suburbs and between suburb and city. Figure 6.1, showing the cruising routes frequented by kids in four different high schools around the Detroit area, gives an idea of the nature of the regular movement of teenagers in and out of Detroit. Evenings and weekends see cars racing or moving slowly up and down these streets, pulling into favorite haunts, some seeking people from their own school, some seeking people from other schools. How far one follows these cruising routes into Detroit depends on how daring one is, and how eager one is to extend one's activities beyond the safe world of Neartown and Belten High.

One can also bypass the streets and take the highway through Detroit and directly to the Windsor Bridge. Across the river, in Canada, there are bars that are popular with Michigan adolescents. There, kids can enjoy an adult-like bar atmosphere without Detroit's special urban dangers. These bars are not safe havens – there are fights and other problems, and going to Windsor is considered sophisticated and daring.

The relation between geography and social practice – the association of urbanness with daring and with trouble – connects suburban kids to the broader social and cultural geography of the urban–suburban area. And the continuum of resources from local neighborhood parks to the cruising routes of Telegraph Road weaves local Neartown geography into the broader geography as well. Ideology is built into this geography, as the urban area stands in stark contrast to the school institution. Inasmuch as the urban–suburban continuum provides a powerful merger of social and geographic space, a crucial aspect of social and linguistic identity in this area is tied up with the way in which kids locate themselves and operate in this space. Contact with urban speakers is not simply a matter of accident or a by-product of other activities. Rather, it has strong social meaning for all adolescents living in the suburban area, and the extent and the nature of contact with others living in that area is an integral part of social practice and social identity. Understanding the relation between urban mobility and other aspects of social practice is crucial to understanding the social meaning of variation and the spread of linguistic change in the urban area.

Milroy (1980) has found that dense and multiplex working class networks serve as mechanisms for the maintenance of the vernacular. The resulting

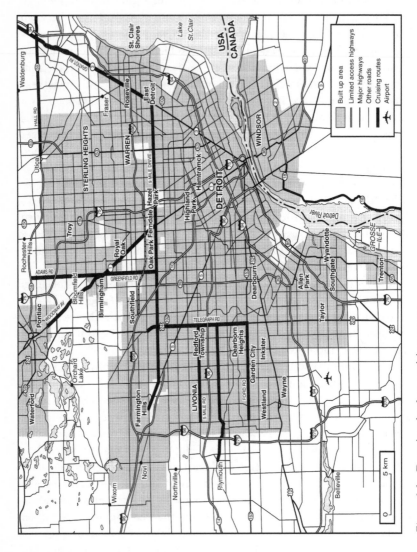

Figure 6.1 Detroit suburban cruising routes

view of these networks as a conservative force has had the effect of opposing participation in dense and multiplex networks to access and receptivity to outside influence. One could come away from this with a view of locally based networks as a kind of a sink, or a limitation to mobility. However, while Milroy's Network Strength Scale assesses the strength of the individual's local ties, it does not preclude important extralocal ties. A person with both strong local and extralocal ties is in a prime position to broker linguistic influence. It is no doubt for this reason that Labov (1990) has found the most innovative speakers in Philadelphia neighborhoods to be those who have substantial contacts both within and beyond the neighborhood.

Local status involves not only solidarity within the immediate area and family and friend networks, but knowledge and contacts in the wider local area. The ability to "get around" the area, knowing people that one can call upon, being able to claim access to resources, involves not only strong immediate ties, but a significant network in the broader local area, into other neighborhoods and into other municipalities. Some emphasis in the sociolinguistic literature (Trudgill 1972) has been placed on toughness as a positive male value associated with working class status and the vernacular. Another important value, for both women and men, is practical technical knowledge – the ability to do things, to fix things, to build things. This ability can come from training in school, observation at home, working with friends, and knowing experts. A person who can deal in the local marketplace is one who knows people who can do things – plumbers, mechanics, electricians, people who are handy – and who can gain access to their work and their skills on an informal basis. People who are not engaged in the local market may have to rely on contractors, or brokers, to coordinate services for them. People who are engaged in the local market are also likely to have knowledge of the kinds of local institutions that facilitate or are problematic in working class life. Knowing how to work the system – the building department, the welfare and unemployment offices, and knowing the people who work there, such as building inspectors, gives crucial knowledge that affords the individual greater independence and local value. The professional who suddenly finds him or herself unemployed will have to talk to the janitor to find out how to deal with the unemployment office. It is important to recognize the role of information and expertise in the local market, and the importance of being able to move around in order to gain first-hand access to information and expertise. Successfully engaged people, therefore, will have to have extensive contacts well beyond the first or even second order zones of their networks. With their emphasis on local engagement, urban-oriented adolescents are not only pursuing excitement, they are laying down a strong basis of local knowledge, experience, and networks. They are learning their way around the urban–suburban area, getting to know the social milieu in which they will function in the workplace, and learning how to act, how to look, and how to talk.

Hines and other parks and cruising strips are not burnout territory. They are urban spaces, partying places, and quite possibly because they are away from the school, they can be claimed independently of school affiliation. They represent adolescent autonomy, adventure, and, to some extent, danger to all the students at Belten, and they draw people regardless of category affiliation. The only category of people at Belten High that does not include regular cruisers is the jock girls.

Cruising, whether it's in Hines or other urban parks (this excludes neighborhood parks in Neartown), or along Telegraph, is a sure sign of urban orientation in Neartown. More kids from Belten go to urban parks than cruise Detroit, for cruising Detroit requires resources that going to a park does not. Above all, cruising requires a car, and gas; but one can hitchhike or bum a ride to a park, and once there, the action is in hanging out rather than being on the move. So while there are many people who go to parks but who do not cruise Detroit, there are few who cruise Detroit but do not go to parks. Both going to parks and cruising Detroit are considered a way of transcending local boundaries, and both represent daring and freedom of association, actively seeking a social life and activity independent of the school, and the excitement of the urban environment.

Table 6.2 shows the variables whose use correlates with urban cruising, which includes frequenting Hines and other parks, and cruising Windsor as well as Detroit. In this analysis, cruisers are the people who regularly pursue leisure activities in urban spaces of the Detroit area that are not reserved for their age group and that are not mediated by institutions. All of the Pattern 2 variables, which are the urban variables, correlate significantly with cruising among both boys and girls. Negative concord also correlates with cruising in both gender groups. Monophthongization, however, continues to show social distinctions among girls only, and, like the other "burnout" variables, correlates with cruising among the girls. The urban practice of cruising, then, is related to the use of "burnout" and urban variables across the population regardless of social category. The non-urban variables also show a more gender-specific relation to cruising. The suburban variable (oh) correlates with cruising but only among the girls. Thus while (oh) fronting is used more by burnouts among the boys as well, it apparently does not have the same urban significance as the Pattern 2 and

Table 6.2 Cruising and six variables

Variable		+Cruising	−Cruising	Input	Sig.
(ʌ) backing	Girls	.563	.458	.422	.000
	Boys	.530	.460	.447	.014
(e) backing	Girls	.544	.464	.331	.029
	Boys	.557	.437	.368	.001
(ay) raising	Girls	.765	.381	.011	.000
	Boys	.636	.295	.009	.004
(ay) monophongization	Girls	.634	405	.036	.000
negative concord	Girls	.777	.294	.106	.000
	Boys	.637	.338	.241	.000
(oh) fronting	Girls	.583	.440	.259	.012
(aeh) raising	Girls	.569	.450	.447	.000
	Boys	.465	.538	.299	.033
(ʌ) fronting	Boys	.419	.606	.027	.009

3 variables. Meanwhile, the suburban variable (ʌ) fronting shows a significant difference among the boys. The strong inverse correlation with cruising further confirms this variable's anti-urban value.

Chapter 5 showed a reverse (but statistically insignificant) pattern in the use of (aeh) raising among boys and girls, with burnout girls leading jock girls and jock boys leading burnout boys. This pattern is magnified in the wider population, as (aeh) raising shows the same reverse effect with cruising among boys and among girls. As shown in table 6.2, girls who cruise lead other girls in the raising of (aeh), while boys who do not cruise lead other boys in the use of the same variable. This is the first evidence of a variable being used in a qualitatively different way by girls and boys. Some of the other variables studied so far have shown girls using fewer advanced variants than boys (Pattern 3) or more (Pattern 1), and some of these variables have shown a greater category difference among girls than boys (Patterns 2 and 3). But in all cases, the category differences among male and among female speakers have been a matter of degree. Only (aeh) has shown a significant difference in direction. This observation builds on the relation found in chapter 5 between gender and category correlations: a relation between female gender and both jock and burnout lead, and a relation between male gender and burnout lead only. While overall the boys are not using the female-dominated variants of (aeh) raising, the burnout boys and

Table 6.3   Cruising and three "burnout" variables. Male jocks and burnouts only

Variable	+Cruising	−Cruising	Input	Sig.
(ʌ) backing	.548	.445	.440	.004
(e) backing	.564	.447	.407	.006
Negative concord	.651	.314	.277	.000

here the boys who cruise are using it less than the jocks or non-cruisers. This variable in particular raises the issue of whether this variable has the same significance among girls and among boys. Raised (aeh) is clearly not a vernacular form across the board, nor is it a standard form – if it were the latter, jock and non-cruising girls would surely use it more than burnout and cruising girls. I will return to this issue below.

Cruising is more of a constraining social issue among girls than among boys – it is not simply "other" but often forbidden. Many parents consider Detroit and urban parks off limits for their kids – some don't go because their parents won't allow it, some go anyway, and some go with their parents' blessing. Of course, this kind of blessing does not come equally to boys and to girls. Urban cruising is more forbidden to girls, it is potentially more dangerous for girls, and it is clearly more of a threat to a girl's reputation than to a boy's. It is not surprising, then, that there are more boys than girls in the sample who go to Detroit and urban parks. And it is not surprising that while none of the jock girls cruise, some of the jock boys do. These are boys who are primarily involved in athletics rather than social activities, and while they hang out with the main groups of jock boys, they court less of a "collegiate" image, and their linguistic behavior is sufficiently different from their non-cruising friends to affect the correlations among the jocks. While the significance of cruising in the overall female population is purely a result of differences among the in-betweens, in the male population it is a combination of differences among in-betweens and of the wedge that this practice creates among the jocks. When only jocks and burnouts are included in the regression, (ay) raising retains the category constraint, but cruising replaces social category affiliation as the most significant determinant of boys' use of negative concord and of the backing of (ʌ) and (e) (table 6.3).

Correlations across the broader Belten High population shows that urban engagement is not only a defining term in the jock–burnout opposition, but an important aspect of social practice across the population. Among the boys, who have greater freedom in their wandering, urban engagement as manifested in the practice of cruising corresponds to linguistic differences within the jock category as well. The use of urban variables thus is a resource for the entire population in the construction of linguistic styles related to engagement in urban practice. These patterns have their complement in engagement in institutional practice.

6.3   Institutional Engagement

Participation in school activities – both academic and extracurricular – is a measure of institutional involvement. For many, the two go together. However, it is not unusual for people to simply keep their academic work under control while throwing most of their energy into extracurricular activities. And there are people, as well, who focus on their studies without paying much attention to extracurricular activities.

6.3.1   The extracurricular sphere

It is the extracurricular sphere that makes the American high school American: sports events, bands, cheerleading, student government, plays, dances, proms, yearbooks, and school newspapers. It is the extracurricular sphere that provides institutional color and visibility – a school's reputation depends not only on its test scores, but on its football scores. Sports, musical, and theater events attract the attention and participation of the community at large. And while parents watch their children perform in the classroom, athletic and artistic events give them an opportunity to watch their children shine in public.

But the extracurricular sphere is not just about athletic and artistic accomplishment; much of it is about coordinating student life in the school. Belten High, like every other public high school in the US, has a system of student government, which includes a school-wide student council, and a structure of officers and cabinet for each graduating class. Regardless of its name, student government has little to do with governing; it does not make decisions about the basic conditions of life in the school. Rather, it provides a student directorate to organize social events.

The extracurricular sphere is not an add-on in the American high school, but a crucial part of the institutional structure. Belten High has a full-time student activities director whose primary focus is student government and its social activities, and advising extracurricular activities is considered an important part of a teacher's job. In turn, many of these activities unfold within a national structure: sports, music, cheerleading, student government, coordination and conception of activities are all supported at county, state, regional, and national levels, by organizations, camps, workshops, inservices, and publications. For both teachers and students, extracurricular activities involve participation in a nationwide profession. The centrality of extracurricular activities is further supported by college and university admissions criteria: a stellar academic record must be supplemented by an equally stellar extracurricular record if one hopes to gain admission to one of the better schools. It is in this notion of an extracurricular record that activities take a particularly corporate middle class slant, as individuals develop careers within the extracurricular sphere.

A career is distinguished from employment by the fact that it has a trajectory, it involves accomplishment, and it is integral to one's identity. The term *career* implies an aggressive stance to employment as a means to a personal end other than remuneration – a development of a self within a community of endeavor. It implies the continual development of skill and accumulation of accomplishment – continual progress to higher and higher attainment. All of these are present in the ambitious high school student's approach to extracurricular activities. Building an extracurricular career, like building a workplace career, requires strong competitive ability, a judicious selection of jobs, knowledge of the domain, cultivation of and attention to professional networks, and a personal identification with the institution in which the career is located. This requires, in turn, a concentration of effort within the institution and within the networks and activities that constitute the center of the extracurricular sphere. In this way, the jocks' lives come to be centered on the school, and their personal networks are brought into line with their professional endeavors.

This is not, however, equally true of boys and girls. The use of the name *jock* to designate the broader category of people involved in school activities, whether athletic or not, is not neutral. Male varsity athletics are still the most visible school activites. Competing as they do with other schools, boys' varsity athletics is the most direct way of establishing and defending the school's status and honor, and the male varsity athlete is seen as working directly in the school's interests. The institutional status and privilege that this brings to the male varsity athlete is considerable; at the same time, it is encumbent upon boys to take the athletic road to prominence. Boys who are not accomplished athletes must work in the social domain to gain institutional status. A group of male athletes, for example, told me that one prominent student officer *had* to do student government because he was not athletic. While they admired his skill, coolness, and hard work, they clearly viewed his activities in school as second best. In general, male athletes see non-athletic activities as something to do casually, as requiring no special skill, but possibly as one's civic duty. Furthermore, the status associated with varsity athletics can be transformed into serious capital in seeking student offices, constituting an advantage that can overturn the candidacy of a girl or an unathletic boy with a long history of experience and service.

There are no school accomplishments parallel to male varsity athletics that lend the same kind of status for girls. Since sports still do not yield the same payoff for girls as for boys, and they certainly did not at the time of this fieldwork, the domain in which girls are expected to achieve prominence is already designated as second best. Girls may receive recognition through prominence in student government and service clubs, through cheerleading and pompon, or through participation in musical or dramatic activities. But for both boys and girls, achieving recognition through these activities seldom if ever evokes the kind of vicarious pride of schoolmates that gives good athletes their special distinction. And while success in sports, music, and theater require clearly defined skill, the relation between outright skill and success in the social-political activity domain is never clear. Even cheerleading, baton twirling, and pompon are mixed in this respect. Although these activities require skill, success in them also requires style. A basketball coach doesn't care how ungainly or ugly a good player looks on the floor, but a girl who does not look good will not make the cheerleading, pompon, or twirling squad regardless of her skill. For girls, who know that skill brings limited rewards, success requires the production of a self[1] – a combination of skill, work, looks, and personality. In this way, popularity, from the late years of elementary school, becomes the domain of the girl. While boys know who's popular, and talk about popularity in relation to others (particularly to girls), girls devote large amounts of time to analyzing popularity, arguing about popularity, worrying about popularity. Girls speak of popularity as something one must construct; boys speak of it more as an inherent property. In other words, girls – because they are aware that they must produce themselves – are social engineers (Eckert 1997b, 1997c).

To correlate the use of linguistic variables with engagement in activities, I have devised an extracurricular activities index, which assesses both participation and recognition in the extracurricular sphere. Participation is represented by the number of official school activities the student participates in. This includes one point for participation in each club, musical organization, student government body, and role in theater productions and other kinds of public presentations (e.g. spoof shows and talent shows). Two points are given for extracurricular recognition as represented by awards for extracurricular participation, such as all school letter, distinguished service award, outstanding young man/woman award. (The latter is separate from the curricular outstanding student awards in various subject areas.) Recognition also includes leadership positions, such as offices in student government and other activities, sports captaincies, and manifestations of visibility in election to such things as homecoming court and yearbook mock elections (e.g. "most popular," "most likely to succeed").

Participation in extracurricular activities for the entire graduating class of 600 falls into four general levels. The large majority of students (348) do not participate in extracurricular activities at all. About a quarter of the students (126) participate in one or two activities, none of whom occupy offices or achieve extracurricular honors, which are given for visible contribution in multiple activities. There are 75 students with activities scores between 4 and 8, and finally 34 students with scores ranging from 9 to 33. The latter group constitute what many refer to as "the super jocks," with scores resulting not just from participation but the accumulation of offices and honors.

These levels have been entered in the data as indices as follows:

Activities Index:
1 – no activities
2 – 1 or 2
3 – 3–8
4 – 9 or more

The relation between category affiliation and activities score is illustrated in figure 6.2. In all cases, there are no significant gender differences, but the jock domination of the extracurricular sphere shows up clearly in the considerable differences between the jocks and everyone else.

A gender specialization in activities does show up when athletic activities are separated from non-athletic activities. Figure 6.3 shows the far greater participation of boys in varsity athletics than girls – reflecting also, of course, the greater number of boys' varsity teams. Figure 6.4 shows the average number of offices held in the non-athletic sphere by boys and girls. The girls show a significant lead in non-athletic offices, but it is notable that

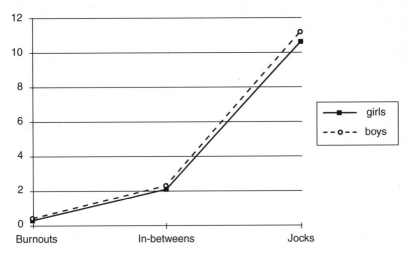

Figure 6.2 Average activities scores by gender and social category

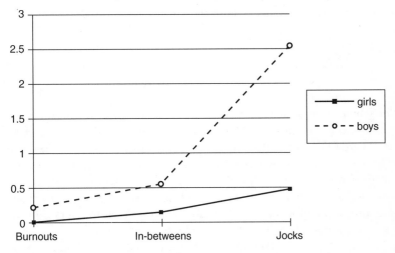

Figure 6.3 Average number of athletic teams per person by gender and social category

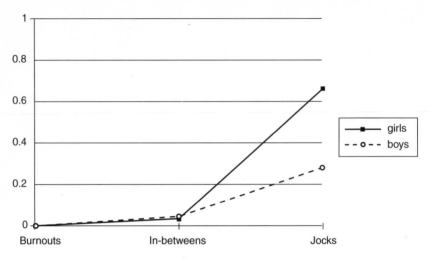

Figure 6.4 Election to non-athletic school office by gender and social category

although girls hold the majority of offices in the non-athletic sphere, they only hold half of the more prestigious offices – those in student government – and the presidents of both the senior class and the student council are boys.

6.3.2   *The academic sphere*

The school offers a range of vocational courses in business education, automotive, electricity, machine shop, drafting, welding, woodworking, family life. There is also a bus that takes students to other sites (e.g. career center and other schools) for additional vocational programs, such as cosmetology and food preparation. Although the family life program, which includes cooking, sewing, childcare, home management, etc., is traditionally thought of as preparation for one's own family life rather than for work outside of the home, a number of the students who take these courses are interested in futures in professional childcare. The traditional gender divide applies in Belten, with girls taking the "homemaking" and business courses, and boys taking the "shop" courses.

While there is no formal tracking in the school, students' course loads tend to bundle, with students taking more vocational courses tending also to take academic courses that are less difficult (Eckert 1990a). Inasmuch as the school has something resembling a vocational wing, academic and vocational students are further separated by geography, since academic students rarely venture into the vocational wing. And inasmuch as academic teachers tend to specialize within their departments (willingly or not) in higher- or lower-level academic courses, vocational and academic students have regular contact with different teachers. Furthermore, since it is primarily academic teachers who advise extracurricular activities, the academic students have greater contact with extracurricular advisors, hence greater access to information and opportunities in the extracurricular sphere.

College and vocational orientations do not spring from simple individual choice, but are built tightly into community practice. The jocks live in a world of preparation for college. Their families, their friendship networks, their school counselors, and their teachers all form a network of assumption and information about college entrance. Choice of college, preparation for college boards, choice of college preparatory classes, and the significance of extracurricular activities for college admission are all daily conversational fare in jock networks – engaged in by parents, siblings, neighbors, teachers, all of whom share the assumption that they will be going on to college. Support for academic activity is also part of jock practice, both in the joint choice of classes and in the limitation of weeknight social activity to phone conversations, building homework into their joint schedule.

Information about college does not flow in burnout networks, as witnessed by the following burnout's account in her senior year of what she was going to do after high school:

Sandra: I think, you know, if I really get my stuff together in art, you know, really get into it I – I probably will try to be an art teacher.

Penny: Um, are you taking courses and stuff that you have to take to go to college?

Sandra: Um, I re – I'm not really aware of, you know, what I have to do to be in college, but I – I think I've got a low grade – you know – grade average pretty much.

Burnout activity schedules also do not leave time for homework. The experience of one college-bound burnout from a middle class family underscores the lack of fit between college and participation in the burnout community. While this girl followed an academic curriculum and applied to college, she did so under her college-educated parents' tutelage, without discussing it with her friends. This is not because she hid the fact that she was going to go to college from her friends, but because college preparation was not part of their practice and as a result not a topic of conversation. For this girl, the difference in cultures was wrenching, as evidenced in her view of the contrast between jock and burnout approaches to the future:

> I can go out, and I can party with them [burnout friends], but then, either right before first hour, or during another class or something, I'm doing my homework. And I get – you know, this last report card was all A minuses and B's. And my friends just looked at me and went, "Wait a minute, you were out with us Friday, why are you getting these good grades?" you know. They're not thinking about after they graduate. And I think, out of those friends, I'm thinking about that. And then there's my jock friends . . . they always have been looking for "What am I going to do for the rest of my life," and "What am I going to do here and there." It's – I'm torn apart again, you know.

But if college information flows in jock networks, workplace information flows in burnout networks. By providing no clear transition to the workplace, and by assuming no interest in college, the high school leaves the burnouts to take it upon themselves to construct a path into the next life stage. This construction is aided by the age heterogeneous friendship networks begin in the neighborhood, for by the time they are in high school, burnouts already have friends who are in the workforce, having either graduated or dropped out. Thus orientation to the local workplace characterizes burnout networks in much the way that orientation to college admission characterizes jock networks.

The opposition between jocks and burnouts, however, is not simply an opposition between academic and vocational orientations. Some burnouts simply hate school and do not apply themselves in either vocational or academic courses. Coming to school high, or cutting school or classes altogether is not uncommon among burnouts, some of whom are indifferent about grades, many of whom get bad grades whether they are indifferent or not. Burnouts overwhelmingly feel that the school is not preparing them for the future, whether because they have a specific occupational goal that the school cannot fulfill or because they simply find school irrelevant. One burnout's evaluation of the school's offerings was particularly amusing to a linguist:

> *Judy*: I don't think they teach nothing. They sh- they should teach us uh, they should teach us everyday things.
>
> *Penny*: Like what?

Judy: Like I don't know, like checking accounts. I don't even know – I don't even know about uh income tax. And I'm supposed to be uh put out in this world. How am I gonna make it? I don't even know about nothing. I don't know about mortgages and shit like that. All they teach you is adjectives, oh, "Right, we're gonna have to go up and have to learn about [laughter] adjectives." I don't – I don't know nothing. I wouldn't know how to go get an apartment or nothing.

Because engagement in the college preparatory academic sphere is an indication of a particular kind of institutional orientation, I have devised an academic index that includes both course selection and academic honors. While academic honors are based on the senior year, course selection is based on courses taken in the second semester of the junior year. The junior year academic schedule is more representative of a student's overall engagement than the senior year, since students who finish their course requirements early may take fewer courses in the senior year but remain quite engaged in school. The index includes two points for each upper-level college preparatory course, three for each advanced placement course, and one point for all other courses. To this is added four points for each formal academic honor: outstanding student awards, membership in the National Honor Society, and Summa Cum Laude status.

The levels for academic involvement, as shown in figure 6.5, are based on the schedules of 182 students, including the speaker sample.

Figure 6.6 shows the average academic score for the interview sample by gender and category. The gender difference that appears in this emerges dramatically, when academic honors are viewed separately, as shown in

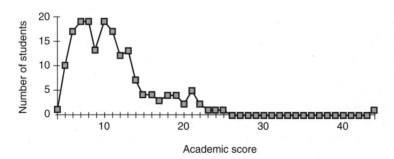

Figure 6.5 Academic scores

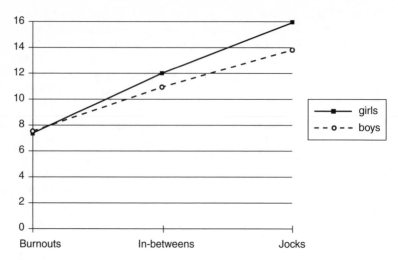

Figure 6.6   Average academic score by gender and category

figure 6.7. (The academic honor score among the burnouts represents an award won by a girl in a vocational area.) It should be noted that while overall academic involvement clearly is an important part of social differentiation, the heightened gender differentiation in academic honors is clearly an indication that girls are far more engaged in at least this aspect of the institutional enterprise than boys. Girls tend to take more courses, and to take more advanced placement courses, than boys. If we assume that this is not a result of gender differentiation in native ability, we are led to speculate that girls are choosing to work harder at academics. While the "good girl" syndrome is one way of explaining this fact, it is also possible that this is part of a broader pattern of women's and girls' greater attention to the production of a self, and in this case academic status is part of that production. The possibility that girls feel their grades will matter more than boys' in the competition for college entrance can probably not be separated from this.

Based roughly on the pattern in figure 6.5, which is precisely reproduced within the speaker sample, I have distinguished four levels of academic involvement, with breaks between 5 and 6, 13 and 14, and 25 and 26. Academic involvement cores of 4 and 5 are minimal, and generally indicate that the student started out the year with more courses but was dropped from one or more because of a problem, such as poor attendance. The large

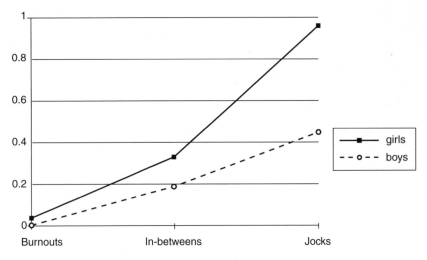

Figure 6.7 Average academic honors by gender and category

majority of students have academic scores between 6 and 13. Scores over 13 generally indicate that the student is taking at least one advanced placement course, and as the scores rise, these courses are supplemented by academic honors of some sort. There is only one person with a score greater than 25. This might suggest a natural division of academic involvement into three levels. However, academic involvement is a gradually cumulative enterprise, and in order to provide greater texture, and to have relatively equally filled cells, I have divided the academic scores into a five-level index:

Academic Involvement Index:
1 <7
2 8–9
3 10–11
4 12–15
5 >15

6.3.3 Variation and school involvement

What is striking about the relation between variation and institutional involvement is the particular balance between the influence of the curricular and the extracurricular spheres. In recent studies, Labov (e.g. 1990) has

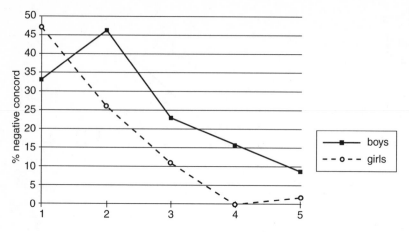

Figure 6.8   Negative concord and academic index

replaced composite class indices with occupational category, claiming that occupation is the best single class-related measure for the analysis of variation. The patterns of variation in Belten High conform to this finding, to the extent that just as education takes a back seat to occupation in Labov's adult population, engagement in academics in the high school takes a back seat to engagement in extracurricular activities in Belten High's adolescent population. This, I would argue, is because occupation is an indication of an adult's actual forms of participation in the standard language market, while education is primarily preparation for this participation. In the high school context, academic activity is preparation for later educational stages or for the workplace, while extracurricular activity is itself a form of engagement in the kind of institutional activity that constitutes the standard language market in the here and now. This is not because the extracurricular sphere is any more part of the school institution, but because it is more highly valued in the community, and generates greater status and visibility. Being a good student does not bring visibility and status in the institution, while being a student government officer does.

As shown in figures 6.8–10, negative concord shows a clear relation to all indices of school involvement. Given the popular connection between education and standard grammar, one would expect this variable to correlate with degree of academic engagement. Figure 6.8 shows this to be the case, but the correlation is not very smooth. However, among the girls, one could view the pattern as distinguishing three levels of academic involve-

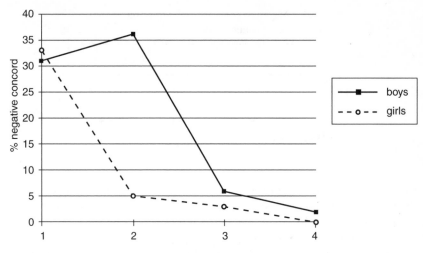

Figure 6.9 Negative concord and activities index

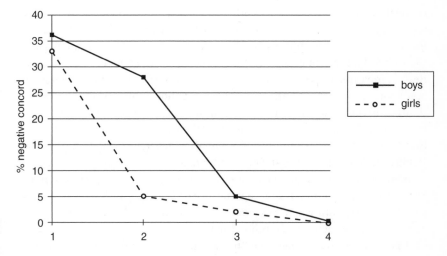

Figure 6.10 Negative concord and non-athletic activities

ment – low (1), medium (2–3), and high (4–5). The correlation with extracurricular activities is even less smooth among the boys, but shows a pattern among the girls that one might well expect: that is, the major difference is between girls who engage in no activities and those who engage in any at all. The difference between none and one or two activities among the boys goes in the opposite direction: those who have one or two activities

Table 6.4 Negative concord and non-athletic activities. Jocks and burnouts only

	1	2	3	4	Input	Sig.
Girls	.831	.346	.123	0*	.159	.000
Boys	.626	.544	.123	0*	.309	.000

* knockout factor

show more negative concord than those with none; and those who do more than two are extremely standard. The explanation for the boys' pattern lies in the kinds of activities boys engage in. All of the boys who participate in just one activity are involved in either a single sport or the boys' choir, for which they get "easy" academic credit. The girls, on the other hand, show a greater mix of activities at each level of engagement. The more gradual correlation for boys comes in both cases when non-athletic activities are separated out, as shown in figure 6.10. This is true to a small extent for girls, for whom the athletic sphere plays a much smaller role. Also, for many girls, the social significance of athletics is similar to other extracurricular activities. Comparing figures 6.8 and 6.10, it is clear that the correlation with academics is weaker than that with social (i.e. non-athletic) activities, even though in this case of a standard grammatical pattern, one might have expected to find academic activity to show the stronger correlation. The fact that social activities are more important than academics suggests that the Belten students associate standard grammar with a corporate image as embodied in the extracurricular sphere. The level of participation in non-athletic activities eliminates the significance of both mother's education and social category, both when jocks and burnouts only are included, and when in-betweens are included as well (table 6.4).

There is no relation between the raising of (ay) and indices of school engagement among the boys. However, the girls show a gradual inverse relation between (ay) raising and academic index (figure 6.11). Activities, on the other hand, correlate in an abrupt fashion (figure 6.12), with a distinction between girls who participate in no activities on the one hand, and any activities on the other (whether social activities or the combination of social and athletic activities).

While the lowered variant of (e) occurs rarely, it shows fine distinctions among the boys according to aspects of jock social practice. As shown in

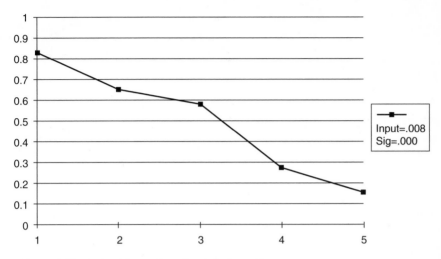

Figure 6.11 (ay) raising and academic index: girls

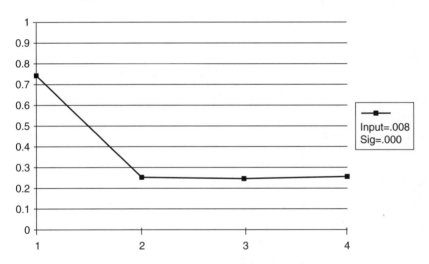

Figure 6.12 (ay) raising and non-athletic activities index: girls

figure 6.13, there is a very rough increase in lowering as academic engagement increases. Figure 6.14 shows a smoother increase in lowering with
increased involvement in extracurricular activities, but it is non-athletic
activities that show the most regular and fine-grained correlation with this
variant. Athletics alone shows no regular pattern of any kind in relation to
lowering, and the boys who lower (e) the most are those who engage pri-

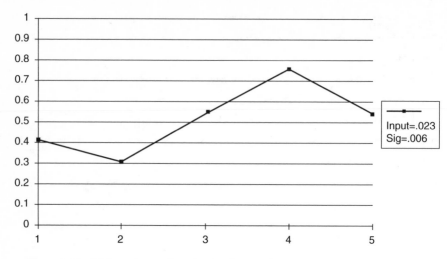

Figure 6.13   (e) lowering and academics: boys only

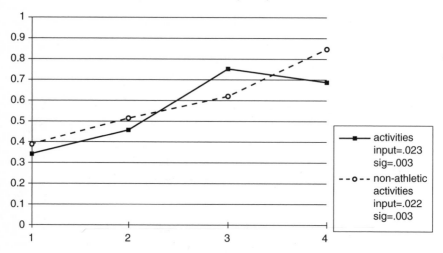

Figure 6.14   (e) lowering and activities: boys only

marily, and intensively, in the extracurricular social sphere. One might think of this variable as constituting a linguistic "preppy factor" for boys. Its restriction to boys who are heavily engaged in the social sphere whether or not they are engaged in the athletic sphere indicates that it is specifically not associated with the kind of masculinity defined by physical prowess. Rather, it appears to be a positive indicator of Connell's other kind of masculinity – the masculinity associated with political and technical prowess, or "technical" masculinity.

6.4   Variation and Urban and Institutional Practice

The correlations discussed above show that the social meanings associated with the polarized jock and burnout categories are salient throughout the student population. The social categories have taken pride of place in this study. Categories reify the polarization of practice. They are constituted by those practices, but they also foreground them. To the extent that we find linguistic differences correlating across the population in such a way that social category recedes into the background, one might ask whether the linguistic behavior of the categories themselves is not simply derivative. One might ask whether, if this study had focused more on in-betweens, the jocks and burnouts would have faded into the woodwork. However, it is also clear that without the jock–burnout opposition, the practices that correlate with linguistic variables would not have the same salience. In that case, would some of these correlations lose their significance? It is no doubt in the interplay between categories and practice that the sociolinguistic dynamics studied here come into their own.

The urban and suburban variables function as symbolic resources associated with local and institutional practice respectively. A somewhat unexpected development is that girls show a more delicate use of urban variables, while boys show a more delicate use of suburban variables. Pattern 1 and Pattern 3 variables are primarily constrained by gender, with girls leading overwhelmingly in Pattern 1 and boys leading overwhelmingly in Pattern 3. In both cases, the gender group that lags in overall use of the variable shows greater differentiation for that variable within the gender group. Milroy has observed a similar pattern in Belfast (1980: 196–7), where men lead in the overall change in (a) but lag in its use as a network marker, and women lead in the overall change in (ε) but lag in its use as a network marker. Emily Bender (forthcoming) argues that if one is a member of a group or category that makes little use of a form, then the use of the form will be more noticeable, hence have greater potential for carrying social meaning in the speech of members of that group or category.

But this does not explain the girls' greater social use of Pattern 2 variables. I would argue that levels of use of suburban and mixed variables carry less significance for girls than for boys, while levels of urban variables appear to carry less significance for boys than girls. In the discussions of gender above, I emphasized that different issues are problematic for girls and boys as they try to make choices about how to live and what to do. For girls, "good girl" issues – issues of "purity" – are central to gender norms, and as a result to social distinctions among girls, while issues of toughness play this role for boys. Thus the use of urban variables is no doubt more marked for girls, and the use of non-urban variables is more marked for boys, reflecting the difference in the sources of threat to girls' and boys' images and reputations. A jock girl who lets her image of purity down will be open to charges of "sluttiness," while a boy's masculinity depends on his ability to maintain an image of autonomy. Hence urban variables pose more of a potential threat to girls, while non-urban variables, and particularly anti-urban variables, pose more of a potential threat to boys. It may well be for this reason that girls are more careful in their use of urban variables, while boys are more careful in their use of suburban variables. Gender groups, in other words, show more delicate use of variables that pose a greater potential threat to standard gender norms.

It is also notable that it is extracurricular activities, but not academics, that have the most regular effect on variables. As shown in chapter 2, there is a relation between engagement in social extracurricular activities and academic orientation. However, a combined index of academics and extracurricular activities as a measure of more general school involvement does not improve any of these correlations. The greater importance of the extracurricular sphere than academics in the use of even the most obviously education-related variable indicates clearly that adolescent variation serves the present adolescent social order. In other words, speakers are not developing patterns of variation in anticipation of adulthood, but for participation in the here and now. This confirms the importance of the *mature-use* perspective in the study of young people's use of variation.

Two variables emerge as the most robust social resources in Belten High: (ay) raising and negative concord. I have argued above that these are the variables that are the most subject to conscious control – negative concord because of its greater accessibility, and (ay) raising because of its relative independence from neighboring vowels since it is not enmeshed in a chain shift. It stands to reason that as a result they would be the most available for fairly specific symbolic manipulation. The vowels that are part of the chain shift may be more limited in their availability for symbolic deployment. I will return to this question in chapter 8.

Note

1   See Eckert (1990b) and Eckert and McConnell-Ginet (1995) for a more thorough discussion of this.

7

Friendships, Networks, and Communities of Practice

Each of the activities discussed in this book – cruising, hanging out in the courtyard, participating in the extracurricular social and athletic sphere, and doing academics – has meaning in virtue of its association with a broader practice, a joint style, a mutual set of values and orientations to the world. The friendship clusters that make up the social network of the Belten High student body constitute the communities of practice in which the most active negotiation of social meaning takes place. While participation in activities and organizations, such as student government, pompon, athletic teams, and school paper may well be important aspects of individuals' identities, the main friendship group is at the heart of one's place in the peer social order. It is in this group that people decide which activities to engage in, construct attitudes and orientations, debate values, and evaluate each other's behavior and that of the people around them. The most intensive work in the construction of social meaning takes place in these intensely interacting communities of practice.

The purpose of this chapter is to locate the isolated social variables of chapters 5 and 6 in the social space in which they are embedded. By discussing the social relations and the history of these relations, I hope to fill out the seemingly rigid boundaries of categories and variables with fluid and meaningful social space. At the same time, I hope to highlight the special significance of certain groups of friends, and to engage in the risky business of speculating about individuals who stand out in their immediate sociolinguistic landscape.

A community of practice is not a unit, like a social category, that exists on one level and to which speakers can be assigned. This is specifically because speakers belong to multiple communities of practice on multiple levels. The significance of the concept of community of practice lies in the way in which it points the analyst to characteristics and functions of social aggregations, and licenses a focus on the kinds of meaning that are being made in a particular aggregation. Thus when I suggest a focus on communities of practice, I am not so much proposing a new social variable to be included in analyses of variation as proposing a different way of viewing the relation between social meaning and human aggregations. Variable rule analysis treats the categories and practices that constitute the Belten social order as properties of individuals, transforming each person into a cluster of activities and categorizations. But the necessities of statistical analysis cannot be confused with the mechanisms of social reality. The social variables that emerge in an analysis of variation are a reflection of what is most important in people's lives together and what connects people to each other. In Belten High, students rehearse and negotiate on a continual basis such things as attitudes about Telegraph Road and Hines Park, about the courtyard, lockers, and the cafeteria, about student government, varsity sports, and choirs, about school dances, marijuana, and chemicals, about studies, college, and work, about individual teachers and other students, the future, family, and the meaning of life and friendship. These are day-to-day topics of conversation and debate in the cafeteria, in the courtyard, in the halls, and outside of school as well. It is not just engagement in these activities but attitudes towards them that make people who they are and that tie people to each other. The individual is not connected independently to the social world of the high school, or of the wider community and urban area, but negotiates that relation jointly within their communities of practice. I would argue that it is within this process of negotiation that linguistic style is constructed and refined, and that patterns of variation are imbued with meaning. The patterns of variation discussed in chapters 5 and 6 reflect orientations to the world, but they come to do so not through each individual's independent negotiations with the world, but in the course of day-to-day interaction among people who are negotiating those orientations together.

The communities of practice based in Belten High make up a vast and interconnected social network, and can be identified in the connections that create different clusters in the network. These clusters and connections have merged and diverged over the years since elementary school, creating a common and very complex joint history. Figure 7.1 is a detailed sociogram showing the general layout of friendship groups among the girls in the cohort. The figure represents a slice of time – individuals' representations of their friendship groups, the "main people they hang out with" in the course of their junior year. Each circle or oval represents one person, and each line represents a friendship tie, regardless of whether the naming was mutual. The length of the lines representing friendship ties is imposed by the limitations of the two-dimensional representation, and is not meaning-

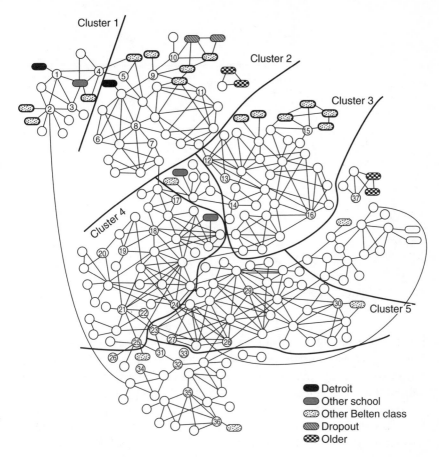

Figure 7.1   Girls' network

ful. Figure 7.2 is a sociogram showing the boys' friendship connections, constructed along the same principles, but in less detail. The clusters in the boys' network correspond roughly to the clusters in the girls' network, inasmuch as the boys in clusters a and b are closely associated with the girls in cluster 2, the boys in cluster c are associated with the girls at the top of cluster 3, the boys in cluster d are associated with girls in cluster 4 and the bottom of cluster 3, and the boys in cluster e are associated with girls in cluster 4 and to a small extent 5.

Since these sociograms are not based on conversations with all the people represented in them, they do not yield accurate information about the

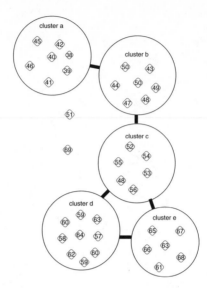

Figure 7.2   Boys' network

detailed structure of friendship clusters or such things as network density. But inasmuch as my networking took a random sample as its point of departure, it covers the population of the class in a general way, and gives a clear indication of the main clusters in relation to each other, the social distances among clusters, and the general nature of the social connections among them. It enables us to locate each speaker in relation to the rest of the class and in relation to networks extending beyond the class and the school itself.

7.1   Interpreting the Sociogram

The borders of a sociogram are imposed by the criteria that govern the selection of data points. While those around the edge may appear marginal, that marginality is with respect to the abstraction that gave rise to that selection. In the present case, that abstraction is the junior class of Belten High. Based as it is on conversations with members of the junior class, this representation constructs centrality and marginality in relation to the class itself. Thus some people appear marginal by virtue of the fact that their friendships extend beyond the graduating class, and those who appear central, by and large, are those who limit their relations to their own graduating class. A student who is quite marginal in her school crowd may be at the center of her church group or neighborhood. And her life in the church group or neighborhood may be more or less important to her than her life in school. Also, based as it is on questions about friendships, the sociogram neglects such things as family ties which, for some, may be the most important.

Once assembled, the sociogram still does not represent homogenous social space except in the limited terms of the abstractions represented by the links. Each sociogram represents a slice of social practice, which fits into the whole quite differently in different communities of practice. While some people have a few close friends, others have a broader group of more casual friends; while some people have one or a few best friends, others eschew the idea of having a best friend at all. Some people spend more time with their peers than others: some go out on weeknights with their friends, while others stay at home doing homework. Some friendship groups see each other only in school, while others spend every available moment together. And the nature of the friendship will determine the kinds of interactions people engage in: whether they share problems, get in trouble together, do homework, ride motorcycles, hang out and talk, go places. It would be impossible to ask enough questions to control for this kind of difference in ties. Nonetheless, it is not unreasonable to assume that these kinds of differences can have an important influence on linguistic behavior.

The separate display of girls' and boys' networks in this chapter is to some extent a reflection of the nature of patterns of relations among and between boys and girls, but primarily a response to the constraints on a small two-dimensional representation. Also, time constraints in the field led me to focus on gathering comparable male and female speech samples, but then to explore the girls' social contacts in greater detail. Thus the girls' network is more complete than the boys', making it difficult to coordinate them, particularly inasmuch as the boys' network is missing the same detail about in-betweens as the girls'. The girls' sociogram gives an overview of "social space" in the cohort, and while boys' and girls' social space do not map neatly onto each other, it is possible to describe the boys' network with reference to the girls' in a general way.

Much thought about the relation between language and gender has been based on observations about the nature of male and female interactions in social networks (Maltz and Borker 1982), and the complexity of the ways in which these networks separate and come together begs for careful study (Thorne 1993). Therefore, the nature of the gender separation in figures 7.1 and 7.2 is worth remarking on. The first source of the separation is in the process of information gathering itself. The school, like the society that it serves, is overwhelmingly oriented to gender difference. Many of the institutional arrangements are gender-segregated – locker rooms, physical education classes, bathrooms, and lockers – and most boys and girls eat separately and hang out separately. People are likely, therefore, to interpret a request for names of friends to be a request for same-gender friends. At the same time, there are differences throughout the network in both the extent and the nature of contacts between boys and girls. A number of the burnouts named members of the other gender in response to questions about who they hung out with and, to some extent, who constituted their main group of friends. The burnouts who named members of the other gender among their main group of friends were members of the major neighborhood-based cluster of burnouts, where boys and girls had been part of gender-integrated friendship groups since childhood. This does not mean that the burnouts necessarily spend more time in mixed gender interactions, but that these interactions are more likely to be based in informal friendship groups. While the jocks virtually never mention members of the other gender among their friends, they are engaged in a heterosexual crowd in which there is fairly constant contact. Much of the time that burnouts spend hanging out, the jocks spend engaged in extracurricular activities, which also frequently involve mixed groups. Although the male and female friendship networks do intersect at a number of points, if "friendship" is the criterion for naming ties, they are to a great extent separate. For most of the kids in this class, relationships with members of the other gender are more casual, or are romantic.

7.2   The Network and its Clusters

The network forms a set of clusters of varying sizes, each of which constitutes an extended friendship set. Each of these clusters is a socially real aggregation. Any one of the members could say who is in their cluster, and this knowledge is activated whenever extended social contacts are needed. For example, because there are three lunch periods at Belten, students cannot expect to eat with their main group of friends. Having a set of people to eat lunch with is key to survival in high school, and working this out has high priority on the first day of each semester – people trade information about who has which lunch early in the day in order to avoid appearing at a loss upon entering the cafeteria. The clusters on these sociograms represent those sets, and are verified by people's actual lunchtime seating. People can also articulate differences among the clusters – different styles, different attitudes, different practices. There is a mutual attention to certain kinds of information, a mutual construction of style, a mutually negotiated attitude towards school and towards the other people in it. In short, people within each of the clusters in these networks are more intensively engaged in the construction of meaning with each other than with those outside. It is in this process – in the meaningfulness of the interactions in which this construction takes place – that the intensity that constitutes "peer pressure," including linguistic pressure, is located.

The top margin of the network has its continuation outside of the class and the school. It extends beyond Neartown, and into Detroit, and beyond the school-based group into networks of people who have dropped out or graduated, and are in the workplace. Clusters 1 and 2 at the top are mutually connected to a number of people from Detroit, other graduating classes, and people who have dropped out of school. These are the self-declared burnouts. While people in other clusters are also connected to people from outside the class, it is notable that these connections are almost always pursued on an individual basis. The burnouts, on the other hand, as locally based communities of practice, tend to share friends from outside the class.

The jocks, mostly located in cluster 4, are connected broadly and almost exclusively with people in their own graduating class. The one exception in cluster 4 was recently a jock in this class but now attends a different local school. While she has remained friends with some of the girls at Belten, she does not have a continued presence in her old friendship network. The jocks say, quite explicitly, that although they might like to, they don't have time to spend with people who are not involved in activities at Belten. The rest of the clusters, representing the majority of the girls in the class, consider themselves "in-betweens."

With the relatively small numbers of people in each cluster, it is potentially misleading to attempt a close comparison of patterns of variation by cluster. Furthermore, the sample for this study was built on a random sample constructed from a class list, and while I kept track of relations among people, I developed the sociogram after the speaker sample had been selected. As a result, the linguistic sample does not include equal numbers of people in each network cluster, nor are they evenly spread through the

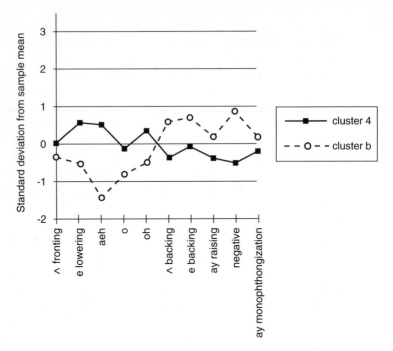

Figure 7.3   Female jock and male burnout patterns

cluster. However, there are some differences among clusters that are suggestive for the study of variation, and I intend the discussion of variation in what follows to be only suggestive. It is already obvious from table 5.10 that the important differences among speakers will not simply be in extent of use of variables overall, but in the pattern of use. This is clearest in the comparison of the jock and burnout pattern, which finds its most extreme form in the contrast between the male burnout pattern and the female jock pattern. Figure 7.3 plots the average use of each variable for female jock cluster 4 and male burnout cluster 2. The values in this figure and in all following figures in this chapter are based on the mean percentage of advanced variants for each cluster, plotting the number of standard deviations by which this mean differs from the sample mean. This figure shows complementary highs and lows, as the jock girls' use peaks to the left among the Pattern 1 variables and the burnout boys' use peaks to the right, among the Pattern 2 and 3 variables.

7.2.1 The burnout clusters

Cluster 2 is the main group of burnout girls. This cluster combines girls from both junior high schools, but many of the members come from a large working class and lower middle class neighborhood serving Rover Junior High. Many of the friendships date back to childhood, when kids gathered in the streets, yards, and parks to play along with their older siblings, yielding an age-heterogeneous neighborhood crowd. Most of the burnouts began to think of themselves as burnouts the summer before seventh grade, when they began to accompany their older siblings and friends to the parks and elementary school playgrounds for initiation into the adolescent leisure world. There, on the long summer evenings, kids hung out, smoked, did some drugs, got into a little trouble, fooled around, and talked. While this cluster is divided into smaller clusters of good friends, they all party together, hang out in parks, and play pickup games in the afternoons, evenings, and on weekends.

The boys in clusters a and b form two friendship groups with some overlap but still a clear division. The boys in cluster b spend more time in Detroit and have more friends in Detroit than the boys in cluster a, and they have a reputation for being somewhat tougher. The boys in cluster a think of themselves more as partiers, and as more mellow. The boys in clusters a and b, and particularly those in cluster a, are closely associated with the girls in cluster 2. They have hung out at the same parks since elementary school, partied together, and participated in the same pickup games after school. Some of the girls in cluster 2 and boys in cluster a are old and close friends, and some are girlfriend and boyfriend. Together, the boys and girls in clusters 2, a, and b constitute the burnout "crowd." This crowd prides itself on its close and supportive character as well as on its independence from adults and its penchant for partying. Personal problems are widely shared in this crowd, and members can count on the crowd for widespread material and emotional support.

The kids in these clusters have a tendency to get in trouble with school and parents, and occasionally with the police and other adults, but mostly from their emphasis on friendship and partying. Margaret (speaker 6) began getting in trouble in junior high school when she first started thinking of herself as a burnout. A tomboy, she had had a difficult time learning how to hang out with girls when the boys stopped wanting her in their games, and partying offered much-needed excitement. When I asked if she liked getting into trouble, she laughed and said:

No. I liked the things that leaded up to getting into trouble . . . staying out later than I should, being with the people I shouldn't have been with. Because it seemed like I had a better time.

In the beginning of junior high school, the jocks and the burnouts constituted two separate visible "popular" crowds. Both participated in school activities, but these activities, nonetheless, were dominated by the jock crowd, and burnouts who participated in them found themselves somewhat isolated, as typified by the experience of speaker 9:

When I joined the pompon squad, you know, when I tried out, none of – none of my other friends made it, so it was just me with, you know, a whole other crowd.

Rather than prolonging this isolation, she did not try out for anything in high school. In addition, participation in these activities required attention to school norms of personal behavior – just at the time when many burnouts were getting into smoking cigarettes and marijuana. Many of the boys withdrew from school sports during that period, either not wanting to spend the time after school, or not accepting the coach's claims on their personal behavior. Others were excluded from school sports because of rule infractions. The importance of school sports in school led to considerable hostility between athletic burnout boys and jock boys: the jock boys resented the loss of talent for the teams and the burnout boys resented the loss of recognition that resulted from the fact that participation on a school team was the legitimized measure of athletic ability. Legendary fights and jock–burnout football games are supposed to have occurred during junior high as a result.

The burnouts' focus on partying presented a problem not only because of the surveillance of coaches, but for attending activities as well. Early on in junior high, both burnouts and jocks attended school dances, roller skating parties, and athletic events. However, the two groups engaged in these activities on very different terms. The burnouts viewed school activities as opportunities to "party," and were frequently busted for drinking or smoking dope outside of dances and sporting events. As these brushes with school officials accumulated, and more and more members of the cluster were banned from activities, the rest of them became disillusioned – it was no fun to do things if your friends couldn't do them with you. In the course of junior high, therefore, the burnouts withdrew gradually from school activities – a withdrawal that was essentially completed by the entrance into high school. But this does not mean that all involved were equally motivated to pull out. In junior high, many burnouts felt a clear pull between extracurricular involvement and participation in the burnout community. Veronica (speaker 8) recalls the pull in junior high between friendship and school activities:

Veronica: I used to go to all the dances. All the roller skatings. All those. But I never got into anything, like I wish I would've like – write in the yearbook, or . . .

Penny: Why didn't you go out for yearbook and stuff like that?

Veronica: Uh, I don't know. I think because I always had so much to do. I was with my friends all the time. Everybody used to hang up at the park. So I did – I didn't really get into it because then I thought, "Oh, school's a drag, school's a drag," you know. I, you know . . . In, in, I don't know, you probably know this, you probably heard this from people too. You know, in, um, junior high everybody was stereotype, stereotype. Like, you hung around with the burnouts, you didn't talk to the jocks. You know. The jocks didn't talk to you. And I talk to so many girls now that I think in ninth grade we didn't talk and stuff because she was a jock and I was a burnout, or whatever. And, um, and they were all on all the activities, you know. So that, sort of – and all – I was the most – out, out of everybody, I'd always go, "Come on, you guys, let's go roller skating," or "Let's go to the dance." And we would, but every – most everybody else was, "Oh, nah, let's go out and walk around instead," you know . . . like, "Well, it's not cool to go to school activities," you know. And then finally they would and stuff . . . I would say, "Let's go," you know. "Let's go." And finally we would, and we'd have a good time. But it was just getting enough people to go to where nobody would get bored, you know what I mean? You had to get a group of us to go. And then, my ninth grade year I got kicked out of all activities.

Penny: Really? What for?

Veronica: Yeah, because, um, alright, there was a group of us standing behind the rink, roller skating, and they were smoking weed. And, um, they took us all in the office, and called our parents. And Mister Jones, okay, he called, and my dad answered the phone. And I had, um, a bag on me, you know. And they didn't search any of us, or anything. And the one kid was such a jerk. He knew he wouldn't get in trouble. He goes, "Oh, we just smoked a bowl man," and oh, he got us all in trouble.

Perhaps it is not surprising that Veronica stands out dramatically among her peers, with a use of (oh) and Pattern 2 variables that is extremely conservative for a burnout. Figure 7.4 compares Veronica's pattern with the average pattern for her cluster, showing a use of Pattern 1a and Pattern 2 variables

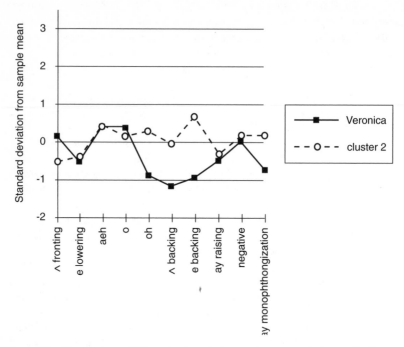

Figure 7.4   Comparison of Veronica in relation to the range of cluster 2 values

that is by far the lowest in her cluster. Veronica is among the less alienated of the burnouts with respect to school and to adults in general, but she has had some very hard times in her life, and the burnout friendship group has provided very essential support – a support that she points to as constituting a lasting bond. It is quite possible that the conservativeness of her pattern reflects a sense of herself that is unrelated to her reasons for being a burnout.

At the other extreme from Veronica, and the least connected to the rest of the class, is cluster 1, Judy's crowd. Other people at Belten point to Judy (speaker 1) and her friends as the prototypical burnouts – the "burned-out burnouts." Some of them do drugs in school on a regular basis (they say that mescaline in the morning helps you stay awake all day), and after school they find a variety of ways to seek excitement in the urban area – skating, cruising, and partying, pulling "all-nighters," picking up guys, etc. – activities that are sufficiently wild to result on occasion in arrest. The burned-out burnouts' networks do not extend much into the school, but beyond, with friends in Detroit and other Neartown schools and other suburbs, whom they've met in parks, bars, skating rinks, through siblings and friends. Judy expresses contempt for most of the students at Belten, considering them weird and "jocky." Preferring older guys, many of them in their twenties, and having many older friends, their social life outside of school is completely independent of the school population and of Neartown itself.

Lucy (speaker 4) comes from the cluster 2 neighborhood, but got to know the girls in cluster 1 in high school after she made a name for herself by becoming a "bigger burnout" than the girls in cluster 2. She describes this to me and her friend Sally:

Lucy: . . .in ninth grade uh we were – me and these two other chicks were the biggest burnouts in the school or whatever, you know.
Penny: How did you get to be the biggest burnouts?
Sally: More partying.
Lucy: Yeah, really. I don't know. We used to get high every day, come to school wasted, just, hey, you know. And people would know that we were wasted. I mean, teachers used to – my one teacher, Mr. DeAngelis, man, he s- "Are you high again?" you know. He used to flip me out. I don't know, we – we, 'cause we knew most, we knew all the ninth graders, and most of the eighth graders, and some seventh graders, and the seventh grade, I think the seventh and eighth graders kind of said, "Wow, I hope I can be like that." And, 'cause, I don't know, 'cause they, I don't know, we got along with everybody. We really didn't have no enemies, in junior high . . . like we got along with everybody and uh we partied every day and that was the cool thing. And uh we'd smoke in school and that was cool. We used to get E's in classes, that was cool. You know? So, I don't know. I guess that's how.

The status of the girls in cluster 1 as the burned-out burnouts shows up in their style, which is extreme in every way. They distinguish themselves from "regular" burnouts not only in their wilder behavior, but in their style of adornment – their extreme dark eye makeup contrasting with light foundation, their long straight hair, dark colored clothes and fringed boots. And nothing is more extreme than their speech.

Cluster 1 is represented in this study by four speakers. These four speakers lead the entire rest of the cohort in the use of variables across the board with sufficient regularity that it cannot be accidental. Table 7.1 shows the rank order for the top eight speakers in the use of advanced variants. (This is the top 10 percent of speakers plus one. I have included the eighth speaker

Table 7.1   Top eight speakers by pattern

Rank	All variables	Pattern 1	Pattern 2	Pattern 3
1	2	2	2	39
2	1	25	6	55
3	4	3	43	2
4	3	15	38	64
5	6	13	7	4
6	25	24	3	1
7	15	21	4	6
8	7	1	1	61

because this inclusion further confirms the pattern established by the top seven). To arrive at this ranking, each speaker has been ranked for the use of each variable, and the rankings have been combined to arrive at an overall ranking within patterns and across all variables. The top four ranked speakers for all variables combined are the members of cluster 1. Judy ranks high for the combined variables because she ranks eighth for Patterns 1 and 2, and sixth for Pattern 3, giving her a high rank across the board even though she does not show up on this table for Patterns 1 and 2. The fifth ranked speaker is a member of cluster 2, leaving two highly ranked speakers who are not burnouts, speakers 15 and 25, whom I will discuss below. The first rank user of each of the Patterns 1 and 2 variables except (e) lowering is from cluster 1. Judy leads all speakers in the use of (ʌ) backing and (ay) raising, and she leads all girls in the use of negative concord. Her best friend Joyce leads the cohort in each of the Pattern 1 variables. All four of the cluster 1 girls lead the cluster 2 girls in the use of (ʌ) and (o) fronting and (aeh) and (ay) raising, and three of the four lead the cluster 2 girls in (oh) fronting and negative concord.

Figure 7.5 compares the patterns for each variable used by the cluster 1 and the cluster 2 girls and the burnout boys' clusters a and b, showing that the cluster 1 girls lead other burnout clusters in the use of every variable except monophthongization. Furthermore, cluster 1 combined leads all other clusters, male and female, jock and in-between, in the use of every variable except Pattern 1a, (aeh) and monophthongization.

It can be noted from figure 7.5 that clusters a and b differ primarily in their use of Pattern 1 variables. The boys in cluster b show the lowest use of these variables in the school, in keeping with their more urban status.

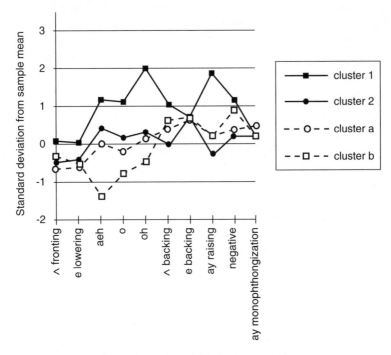

Figure 7.5   Average values for each variable for burnout clusters

7.2.2   *The jock and in-between clusters*

It is the general consensus in the school that the most powerful girls in the
school are the girls in cluster 4. While they come from both junior highs, it
is generally felt that the girls from Rover dominate. This is not without its
bitterness. Most of the girls in cluster 3 came from Finley junior high, and
constituted the main body of jocks in that junior high. When Finley, Rover,
and Bolder (a junior high that sent a very small number of students to
Belten) came together, the jock groups merged to some extent, but many
felt that the jocks from Rover ended up predominating. The girls in cluster
3, all from either Finley or Bolder, view cluster 4 with some resentment,
commonly referring to them as the "Rover gang." Although most of the
people in cluster 3 were heavily engaged in extracurricular activities in
junior high, heightened competition at Belten turned those at the top of the
cluster closer to cluster 2, away from activities in high school. One of them
traced her withdrawal to cheerleading tryouts:

.... in ninth grade I was a cheerleader. And then when I came here I tried out for cheerleading. And I didn't make it. And after that I just haven't tried out for anything after . . . That, it really hurt me, so I never tried out for anything, and then – like I'll go to a football game or a basketball game, but I can't do it myself.

Janice (speaker 12) is said to have been the most popular girl at Finley. She says that when she came to Belten, however, shyness made it it hard for her to get to know people. At the same time, she was eager to get a job and earn money, and now the job is more important to her than popularity or school involvement. Sarah (speaker 13) also stopped doing extracurricular activities:

Sarah: I was pretty all-around in junior high. Like I did everything. I sang, I was in an office, ran track, did volleyball. I mean I was just after school every day. Every single day. I mean, every teacher knew me. That's just because I always was coming in the office, "Can I have the keys?" You know, just – and I was making posters all the time.
Penny: And when you came in the high school how did it change?
Sarah: Oh, it changed a lot. When I ran for an office last year I don't, I didn't do anything. . . . I ran for office because I love being in the student council, but none of my friends were in it, you know. Like Harriet Murdock went to Calhoun for the first half, and Janice Robertson ran but she didn't win. And Ann Teller ran but she didn't win.
Penny: So who did you find yourself with?
Sarah: Uh, the Rover gang. And I didn't know them, any of them. You know, I – they were all nice, but just, it seems uh – . . . there wasn't much for me to do, you know. I used to come to meetings and stuff, but we didn't do that much in our sophmore year, really. We didn't support any dances or anything, you know, like that, you know. Float I got into, Banner I was there, you know, but it just wasn't the same.

Many of the members of cluster 3 who did not join cluster 4 developed a joint sense of being "on the outs." The continuation of Sarah's account explains another important distinction between clusters 3 and 4, and one that adds to a differentiation of practice accompanying the withdrawal from activities:

Rover girls were a lot different than the Finley girls, you know, like, it seemed like they thought we were so, "wow, man, we party and everything," you know – it just seemed like they just didn't like us, they thought we were too loose

or something . . . Even, what did they used to say, uh, like none of them –
this is just what people used to tell me – that they used to think it was really
gross to French kiss in ninth grade and when they found out that we did it
in ninth grade, they just thought that was disgusting, you know. And I almost
died, you know, I just went "Noooo."

The girls in cluster 3 have been referred to as the "partying jocks," not
so much because they are wild partiers but in contrast to the squeaky clean
image fostered by people in cluster 4. According to many, Finley junior high
was more of a partying school than Rover, which was considered to have a
sharper division between jocks and burnouts. Sarah's following portrayal of
the Rover gang as not only prudish but inexperienced is reminiscent of
many burnouts' characterizations of jocks in general:

I still don't get along with anybody from Rover. I mean, I get along with them,
"Hi, how you doing?" But I just never would hang around them. They're just
not my kind of people. See, like, I don't know. Maybe we're di – we are, totally
different people. Um, oh it's weird, we just do not feel comfortable. . . . we've
gotten to parties together but very rarely do we uh like mix, you know. And
just I think we all act pretty different at parties. Like, when they get drunk
they scream and they go wild. And they dance and they yell and they, some
of them cry. Just do weird things, you know, like freak out. And then when
we're at a party and we're watching them do this we just think, "Give me a
break," You know, it's like, "Cut this out, that's terrible" you know. And "how
embarrassing," you know, just like, "how can they be doing this stuff? People
must think they're weird," you know. I always think they're really weird when
they do that.

As Sarah's group of friends withdrew from school activities, and began
to think of themselves as in-betweens, they turned away from the jock networks, and questioned the entire jock–burnout split. Janice started going
with a burnout, a member of cluster b, and Sarah started going with Dave
(speaker 52), an in-between whom she avoided in junior high. The
in-between status of Dave and his friends in cluster c is very much related
to their transitional status between the jock and the burnout clusters in
the network, which is far less abrupt than in the girls' network. Sarah credits
Dave with having gotten her out of the social straitjacket she was in in junior
high:

Ever since I met Dave I changed a lot. Just because he's the type of person
– I used to be, I'm like really paranoid about what people thought about me.

It was really important to me that I should try and impress everybody. But you can't do that. You know, I should try to make everybody think I'm cool, or like me, or be nice to everybody. But you can't always impress everybody. You know, you can't worry constantly about what everybody thinks about you because everybody thinks something anyways, you know . . .

Sarah and Janice and their friends began to smoke pot in junior high, and Sarah and Janice and their friends have also started spending time with some of the girls in cluster 2:

There's another group of people from Rover, though, you know, that I like. . . . They party. Like, I think they were considered the burnouts at Rover when they went there. And I – they're not burnouts at all. I mean, they don't even smoke weed, any of 'em. They like to drink and stuff, but they're all really nice, you know. I really like those guys a lot. But see, then the Rover people that I'm talking about just a minute ago, they don't like them at all, you know what I mean, it's just like, "get away."

Since their move away from jockdom, Sarah and Janice have formed a transitional zone between the jock and burnout end of their cluster. This has not escaped the notice of others, who view them as having become burnouts. Speaker 15 talked about how some of the girls in cluster 3 have changed:

. . . . it was like, God, you know, if you were with Liz, you, you know, had a chance to get into that, you know, big crowd. . . . And then lots of them turned out to be burnouts, you know. Turn out, out, now are burnouts and everything. You know, they're not really burnouts, but, you know, they all smoke and everything now which you wouldn't think they would.

It is interesting that she should characterize them so, since she herself is an avid partier, and enjoys alcohol, marijuana, and cruising with her friends. It is no doubt the fact that she is an athlete involved in school sports that keeps her from being a burnout.

The cluster 3 girls are in-between in the socio–geographic sense: they actually occupy the social space between the jock and the burnout clusters. Their linguistic patterns, however, are not strictly transitional between the two (figure 7.6). Rather, they show higher values for the Pattern 1 variables than cluster 2 or 4, and values very much like those of cluster 4 for the urban variables.

Just as girls in cluster 3 are connected to the burnout cluster 2, so are

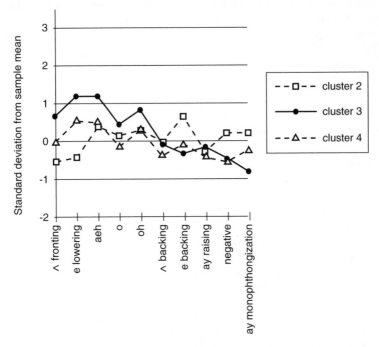

Figure 7.6   Average values for each variable for clusters 2, 3, and 4

the girls in cluster 4. However, in this case the ties are more historical than current. A few girls at the very top of cluster 4 (speaker 17 and her close friends) are transitional in practice as well as in social space. They firmly consider themselves in-betweens: they like to party, but do not consider themselves burnouts. These girls come from the same neighborhood as the people in cluster 2. They have been friends with each other since first grade, and with other people in the neighborhood, but these friendships started breaking up in junior high. One friendship, between Margaret (speaker 6) and Denise (speaker 19), broke up in eighth grade, when Denise felt that Margaret was getting into too much trouble. Margaret sees the choice at the time as having been between excitement and boredom. A tomboy holdout into sixth grade, Margaret talks about how hard it was to start hanging out with girls when the boys didn't want her around anymore. She found the girls' pursuits silly, but recognized the necessity of accommodating to the group:

Um, it was hard – well, I still wanted, you know – go out and play baseball and stuff, and they'd rather – "Well, let's go to a show," or "Let's go shopping." Shopping was a big thing – "Let's go shopping, let's buy these, buy this" and, you know, I – "OK, maybe tonight, but let's play baseball today" or something, you know, and it was kind of hard for me to, you know, to steer their way.

Coming from an educated family, Margaret decided to stay with the burnouts, despite pressure from her parents:

Margaret: That's, that's where all the, the jock–burn, or the jock–jelly thing started, beause I didn't hear anything about it in elementary school. But once I hit Rover, you know, that's all you heard was, "She's a jock," "She's a jell," you know. And that's all it was. You were either one. You weren't an in-between, which I was. I was an in-between (laughter) because here I was, I played [sports] . . . so I get along really good with, quote, jocks, ok. And I get along really good with jellys, because I'm right, I'm stuck right in the middle. And in my ninth grade, and tenth grade year, that kind of tore me apart a little bit too.
Penny: Why?
Margaret: Because I didn't –. My parents wanted me to make a decision. "Now which way are you going to go?" And here I was, you know.
Penny: Why?
Margaret: Because I was getting in trouble, and yet I'd always come back with them, "Well, you know, I'm trying to do the good things. Here I am, I'm getting, you know, A, B's, and C's," and this, that, and the other thing. I'd bring up arguments, and "Why can't I do what I want" every once in a great while, and –. So, I'd – uh, I was getting torn apart (laughter).

Irene (speaker 18), another girl from the same burnout neighborhood and arguably the most visible girl in cluster 4, describes how she pulled away from her neighborhood friends and became best friends with Denise:

It was around, um, when junior high started. . . . Because, like, I discovered other friends . . . it's not so much they changed though, I guess. Maybe I've changed too, or. . . . It's not so much you change it's just you grow up, whatever. You just decide. I don't know. If everybody was the same, the world would be so boring.

Nonetheless, Irene retains a friendship from the neighborhood with a girl from the top of cluster 4, Alice, who is a partier and not at all involved in school. They drew apart in junior high because of their very different desires, but when I asked if that had put an end to the friendship, she said:

> No, no, i – it had a break, you know. We didn't do things with each other as much or anything. But now, like now . . . we just keep in touch, but it's not like we enjoy the same things.

Alice and Irene still list each other as among their best friends. It is highly unusual for a jock girl to retain a close relationship with someone outside the jock circle, and Irene's relationship with Alice is among other things a sign (and perhaps a source) of Irene's social confidence. Irene is the only jock I met who is self-consciously working class, and who is proud of being able to cope with personal difficulties. She prides herself in being outspoken, and is one of the few girls to clash openly with an unpopular faculty advisor. Irene has the highest value for (Λ) of any jock or in-between girl, and in fact her value is above average for a burnout. The rest of her pattern, however, is more like that of a jock.

Cluster 4 and clusters d and e together constitute a heterosexual crowd. They dominate student government, varsity sports, elected offices, and the popularity market. The boys in cluster d are primarily involved in sports, but some of them are also involved in student government. The boys in cluster e, on the other hand, are almost all involved in non–athletic as well as athletic activities. This part of the social spectrum is hierarchical, and while Irene and a few girls around her appear secure in their status, many of the cluster 4 girls are concerned about their popularity. There is a similar, but nowhere as extreme, sense of hierarchy among the jock boys. One boy (speaker 61) who says he began to taste popularity through football, talked about his and his best friend's aspirations:

> You've heard the expression, "I'm on cloud nine." And we've labelled certain people that are cloud nine people, that are really up people, and then there's us on cloud eight, we're just below them, we gotta work our way up there to be accepted in school and then have a good time on the weekends I guess or whatever, go out with them, and get accepted by them.

The girls in clusters 4 and 5 are separated socially but intensively engaged together in activities. The girls in cluster 5, however, are not part of the heterosexual crowd of clusters 3 and 4, and many of them do not date at all. Most important, the people in cluster 5 emphatically do not think of themselves as jocks, and view the popularity market of cluster 4 with cynicism. While there are as many serious students in cluster 4 as cluster 5, the cluster 5 girls pride themselves on their sophistication, and participate in more intellectual school activities – newspaper, yearbook, debate club. Annette (speaker 27), a particularly outspoken member of cluster 5, sums up many of her friends' attitudes:

> I live in the real world. I don't, I don't think any of those people really do. And I'd be interested to see them at a reunion or something, see where they've gone – they'll probably all be bald and ugly.

Like most of the girls in cluster 5, she considers the popular crowd shallow, manipulative and two-faced:

> *Penny*:   Um, what's involved in being popular?
> *Annette*:   Uh, acting the way the populars do, or whatever, I mean, hating the right people (laughter) and liking the right people. Wearing the right things. Liking the right things.

In discussing how one particularly visible class project succeeded, Annette described how the popular crowd creates what she calls "branches," which can be activated as needed:

> *Annette*:   They needed them because they were good artists, so they, they let them in for a few days. (laughter)
> *Penny*:   So there are really branches of the elites.
> *Annette*:   Yeah. . . . They make them themselves, whenever they need it. Like the artists, o.k. I guess Carolyn and this Jerome kid would, would be one of the hangers on, but they can come into the popular group when they need them. (laughter) . . . or when they're having – one of the hangers on is having their party, they can come into the popular group when the popular group wants to go to their party.

Figure 7.7 compares the pattern for cluster 5 with that for clusters 1–4. It should not be surprising that the speech of the girls in cluster 5 is more conservative than that of any of the clusters discussed so far. Thus it is not the jock girls who are the most conservative overall, but the girls who are intensely engaged in the institution but less engaged in the social scene. This cluster does show a relatively high value for one variable, (o), which I will return to in section 7.5 below.

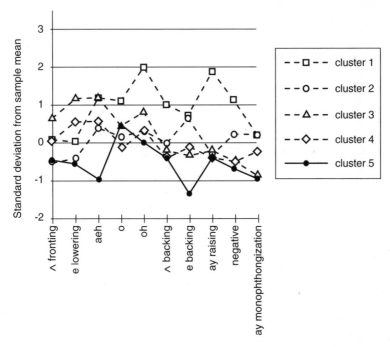

Figure 7.7 Average values for each variable for girls' clusters 1 to 5

7.3 The Social Continuum

When one moves from girls' cluster 1 to cluster 5, one moves through people with palpably different styles, activities, and orientations: from the burned-out burnouts of cluster 1 to the "regular" burnouts of cluster 2, then through the partying in-betweens in cluster 3 to the main group of jocks in cluster 4, and finally to the in-betweens in cluster 5 who are actively engaged in school activities. Moving from cluster 1 to cluster 4, the girls become increasingly school-oriented, decreasingly urban-oriented, increasingly "clean-cut," increasingly oriented to school-based popularity and visibility, decreasingly party-oriented. Moving from cluster 4 to 5, the girls become decreasingly involved in a heterosexual crowd, and decreasingly oriented to popularity and visibility.

The boys' network offers a similar continuum. The two burnout clus-

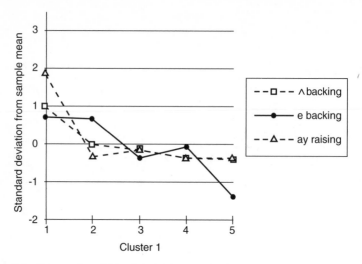

Figure 7.8   Pattern 2 variables by girls' network cluster

ters, a and b, do not correspond to a transition from more to less extreme burnouts, but to a transition between emphases – from "mellow" to "urban" burnouts. From then on, there is a continuum of increasing engagement in the school enterprise, from cluster e which includes several boys who are engaged in musical activities and a number of athletes, to cluster d, consisting primarily of athletes, and finally to cluster e, most of whom are heavily engaged in sports and other kinds of activities.

These continua show up in the following figures which show, cluster by cluster, the use of advanced variants for each variable. Figures 7.8 and 7.9 show the Pattern 2 and 3 variables among the speakers of the girls' main clusters, 1–5. The use of advanced variants of these variables shows a fairly regular decrease as one moves through this social continuum from cluster 1 to 5.

The somewhat weaker nature of the social correlations for boys' use of Pattern 2 variables and the complete lack of correlation for (ay) monophthongization found in earlier chapters shows up in the network patterns as well (Figures 7.10–11). The main difference for (ʌ) and (e) is between burnouts and non-burnouts, with little distinction within categories. While monophthongization continues to show little differentiation among boys, negative concord shows a fast decrease among the non-burnout boys from

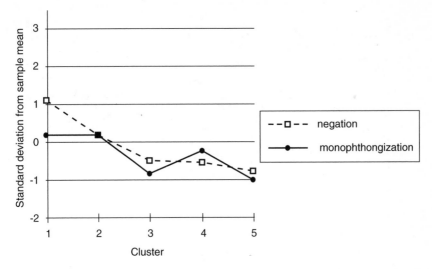

Figure 7.9 Pattern 3 variables by girls' network cluster

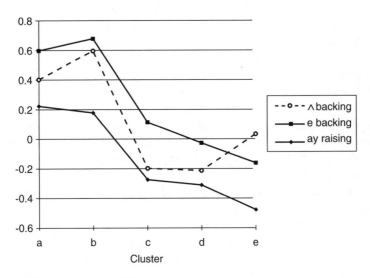

Figure 7.10 Pattern 2 variables by boys' network cluster

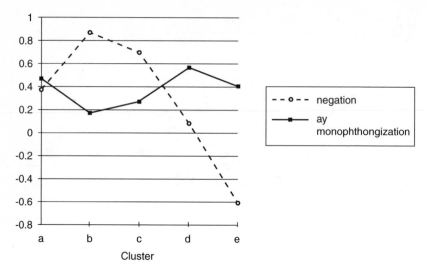

Figure 7.11   Pattern 3 variables by boys' network cluster

cluster c to d to e. The difference between the primarily athletic jocks of cluster d and the social jocks of cluster e, corresponding to the correlation with non-athletic activities found in Chapter 6, shows up in two of these cases. The athletes in cluster d show a level of (ay) raising comparable to the cluster b burnouts, while the in-betweens in cluster c and the jocks in cluster e show the lowest values. These latter boys also show the lowest use of negative concord.

While the Pattern 2 and 3 variables show a more robust correlation for girls than for boys, the reverse is true for Pattern 1b variables. This difference shows up in the network patterns as in the correlations in chapter 6. Figures 7.12 and 7.13 show the use of 1b variables along the boys' and the girls' network clusters respectively. Most particularly in the lowering of (e), there is a steep increase in the use of advanced variants as one moves towards the preppy end of the boys' network, while girls who show the greatest use of the Pattern 1b reversals are the partying in-betweens and the main cluster of jocks. The latter may indicate that the meaningful use of these variables is developing among those most centrally engaged in the school's central crowds, and that their significance has not been picked up elsewhere.

Among the boys, there is no discernible network pattern for Pattern 1 variables (figure 7.14). Among the girls, however, Pattern 1 variables show a similar pattern to 1b (figure 7.15). The network figures repeat the

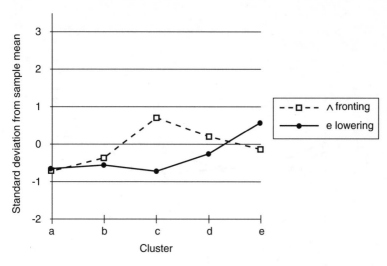

Figure 7.12   Pattern 1b variables by boys' network cluster

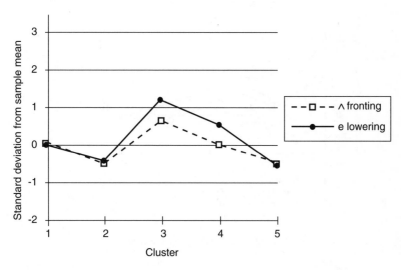

Figure 7.13   Pattern 1b variables by girls' network cluster

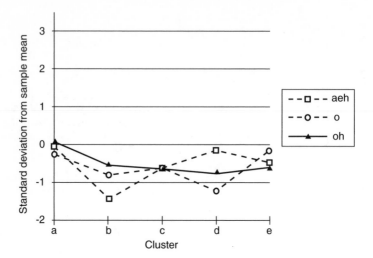

Figure 7.14 Pattern 1 variables by boys' network cluster

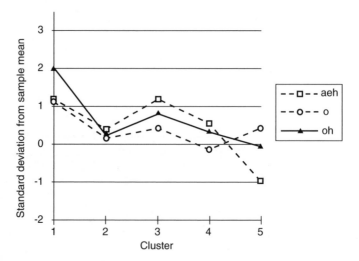

Figure 7.15 Pattern 1 variables by girls' network cluster

findings of chapter 6, that girls tend to differentiate among urban variables, while boys tend to differentiate among suburban variables. There remains a puzzle about girls' overall greater use of the Pattern 1 variables. The lead of clusters 1 and 3 in the use of Patterns 1 and 1b may be clarified below.

7.4   Extreme Speakers

As I have discussed at length above, the burned-out burnout girls of cluster 1 are by far the most extreme speakers in the entire cohort. But there are other speakers who stand out in their extreme use of certain variables as well. I return to table 7.1, to discuss the leading speakers who are not burnouts. The top users of all variables are burnouts, followed by a jock (speaker 25) and an in-between (speaker 15). These latter two speakers owe their lead in overall use to their extreme use of Pattern 1. As table 7.1 shows, the leaders in the use of Pattern 2 variables are all burnouts, with the burned-out burnout girls all among the top eight. This requires no further explanation, since the urban and burnout significance of these variables has been clear throughout the study. What is more complex is the deployment of Pattern 1, which has shown a gender difference, but an unclear difference within gender groups. As mentioned above, the cluster 1 girls make extreme use of these variables along with the other patterns, setting them starkly apart from the burnout girls of cluster 2. The rest of the girls who lead in the use of Pattern 1 variables are at first sight quite a heterogeneous group, including jocks and in-betweens from a variety of places in the network. Consideration of these speakers suggests strongly that the older changes, which are advanced throughout the suburban area, constitute a generalized stylistic resource for speakers at large. Because they are present in the speech of older generations as well as adolescents, and because they are present throughout the metropolitan area – even the midwest – rather than limited to urban areas, these variables are a kind of linguistic public property. The question is, what kinds of people choose to make extreme claims on this property?

The non-burnout leaders in the use of Pattern 1 are all in clusters 3 (speakers 13 and 15) and 4 (speakers 21, 24, and 25). The extreme users in cluster 4 are all at the edge of the cluster and all have broad connections within and beyond that cluster. Given their place in the network, close to cluster 5, one might expect these speakers to have more conservative patterns. However, their place in the network appears to be crucial to their extreme uses of Pattern 1 variables. All three of these speakers deny having one main group of friends, but cultivate a variety of friendships, which shows up in their connections in the network. Only one other member of the speaker sample makes the same claim – speaker 23 who, like speaker 24, connects clusters 4 and 5. The significance of the Pattern 1 variables may be apparent in the difference between speakers 23 and 24. Speaker

23, who makes relatively conservative use of all the variables, has been friends with speakers 21 and 22 for some time, but aligns herself primarily with cluster 5. She is a top student, and vehemently distances herself from the popularity market, hanging out with people she meets in AP (advanced placement) classes, including a number of boys who constitute an "intellectual crowd." Speaker 24 (Gloria), on the other hand, is much more of a "social animal." Connecting clusters 4 and 5, Gloria has more connections (10) overall than anyone else in the network except for Eunice, the girl directly above her in the sociogram, who has 12 connections. Eunice shows very high values for the use of these variables as well, but was not included in the linguistic sample because she moved to Belten from Detroit in junior high school. Gloria and Eunice are important brokers. They pride themselves in having many friends, and no best friends, and they are both well known and well liked. Gloria in particular stands out in Belten High as flamboyant and outgoing, and describes herself as a flirt. She is known as an enthusiastic gossip (but not a malicious one) and a character. She emphasizes the importance of getting to know people, and when I asked her about how people become popular, she answered as follows:

> Beats me, I'm still working on it (laughter) . . . Like, well, you know, you, you just talk, like try and meet a lot of people, and talk to l – people in class and stuff, like we got our new classes, and – mainly like don't s – like a lot of times like people will go into classes, they'll see one person they know, and they go and sit by them. And, you know, they'll never know anybody else if they don't sit by somebody (laughter) they don't know . . . You know, if – you don't have to be best friends with all of them, but just even to say "Hi" and . . . you know.

These personality traits make her generally visible, and a valuable connection for the girls in cluster 5. Because her connections plunge fairly deep into cluster 4, she has access to information about people and activities in that cluster, making her a perfect broker for cluster 5.

Speaker 21, Natalie, plays a similar role for her cluster of friends, who are deeply engaged in school activities but consider themselves not to have quite "made it" in the popularity market. With the exception of speaker 23, Natalie and her friends are concerned about popularity. One of them, Bertha, talked about the concern with popularity when they entered high school:

> . . . . as soon as you get into high school, it's like "popularity, popularity" – everybody's like, you know, you have to be popular, that's what – that's what's

in, you know, so you have to try to get the popular friends, the people who are really popular. . . . I thought that Irene Castagno was really popular, I had to get to know her. Then when I made it on pompon squad, I got to, you know, know a lot of really popular girls. But then you find out that they're not really – they're popular but they're just like everybody else, you know, and that's what I was really glad, because now they've become, you know, re-good friends of mine and I don't, I don't care whether they're popular or not.

Nonetheless, she still finds popularity intimidating:

Penny: Are there people that make you really tense?
Bertha: Yes!
Penny: Like who?
Bertha: Um, boys in particular. Really popular ones. I get really tense around them. I'm not, I don't know. The boy atmosphere is just kind of (laughter) I've really been close to girls all my life. I've really had really close friends, so it's kind of hard for me, I get really tense around people like that. But even still, really popular people I'm still really tense around – maybe I'll say something wrong, maybe, you know, I'll do something wrong, and then they'll hate me, and then (laughter) you know.

Of all these girls, Natalie is known for seeking popularity and trying to get "in" with Irene (speaker 18) and her friends. Her best friend, Jamie (speaker 22), accepts this, and figures that she benefits from it: "Natalie's like trying to be in the popular crowd, so I meet some of the more popular kids." Jamie contrasts her more reticent style with Natalie's:

She talks to (laughter) me a lot on the phone, and I, sort of, listen. . . . I don't know, I, I feel kind of, when I call somebody I don't really know, I have to call for a reason, I can't just call to talk. Like I know Natalie can. She'll just call anybody that she doesn't really know and she'll just talk to them. And I always feel like I'm interfering with something, so I never have done that.

Over and over, I heard Natalie's closest friends, as well as girls in cluster 5, joke about her overwhelming upward mobility, and about her energetic networking. Natalie emphasizes that while Jamie is her best friend, she also has many friends that she meets in her activities:

I'm not trying to say I'm Miss Popular and I know everybody, but there's no defined circle. I just kind of have a lot of different friends . . . I have friends from track, and I have friends from cheerleading. And we share, we share different interests, while me and the ch–, my cheerleading girlfriends share other interests. Or, me and my physics buddy share different interests. Where, if these two people met, they don't really have anything in common as my friend and myself do.

Speaker 25, Beth, is not tightly integrated into any cluster, but is friends with a variety of people in school, in her neighborhood and in her church group. Until junior high school, she was best friends with a group of burnouts from cluster 2, who live in her neighborhood, but she pulled away in junior high school because of her involvement in school activities:

> *Beth*:   It's funny, it makes me laugh to think of these people now . . . it's funny because these people are so different right now, I can't (laughter)
> *Penny*:   Really, how are they different?
> *Beth*:   They're – well, they'd be classified as the, uh, quote burnouts, you know. They're just totally different. And now, you know, when I see them in the hall, we, you know, sometimes we'll say "hi," but that's completely it, you know, and I think that we were really, all of us, we had like a little group, you know, we were all really close, you know, every weekend it would be a pajama party at someone else's house, you know, and something like that. And now, it's just, you know, just over junior high, like between sixth, sixth and seventh grade really, it's just a big change (laughter).
> *Penny*:   Really. Uh huh. And do you remember how it happened? I mean were you still friends when they started becoming different from you?
> *Beth*:   Not r–, well, it was like over the summer I think really, of sixth grade. And um, I'm not exactly sure how it happened now that I think about it, but just like in junior high, for a little bit, we were friends, you know. And then we just, I think a lot of it was our interests, you know, they just had, I was in a lot of [activities], and you know, I was more interested really in school, and they just, and, oh, they were more interested in partying and stuff. And I wasn't really. At that time, I think in seventh grade, I was just more afraid, you know, I just didn't, you know, the thought of smoking and stuff didn't really, I didn't want to, and so –

With the loss of that friendship group, she entered high school making friends with a wide range of people through her church and school activities. She is highly visible in the school for her intensive and enthusiastic participation in activities, particularly in theater and music, and rather than participating in a tight group of friends, she tends to pursue individual friendships through her activities. Beth is the only extreme speaker in this sample who is not flamboyantly outgoing. In fact, she was plagued with shyness in elementary school – a problem that she worked hard in junior high to overcome. It may well have been this effort and her status as a free social agent that has moved her to develop an extreme speech style.

The two other non-burnout speakers who make extreme use of variables are in cluster 3. I have already discussed Sarah (speaker 13) at some length above. She is known as the most outgoing member of cluster 3, and although she no longer participates in school activities, she is known as "crazy" and funloving and is a very visible member of the cohort. Less outgoing, but ranking in the top 10 per cent overall is speaker 15, Angela, whose high overall values stem from her extreme use of Pattern 1 variables. This seems to fit in with the patterns of her social activities. As the sociogram shows, Angela is not tightly integrated into her class, but hangs out with older girls, and together they socialize with people from other towns. Angela's middle class parents expect her to go to college, but she plans to be a secretary directly out of high school. While she drinks, smokes dope, and parties, she is a reasonably good student and vehemently does not consider herself a burnout. However, she is one of only two non-burnouts in the speaker sample who have the kind of non-school connections that are characteristic of burnouts. Angela and a couple of Belten friends have been hanging out at a skating rink in another suburb since junior high. The social scene at this rink spans suburban schools, and Angela and her friends orient to this social scene rather than to Belten, attending parties in other suburbs and looking upon the Belten scene as less sophisticated. This is not an urban crowd, however, but a crowd primarily from suburbs farther from Detroit.

The other person in the speaker sample who has broader suburban connections is speaker 37, Cindie. Like Angela, Cindie has distanced herself to some extent from school networks since junior high. Two of Cindie's closest friends moved from Neartown, and rather than making new friends in school, she and the remaining member of their group concentrated on external networks. Unlike Angela, though, Cindie has moved into an older crowd, socializing almost exclusively with people who are out of school, frequenting the bars in Windsor on weekends. While she and her best friend attended school functions in junior high, they lost interest in school things in high school and saw high school as a time to break away from the limitations of home and school:

When you start going to high school, you start looking forward more to the weekends, I think, and going places farther from home, and doing, you know, things that you've never done before.

While Cindie does not rank in the top 10 percent of the class in the use of grouped variables, she does rank eighth in the use of advanced variants of (ae).

The extreme users of Pattern 1 vowels are all known for their sociability, but so are other people in the sample. The difference is that the extreme users are known also for for being navigators of broad networks, and most of them are known for flamboyance in that enterprise. Speakers 1, 2, 3, and 15 (and 27 as well) are primarily engaged with people from outside of Belten High, most of them older. Speakers 1, 2, and 3 are particularly focused on being outgoing in that arena, meeting new people and partying on a continual basis. They are consciously flamboyant, distinguishing themselves from what they see as the drab norm of Belten High. Their extreme use of Pattern 1 as well as Pattern 2 vowels, I would argue, heightens the overall effect of their style. Speakers 13 and 24 are known throughout clusters 3, 4, and 5 as the most outgoing girls in the class, and are both credited for having flamboyant personalities. They both pride themselves on this character as well. Speakers 24 and 25 stand out for their diffuse networks and their functions as brokers, and speaker 21 stands out for her relentless networking and her eagerness to take on this function.

While these speculations are after the fact, I would argue that they are not entirely ad hoc. However, they are simply speculations, and could only be confirmed through in-depth study of their use of variation in interaction. I would emphasize here that while I believe that no speaker's patterns of variation are accidental, their development is so embedded in individuals' histories that the analyst cannot hope to have access to explanations at the level of the individual. However, there are kinds of linguistic practice that are integral to certain ways of operating in the world, and defining these ways of operating is as important to the sociolinguistic enterprise as identifying categories and aggregations. Many ways of operating are specific to class, ethnicity, and age. But they are perhaps most basic to gender. While I would not overemphasize the view of women as connection oriented (e.g. Belenky et al. 1986), I would also not discount it. It is unquestionable that personal networking is a far greater preoccupation for girls in high school than it is for boys, precisely because it is the primary means that girls have for gaining visibility and influence. But working on connections and status is a delicate operation in high school, because of the strong sanctions on serious social competition (Eckert 1990b). The development of strategies for being socially aggressive without appearing too serious is crucial to girls' social networking, and distinguishes it from the kind of serious aggressiveness associated with professional networking.

7.5   On the Margins

Sociolinguistic studies tend to focus on speakers who are "typical" in some way. Labov's study (1972a) of the "Lames", however, offered a picture of speakers whose marginal position in network clusters correlated with unusual linguistic patterns. There are several people in the Belten speaker sample who are truly on the margins – who do not feel that they fit in, who consider themselves "loners." Donna, speaker 34, is not a loner, but sees herself as on the periphery looking in, and doesn't like what she sees. She views Belten as a very divided school – as a school dominated by a snobby jock crowd, and in which people cannot afford to be different:

> Yeah. There's, there's like a lot of loners in this school, you know, who, like will come out in the courtyard and look for somebody to talk to, and I'll talk to them, you know, and then, and then you get like a label, you know, like "Oh, you're weird," you know, and – and this. And I just don't pay any attention to those kind of people, because, again, it's the people that are popular, you know. If you're not in just with them, then, you know, you're nobody to them.
>
> . . .
>
> They just – like, when they're not with their friends, they'll talk to you. If they're –, like you're the only person, or something. Or they see you shopping, or something, they'll talk to you, and everything. But, and then like you'll, you'll come to school the next day and you'll say "Hi" to them, and they just, "Oh, who are you?" you know, "I don't know you," "I don't talk to you," "You're not my friend," or whatever. I just –.

Several people with patterns that stand out are what are commonly called "loners," people who are only loosely integrated into the peer social fabric. It is not surprising that such people might not develop delicate linguistic patterns in concert with major clusters, since they lack the opportunity to participate on an ongoing basis in the process of meaning-making with a consistent set of peers. However, the ways in which loners' patterns stand out are not all the same. The emphasis so far in the discussion of people with extreme uses of Pattern 1 variables has been on a general outgoing-ness. At the opposite extreme are people who are painfully shy.

The most conservative speaker in the sample across the board is speaker 28, in cluster 5. Trailing just behind her are Ann (speaker 33) and Harold (speaker 69). Placed between clusters 4, 5, and 6, Ann suffers from extreme shyness, and finds it difficult to make and keep friends. During her sophomore year, she was friends for a brief period with some girls in cluster 4. She felt, though, as if she didn't belong, because the others were better friends with each other than they were with her, and because she found herself incapable of being sufficiently aggressive to keep up her part of the friendship. In her junior year, she spent time in school with cluster 6, who welcomed her at their lunch table, and with whom she occasionally went to school events.

> Oh, well I've always wished I could go to a, a dance. Or, uh, just someone call me and say "Did you want to go to, uh, the game" or, something. . . . I've always been quiet, and I think some people are turned off that I'm quiet and shy, and they don't try to talk to me. Uh, I've been trying very hard to make more friends, but it's hard to just say, "Be my friend" (laughter). . . . I don't see why I'm not involved with friends and have some close friends, or – like other people, not everybody, but most people have a group of friends that they do things with, and they can talk easily with them, and I have a few friends but not a whole group of friends. And sometimes I wonder is there something I'm doing wrong.

While she feels lacking because she can't integrate herself into the peer culture, she does not lack for social involvement, which she finds in her church group and with her extended family. It is particularly with her family that she is able to live without insecurity:

> Oh, I'm different than I am in school. Um, I have more of a sense of humor with my family, and um, I feel more relaxed, and I'm not really worried about anything. I'm not worried about what they'll think if I do something. Or that I have to do anything toward keeping my family, because I'll never lose them. It's different than with my friends.

Harold is another loner in school, but he is closely integrated into his church. While Harold and Ann are both shy, and while they feel somewhat inept in relations with their peers, they each have long-term and consistent participation in communities of practice outside of school, and communities of practice that are dominated by adults. Given the nature of these communities of practice – Harold's church and Ann's family – it is not surprising that Harold's speech is the most conservative of all the boys in the sample, and Ann's speech is the second most conservative overall of all the girls in the sample.

There are two other people on the margins who are neither the most advanced nor the most conservative speakers, but whose patterns are noticeably anomalous. While the leaders in the use of Pattern 1 variables discussed

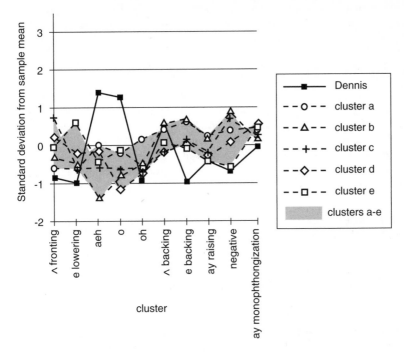

Figure 7.16   Comparison of Dennis with major boys' clusters

above all rank high in the use of each of these variables, these two speakers rank very high in the use of individual Pattern 1 variables. In both cases, these are the oldest variables, (aeh) or (o). Both of these speakers are outside of the mainstream in the school. Dennis (speaker 51) ranks fifth overall in the use of advanced variants of (o), and seventh in the use of advanced variants of (aeh), but he ranks close to the bottom in his use of (oh), (e) backing, and (ay) raising. As shown in figure 7.16, Dennis's high use of (aeh) and (o) make him completely unlike any other male speaker, since these are both variables used primarily by girls. And although the people he spends time with when he does socialize tend to be burnouts, his speech is more like a female jock's than a female burnout's. Dennis is extremely self-conscious, both in demeanor and by his own report. He has not had a good friend since elementary school, when his best friend changed schools:

> I didn't really – since – since then, I never really did hang around with anybody that you could call a friend. Except for the neighbor – neighbor kids around the block . . . most of the time, most of the time, I don't even hang

around anybody, most of the time. I'm either at school, you know where it's everybody, I'm "oh hi what's going on," and stuff, or people like that or, I'm at work where I just know the guys that I work with.

He attributes his lack of friends to his shyness:

> *Dennis*:   Just like some people got it where they could go out and get their friends. They – they got the knack, they got the magic. I'm not one of those people.
> *Penny*:   Why not? I mean do you have any idea why?
> *Dennis*:   I don't know, maybe I'm, maybe I, I just don't strike up a good conversation, I don't know.

He describes himself as overcome with fear of doing something wrong, and as a result reluctant to be with people:

> I'm just kind of like, oh I don't want to, you know, maybe it's somebody that I think more of, or something. Oh, I don't want to stick around with [xxx], I'm going to do something wrong or something where they, they, they, they won't think so, so hot of me. So I think I'll just uh, just kind of make my way out of the way, and then, you know, uh . . . I'm afraid I'm going to screw up or something. Um, oh, if I do, I just kind of, just forget about it you know. . . . but then you get those, those people that, that, uh, never, never let something go. They, they got something on you, "oh, yeah, we seen you trip down that step, yeah. Oh, yeah, you really made a fool out of yourself," they you know, next time you run them, "hey how you doing, yeah are you going to trip down the step again? Uh, let's see, watch."

Dennis does not hide, however. Rather, he moves around the world on his own, projecting a carefully constructed "Fonzie" image, striking a confident attitude, all the time keeping people at arm's length.

The other speaker with an unusual pattern is Alicia, speaker 35. Alicia is not as isolated in school as Dennis. However, her group of friends are less integrated into the rest of the class, and have few connections outside of school as well. Some of them are thought of as loners, and some of them think of themselves that way as well. The girls in Alicia's cluster are not shy, but they are notable both in their relative disconnect fom other clusters, and in the nature of their own connections. A number of the girls in these clusters talk about their friendships as problematic, or having been in some sense foisted upon them, or as existing out of necessity. These friendships date back to elementary and junior high school, but the girls reflect a

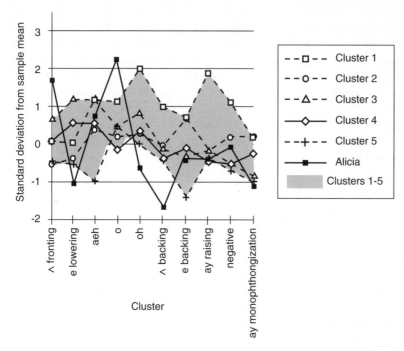

Figure 7.17 Comparison of Alicia with major girls' clusters

sense that they are friends because they haven't made many new friends in high school. Many other kids in the class point to the girls in cluster 6 as the "weird people," and many single out Alicia for particular ridicule as someone who is "clueless."

Alicia is ranked seventh on the Pattern 1 list, but her place in this ranking is due to an extremely high use of (o), placing her second for that variable in the entire population. She ranks 14th in the use of (aeh), but ranks quite low in the use of other variables, and is the lowest ranking user of (ʌ) backing. This gives Alicia's vowels an unusual spiked pattern, as shown in figure 7.17.

Alicia is very outgoing, but in a way that strikes many of her peers as "goofy," while Dennis carefully constructs a "cool" persona to serve as a kind of mask for his insecurity. The fact that both of these speakers make a kind of extreme use of Pattern 1 vowels that differs from general patterns in the school suggests a relation between integration into the social fabric and the "appropriate" use of variables. It also suggests that Pattern l vowels, the oldest variables in the chain shift, are available to all speakers as generalized expressive resources. I will discuss this further in the concluding chapter. It is particularly interesting that (o) is the one that has been found in this study to have the least clear social meaning. One might speculate that inasmuch as Alicia and Dennis are isolated from the mainstream of meaning-making activity in the school, they have constructed their expressive patterns pretty much on their own. In both cases, they have drawn on the oldest variables, the ones that are most widespread throughout the community, using them disproportionately in relation to community norms.

7.6   Conclusions from the Network Study

The knowledgeable construction of local styles is a function of integration into local networks and access to local information. The importance of information is clear at the level of clothing style. For example, in the middle of senior year, there was a dance – a battle of the bands, in which a local punk band challenged a local heavy metal band to a musical duel. Punk was an important issue at the time. There were clusters of in-betweens who were into punk style, a few people were coming to school in clothes bought at second hand stores, and school officials were beginning to send them home to change into more conventional dress. Jocks and burnouts alike found the punks bothersome – presumably because the punks represented a progressive trend rejecting the conservative class-based opposition between jocks and burnouts.[1] At the same time, Belten High was known among local schools as being "punk," and the students at Belten recognized that this gave their school distinction – a bit of a reputation as ahead of the other schools. And after all, punks were being highlighted in the news and adult media as representing the latest in adolescent trends.

The jocks decided to dress "punk" for the dance, and the word went around the school – not all around the school, but to those close enough to clusters 3, 4, and 5 to hear it. Plans were made for outfits at lunch, on the phone, at people's houses. The night of the dance, I arrived before any students, and watched as people began to filter in. Some of the earliest arrivals, people who were not very central in the school social network, were not dressed as punks. They were surprised to see some other students arrive, dressed in quite flamboyant punk outfits – somewhat shredded clothes held together with safety pins. But an hour later, when the main cluster 4 jocks arrived, much of the rest of the room stopped to watch their entrance. No safety pins or tatters for these jocks; they were dressed in mod style, after *Clockwork Orange*, subdued and dapper. Nobody failed to notice and comment on the jocks' punk style, for it was the most visible, and given the structure of institutional meaning-making rights (and a school dance is an institutional function), it was also the most authoritative. Together, the jocks had agreed on a particular spin on the punk look – one that marginalized the "true" punks. And regardless of the hierarchical aspects of the various styles at this dance, it is clear that the negotiation of style was accomplished within, and confined to, the network clusters that constituted basic communities of practice in the school.

Certain aspects of linguistic style are also negotiated consciously. I can recall explicit discussions in my own high school crowd of "cool" ways to say things, generally in the form of imitations of cool people with explicit references to foregrounded utterances. But in general, linguistic influence takes place without explicit comment and all the more requires direct access to speakers. The adoption of a way of speaking, like a way of dressing, no doubt requires both access and a sense of entitlement to adopt the style of a particular group. Information is at a premium, and the above discussion suggests that those without access to information from the dominant crowds in the school social order are likely to be either conservative or anomalous in their linguistic usage. But in addition, and perhaps most crucial to a consideration of the social spread of linguistic change, the general accessibility of a particular variable depends on the extent to which it has spread through the population.

The most striking result of the network study is the overwhelming community lead of the burned-out burnout girls in the use of almost all variables. These girls' use of all variables, not simply the "burnout" ones, makes every single utterance stand out. Thus the flamboyance of these girls' personal style is manifested in their speech as well as their dress, attitude, and action. They are linguistic icons, representing in the school what is the farthest out from the institutional, and placing a big red flag on the social and linguistic map. As icons, they constitute a local nexus for the construction of social and sociolinguistic meaning. Other speakers who lead in the use of Pattern 1 variables appear to stand out for their networking and flamboyance. It appears, then, that the Pattern 1 variables, carrying no urban associations and widespread in the region, constitute a more generalized kind of stylistic intensifier. These are available, by virtue of their widespread distribution, to all speakers no matter how marginalized in the age cohort. The female lead in the use of these variables, then, stems from girls' greater inclination and/or freedom to engage in flamboyant stylizing. And the most conservative speakers will be those who are constrained, whether by male gender norms or by shyness, to avoid a flamboyant style.

Note

1   The status of punks as a progressive group is discussed in Eckert 1989.

8

Style, Social Meaning, and Sound Change

The correlations found in chapters 5, 6, and 7 relate the use of variables to social categories and to the practices and groups that constitute these categories. Ultimately, they point to the stylistic work of the communities of practice in which the students of Belten High participate, and in which they negotiate their relation to, and the significance of, these practices. While the individual variables available in a dialect may correlate with various aspects of social membership and practice, most of them take on interpretable social meaning only in the context of the broader linguistic styles to which they contribute, including both the inventory of variables and their use. When we view each variable in isolation, thinking of speakers as leading or lagging in the use of advanced variants, we miss the overall effect of speakers' choices. What distinguishes speakers in Belten High is not simply the extent to which they use variables, but the way in which they combine frequencies in the inventory of variables.

Social meaning is not incidental to style, but it is very much what style is about. One might say that style is the terrain upon which social meaning is constructed – that people are able to work with social meaning partly by virtue of its attachment to the concrete material of style. Rethinking social meaning in variation requires rethinking our approach to style as well. So far, research on style in variation has focused on intra-speaker variability, viewing that variability as a negotiation of one's relation to the social world – particularly to the immediate situation. With the traditional focus on variables in relation to the socioeconomic hierarchy (Labov 1966, Trudgill 1974), stylistic variation has been treated in terms of the speaker's negotiation of that hierarchy. Viewing variation as a function of attention paid to speech, Labov (1972b: chapter 3) treats stylistic variation in terms of applying constraint on the more automatic, vernacular, variants in situations that call for more standard speech. This places an emphasis on poles of prestige and stigma. Bell (1984) views stylistic variation in a somewhat less constrained way, but as accommodation to audience, whether real or imagined. In both cases, the relation between style and identity is purely reactive – speakers style-shift in order to form a presentation of self in relation to their interlocutors. I am not the first to argue for a view of style as a more creative process. Coupland (in press) and Rickford and McNair-Knox (1994) have moved beyond the view of style-shifting as purely reactive, and explored the notion of style-shifting as performances of personae. Indeed, Coupland has long viewed style as involving the active construction of a persona through the use of a range of dialectal resources. In both of these cases, the resources are accessible and come with ready-made meaning by virtue of their association with well-defined dialects (Cardiff English in Coupland's case, and African American Vernacular English in the case of Rickford and McNair-Knox).

I wish to take this approach to style a step further in a direction set out by the California Style Collective (1993). In this view, style is a process of bricolage – an appropriation of local and extra-local linguistic resources in the production not just of a pre-existing persona but of new twists on an old persona. One particularly striking example of the conscious construction of meaning in style – in this case clothing style – comes from a conversation I had with two high school girls in California in 1985. These two best friends were part of the main preppy group (more or less equivalent to a Belten High jock). However, they felt some admiration for the new wavers, who were a prominent counter-cultural group in their high school, because of their autonomy – their unwillingness to be dominated by "the school thing." The new wavers wore dark eye makeup and black clothing, most notably black pegged jeans, while the preppies stayed away from dark colors and wore straight legged designer blue jeans and light or bright colored name brand shirts and jackets. These two girls found a way to align themselves slightly with the new wavers without moving too far from the preppy mainstream, by pegging their blue jeans. This stylistic move was completely conscious and completely rational. The girls saw it as a social strategy, and were able to tell me about it unselfconsciously, and to tell me what each element represented. Certain aspects of linguistic style also work this way – those aspects of style that are most easily controlled and most easily associated with parts of the social landscape. Thus people adopt lexical items, expressions, intonation patterns, and pronunciations, at least of particular words, in a quite conscious construction of style whether momentary or as part of a trajectory. One might, for example, combine uses of "cool," "dude," or "whatever" with otherwise fairly standard English to achieve a "with it" image – to show that one is in tune with, but not limited to, vernacular culture.

One might venture to say that speakers can mix and match variables in the construction of local meanings just as they might mix and match items of adornment. The patterns of variation shown in chapters 5–7 suggest that while this process of mixing is constrained, the speakers of Belten High are actively and selectively using the resources offered by the variables under study in a way that yields a variety of styles. But this production of style and social meaning is above all a collaborative effort. Styles are developed within communities of practice as part of the community's efforts to make meaning of themselves as they jointly interpret the social landscape, and jointly carve out a desired place for themselves in that landscape. While individuals can, and certain individuals do, invent styles of their own, these new styles are meaningful to the extent that others can interpret them. Thus they must be placed within a landscape of stylistic meaning. Furthermore, their effect on that landscape depends on others' willingness to engage with those meanings. Marginalized people, therefore, no matter how much stylistic activity they may engage in, are unlikely to set trends except in the case of humorous backlash.

One member of cluster 5 was known for her fashionable clothing. An avid reader of *Seventeen* magazine, she was always the first person to arrive in school with the latest fashions appearing in that magazine and in the department stores. But this won her scorn rather than admiration or even approval. Her friends thought she was silly for following *Seventeen* slavishly, and she herself told me that the other people in school didn't like the fact that she came in with the latest styles because she didn't have the social status required to introduce new styles. She could even point to the girl in cluster 4 who was known for introducing new styles into the school, and who would be licensed to introduce the styles that she was wearing prematurely. While none of her peers would deny that she was fashionable within the global context, she was not locally fashionable. She was violating the local order by reaching out as an individual and making a direct connection to the world at large, without the mediation of the local community. And by making this move, she was in effect rejecting that mediation, hence rejecting the supremacy of the local social order.

While stylistic activity involves reaching out into the social landscape to assess the use of resources, and to seek new resources or new ways of deploying old resources, this activity is anything but random. I emphasize creative agency, not because I believe that speakers are constantly looking for new ways to speak or that they are completely free in their adoption of new elements of style, but to counter the prevailing emphasis in the literature on norms and on the constraining effect of social groups. Innovation does not come in through accident and inattention, or through the chance encounter. It comes in through very much the same mechanism, no doubt, as the basic acquisition of language – a process of analysis of the relation between linguistic form and its effect in the world. In fact, I am inclined to think of language acquisition as a process that continues throughout life, but focuses on different aspects of language through the life course as speakers construct and revise their theories of the linguistic behavior of others and of the effects in the world of their own linguistic behavior.

8.1   Sociolinguistic Icons

In my discussion, I have referred to urban variables as urban symbols, speaking of them as if they were comparable to wallet chains and Detroit jackets. It is clear that phonological variables are not as manipulable as features of clothing, and it is clear that for the most part, speakers are not accustomed to overt strategizing about their pronunciations. However, certain features of linguistic style are consciously negotiated and rehearsed.

Certain intonation contours are a linguistic resource that people can consciously adopt. Much of the perception of "valley girl" speech is based on intonation, and the spread of new intonation patterns can be extremely rapid. Undoubtedly, the value of linguistic elements for stylistic purposes derives from their ease of adoption, and new expressions, lexical items, discourse markers, and intonation contours can be adopted in at least stereotypic fashion with little contact with their native speakers. And the properties that make them easily adoptable also make them easily identifiable and available for meaning negotiation. The inventory of sociolinguistic resources is heterogeneous, not only in social meaning, but in simplicity and clarity of social meaning, and it may be that simplicity and clarity are related to the extent to which the variable is separable from the rest of the grammar. Of all the variables covered in this study, the ones with the most stark social distributions are those that are not part of the Northern Cities Chain Shift: negative concord and (ay) raising. As arguably the most common stigmatized variable in the English language, negative concord is bound to show stark social distributions – it is almost a touchstone of variation. Unlike the vowels in the chain, whose pronunciations are linked to some extent by their coexistence in vowel space, the raised diphthong (ay) can overlap only with /oy/, which occurs rarely but most commonly word finally and before /l/ – both environments that turn out to highly disfavor (ay) raising. Speakers may be freer, therefore, to vary this vowel. In addition, the diphthong pro-vides a clear contrast between nucleus and coda, possibly making increased differentiation more salient than the movement of a monophthong. On the other hand, the vocalic variable that has the least identifiable social meaning is (o) fronting. As I will discuss below, this could well be related to its middle position between two pivotal vowels, as well as its considerable overlap and perhaps incipient merger with (oh). While the other vocalic variables show sometimes delicate, and always significant patterns of variation, (ay) raising and negative concord have a kind of iconic status. Their use as part of a speaker's style serves as a kind of road map for certain key social concerns.

While styles are constructed within communities of practice, the success of the global stylistic enterprise depends on the clear establishment of social meaning. As speakers reach out into the sociolinguistic landscape, inter-preting what they hear in terms of whose mouth it is coming out of, there need to be clear places in the linguistic map. This map is populated not only by iconic variables, but by iconic speakers. Judy and her friends in cluster 1 are cultural and linguistic icons in Belten High. Collectively, they lead the rest of Belten High in the use of extreme variants of every variable except negative concord (in which they do lead among the girls) and the preppy changes – the reversals of (e) and (ʌ) backing. As local icons, the burned-out burnouts are in a position to make meaning for the rest of the commu-nity. In their extreme speech, they are not just using phonetic variants with a set meaning; rather, their very use of those variants produces a social meaning. In their position as prototypical burnouts, their every utterance creates meaning for variables and for being a burned-out burnout in the inseparability of the use of phonetic variation and the construction of identities.

The potential of the iconic individual for making sociolinguistic meaning is inseparable from the situations in which that meaning is made. This is where the ethnography of speaking becomes crucial for the understanding of variation. Bauman, in his discussion of market calls in San Miguel d'Allende (in press), illustrates and points out the intersection among social categories, situations, genres, and linguistic styles in the establishment of social meaning in variation. Bauman points out that vendors' market calls are tied to a recurrent context, the market, to a category or categories of speakers, the vendors, and to the specific content – the nature of the wares being hawked. He argues that as children grow up, hearing these calls must be an integral part of their sociolinguistic development as they foreground linguistic form and provide a stage for the performance of unusual linguistic variants. This foreground is in turn enhanced by the poetic structuring of the calls, which involves lexical repetition and phonological parallelism.

Foregrounding can be found in different kinds of interactions, both public and private, in which speakers perform language and identity. The jocks have a stage in the literal sense for the presentation of their style, in public appearances such as student government campaign speeches and award ceremonies. Such things as public teasing, arguing, flirting, etc., often involve stylized linguistic forms, as do small utterances that come to be iconic of certain groups, and that have particularly stylized forms. People can be heard working at the particular front rounded or fronting diphthong that is currently trendy in the lexical items "dude," or "cool." The situations in which they are said, the people who say them, and the intonations and voice qualities that accompany them all conspire to imbue the fronted vowel with social meaning. In Belten High during this study, burnouts' use of *right* with a particularly raised nucleus, and *excellent* with a backed stressed (e) has an iconic quality, both uttered slowly and in specific discourse contexts. Burnouts also have distinctive ways of using profanity, such as *damn* with a raised (aeh), and *fuck* with a backed (ʌ). This combines the effect of the extreme vowel with the force of profanity, and with utterances and situations that call for profanity. This combination emphasizes aspects of burnout culture, as the use of profanity signals independence from adult norms and the topic frequently reveals a sense of unfair treatment, anger, danger, or excitement, hence combining identity with both form and content. This merging of variable form and content is particularly striking in the case of (ay) raising. It is only the extreme variants of this vowel that carry social meaning in Belten High, and they appear to carry heightened meaning in the other suburbs as well. Tracing the individual occurrences of extreme raised (ay) back to their context in the interviews, I have shown (Eckert 1996a) that they occur virtually exclusively in utterances that are directly related to key burnout cultural themes: alienation from school, restricted substances, trouble, fights and disagreements, and social categories. In other words, the use of extreme raising is inseparable from the construction of burnout identity.

The notion of sociolinguistic icon can also be extended to a more macro level in the analysis of the general sociolinguistic order. Just as iconic individuals are the most extreme users of advanced variants in the peer social order, adolescents in general are the most extreme users among all age groups. I have already suggested that this is because adolescence is the most intense locus of the emerging peer-based social order as it moves away from childhood and towards adulthood. This social order is the result of several years' work appropriating social control into the cohort itself, and separating itself from direct adult control. There is a tremendous amount at stake in the emerging moral order – both the jocks and the burnouts are competing for what's "right," as are in-betweens of all kinds – frequently in their rejection of the polarization that forces them to be in-between. But in addition, adolescence is a cultural focus – it is an iconic life stage. Adolescents are put on stage, scrutinized, judged, satirized, and, generally, stigmatized. While adolescents may be constructing a complex and meaningful social order, adult society still controls institutions, including the schools that house them and the media that represent them. In some sense, adolescents are in a panopticon (Foucault 1977), consciously under the constant regulatory gaze of the adult world.

8.2   The Progress of Sound Change

The patterns of variation in Belten High conform to some extent to Labov's outline (1990) of the interaction of gender and social class in the progress of sound change. Labov has argued that sound change is constrained in its early stages primarily by class, but with a consistent gender effect, with women generally leading. As changes become more vigorous and move towards completion, there is a shift to an increase in gender difference and to greater interaction between gender and class. In these latter stages, Labov shows in some cases a gender crossover in the lower middle class, as women at the lower end of the occupational hierarchy show more vernacular use, while women at the upper end show more standard use, than men. If one were to take Belten's Pattern 2 variables as evidence of the social constraints on a current, vigorous change, we see very much the crossover pattern that Labov discusses. The burnouts, and particularly the burnout girls, lead in the use of advanced variants; and the jocks, and particularly the jock girls, lag in the change. Although gender differences within either category are not statistically significant, the general pattern clearly shows a gender crossover with girls leading the boys within each social category, in their overall relation to the change. Thus, with the burnouts leading in the use of advanced variants, the burnout girls lead the burnout boys; and with the jocks lagging in the use of advanced variants, the jock girls show a greater lag than the jock boys. The pattern also holds, with significant gender differences, in the case of (ay) raising which, while not part of the chain shift, is arguably a recent development in the Detroit area. However, although this pattern also shows up in older changes in Labov's data (e.g. (aeh) raising in Philadelphia), it does not in the older changes in Belten. As the changes get progressively older from (oh) to (o) and (aeh), the gender difference increases, but the relation between gender and social category becomes less clear. It appears that in the oldest changes, (aeh) and (o), the relation to social category breaks down.

It is difficult to compare results from studies of primarily adult populations, as those on which Labov's conclusions are based, with studies of a single age group. Most particularly, the social system in which the Belten High adolescents function is different in a number of respects from that of adults. The question is how different is it? To what extent is the lack of social category differences in the old variables in Belten a function of differences between the adolescent and the adult social order? Of course, differences in age-group sociolinguistic patterns due to life stage would have to be within the tolerances of change within the individual's system over the lifetime. Labov (1990) argues that the interaction between gender and social class cannot be studied with fewer than four class distinctions, and certainly the gradual crossover that he shows in his adult data is striking. The crossover shows up strikingly in the Belten data as well, though, when only the two class-based groups, the jocks and the burnouts, are taken into consideration. And chapter 6 shows some instances of gradual differentiation along lines of institutional engagement that are similar to differentiation in adult occupational categories. But I would be inclined to argue that Labov's conclusions about details of the development of social constraints over the life of a social change are premature. While the vigorous urban changes in this study conform well to Labov's account, what appears to characterize the older changes, (aeh) and (o) and even (oh) fronting, is a greater flexibility of deployment. I would speculate that this is related to the possibility that these are not just advanced changes, but moving toward a stable pattern, and that the explanation for the use of these variables lies not simply in the speech community itself, but in the broader sociogeographic context.

Because variables representing sound change in progress show similar general socioeconomic distributions to stable sociolinguistic variables, we have come to conflate them when we talk about the social dynamics of variation. At the same time, there has been discussion of the differences in the distributions of the two, such as the lower middle class crossover found by Labov (1966) and the frequently greater gender difference in correlations of sound changes in progress (Labov 1990). Haeri (1997) argues for viewing the social meanings of stable variables quite separately from those of changes in progress, claiming that stability allows variables to develop more conventionalized social meanings. I would add, further, that the widespread variables that are commonly viewed as stable in the study of English variation also show little regional differentiation in their social meaning. This pattern may well reflect that the significance of these variables is shared across the population, whereas the significance of changes in progress is still more local. It is both possible and intuitively compelling that variable reduction of (-ing) reflects and constructs simple formality and informality – the kind of formality and informality that anyone would be proud to engage in – and that it alone does not attach to prestige or stigma. The socioeconomic stratification of this variable, then, may be more associated with class differences in formality and attitudes about formality. Of course, some groups' greater informality may be stigmatized, and the greater use of -in may be an easily identifiable sign of that informality. However, a single -in does not carry the negative judgment of a single use of negative concord, which is stigmatized regardless of region, and is associated quite consciously with class and education. (th) and (dh), I believe, are quite widespread in US urban areas as emphatic and connoting toughness, and their urban character most likely derives from its association with European immigrant groups. These variables have been found in New York (Labov 1966), Detroit (Edwards 1991), Northern California (Mendoza-Denton 1997), and Chicago (based on work done by my students at the University of Illinois at Chicago in 1986) to be used most by members of large local immigrant communities. In this case, it is quite probable that the substrate effect of Italian (in the case of New York and Chicago), Polish (in the case of Detroit), and Spanish (Northern California) introduced the fortis variants of these variables into the community, to be picked up and deployed by the native English-speaking generations as markers of ethnic/class identity.

I would speculate that as a change gets older and spreads more widely, and as it becomes more of a common resource across widely diverse areas, it loses its value as a local symbol, becoming available for the negotiation of kinds of meaning that are common to a wider population. The older changes of the NCCS are still regionally specific, but within the region, they have come to constitute a widespread symbolic resource. The discussion of the relation between the stage of change and social meaning, therefore, must take the socio-geographic picture into account.

8.3   Sociolinguistic Geography: the Local and the Global

It has been my purpose in this book to establish that variation carries social meaning that is very local, but embedded within a socio-geographic context, and systematically related to global patterns. I have brought these local meanings into the conversation about variation not in order to dispense with global categories, but to attach them to personal and community experience in such a way that the structure of variation makes everyday sense. The link between the local and the global is the semi-local – the immediate geographic area that provides a concrete context for the local. This concrete context is not simply spatial, but brings together social geography and local social and sociolinguistic practice and permits speakers to locate themselves and their speech in a wider landscape of sociolinguistic meaning. In doing so, speakers position themselves with respect to the progress of linguistic change. The question of how sound change spreads outward from urban areas finds its answers in the sociolinguistic dynamics that I have shown in Belten High and neighboring high schools. It is precisely in the con-struction of local social meaning through language use that speakers connect to, and make sense of, the surrounding communities, and that they come to deploy the linguistic resources offered in those communities.

If social geography explains the spread of new changes outward from the city, it also explains the evening out of older changes in the metropolitan area. The relation between the urban distribution of the variables and the local deployment of the variables in this study suggests that the change in the social distribution of variants over the life span of linguistic change is directly related to speakers' recognition of the urban distribution. The jocks and burnouts live in a socio-geographic landscape that is peopled by other jocks and burnouts. When they leave their school and look to other people their age, they look to very different places and very different groups of people, and in very different situations. Both burnouts and jocks are constant networkers, but in different domains: the burnouts in the local urban domain, and the jocks in the institutional domain. Jocks are outgoing in school, making a point of getting to know their constituencies and fos-tering an open and friendly demeanor. Burnouts consider this phony, and politicking. However, they tend to be outgoing in public places, taking pleasure in starting up conversations with strangers, including the senior citizens with whom they share fast food places, and young people who appear to be like them.

Jocks, by and large, come into contact with people from other schools in institutional contexts, and in which their relations with these people are structured by their institutional roles. At athletic events, cheerleaders, pompon girls, band members, and athletes may get to know their counterparts at the rival school. But they get to know them as counterparts and as rivals. The demands of their own intensive lives at school, which constrain them from making friends with people from other schools, also shape their stance towards the people they meet at such events, making it unlikely that they will try to become friends. Burnouts, on the other hand, meet people from other communities in the regular course of their peer-organized social lives, and they view them not as institutional counterparts, but as potential friends. Cruising and hanging out in parks is both a way to pass leisure time with one's local friends, and a way to encounter like-minded people from other communities. There is a strong force among burnouts to expand the network, to keep meeting exciting people, and to gain access to new resources. New people, particularly new urban people, are potential sources of information, urban connection, and excitement. The burnouts readily absorb newcomers to Belten who look or act like burnouts, while the jocks maintain their tight hierarchy by making entrance extremely difficult. As a result, there is a regular influx of urban newcomers into the burnout community – an influx of people who are viewed as important cultural sources, who bring both connections to urban networks and new knowledge, both of which make urban activity more accessible.

The newer changes in the Northern Cities Chain Shift, the backing of (ʌ) and (e), as well as (ay) raising, are more intense in the urban area and appear to be spreading through the suburban area. This spread is being carried out by adolescents who are engaged in what one might want to call a vast informal metropolitan youth network, in which urban symbols of all kinds are a prime means for establishing connection. Most every kid who cruises is drawn to something that goes on in these venues, whether it is the excitement, the sense of larger community, the feeling of autonomy, the access to controlled substances, the feeling of shared anger, or something else altogether. Without this sense of affinity, it is likely that they would not adopt the linguistic patterns associated with the urban milieu. Thus cruising involves not simply urban–suburban contact, but an active engagement that provides the motivation to develop an urban speech style. The potential for urban linguistic influence, then, is deeply embedded in the social practices of local communities of burnouts. While many isolated instances of contact with urban individuals may take place in the course of urban cruising, it is not these contacts that constitute the primary contact with urban speech. Cruising is one activity in a wider range of practices that orient and expose burnouts to urban speakers, and the brief contacts that may take place in forays to the city are embedded in contacts that range from the somewhat less brief to the fully substantial. Another way of looking at these variables and other urban symbols is that they signal local ownership. Burnouts use all kinds of local geographic resources, from parks to street corners to dirt bike tracks to roller rinks and bowling alleys. The burnout network itself reaches out to the city and brings the city into Belten High – and brings Belten High out to the city. It is for this reason that there appears to be no relation between the use of urban variables and the actual amount of contact with urban speakers, but rather between these variables and the extent to which one engages in urban practices.

The older changes, the raising of (aeh) and the fronting of (o) and (oh) have already spread intensely throughout the metropolitan area and beyond. As widespread changes, they may have general regional value, but they no longer have the potential to serve as urban symbols. A linguistic change that is originating in the urban center is local both by association with the activity of local groups in that center, and by association with its relative rarity within the wider metropolitan center. The definition of "local" that I have arrived at through this work is not simply geographically local, but local in the sense of consciously affiliating with locally based culture. This is opposed to the sense of affiliation with institutions that consciously transcend this culture. Thus while the burnouts are not necessarily primarily engaged in their neighborhoods, since their orientation becomes increasingly urban as they move through high school, they are in some sense becoming increasingly locally oriented as they engage seriously with the center of the local metropolitan area. The contrast between urban and suburban variables, then, is a contrast between a focus towards and a focus away from the urban center. There is no suburban or rural center that serves as the focus for suburban variables. Jocks do not cruise an "anti-urban" extreme while the burnouts are cruising the urban center. Rather, they focus on their institution and on its relatively homogeneous connections to other institutions in the metropolitan area. They do not need suburban contact to support their status, because their status is institutionally, not locally, based. But their use of variables that have spread well beyond the urban area does not distinguish them from the other jocks that they meet through institutional networks, but provides them with a linguistic resource that they can be sure they share with those jocks.

The changes that have been around long enough to lose their usefulness as urban symbols, then, take on a different life. When the overall use of advanced variants is high throughout the metropolitan area, the significance of these variants cannot be local, yet it distinguishes residents from somewhat more distant areas. Certainly, metropolitan Detroit variables distinguish speakers from other clearly different regional dialects, and certain differences among metropolitan areas in the midwest are sufficient to attract speakers' notice. Callary's finding (1975) of a correlation between the height of (aeh) and the size in population of the speaker's home town suggests that there can be a perceptible difference between metropolitan and rural status. There is a clear difference between Detroit suburban speech and the de-regionalized speech heard on the media. Thus it is possible that this variable provides a generalized metropolitan resource that makes no particular local statement, but that locates the speaker within a less locally differentiated landscape. The potential social meaning of such widespread variables cannot be very specific, and I would argue that when a variable gets to this stage, it serves not so much as a social marker as a marker of quite general engagement or as a stylistic intensifier. The social distributions of the use of such a marker depend on the extent to which speakers wish to display such expressiveness. Such an account has the advantage not only of explaining the substantial female lead in the use of the older changes in the Detroit suburban area, but of explaining the fact that the burned-out burnout girls make as high a use of these variables as other girls. Chapter 7 suggests that the greatest users of Pattern 1 variables are the girls generally known for flamboyance, regardless of the nature of that flamboyance. It is possible that these older changes, with no particular urban associations, are resources available to all for the general enhancement of style. Within the context of heightened Pattern 2 variables, this enhancement is of an urban style, while in the context of lower Pattern 2 variables, the enhancement is of a more suburban style. This kind of enhancement is found almost exclusively in the speech of girls, then, because boys – particularly boys who are especially eager to associate themselves with physical masculinity – may be constrained to avoid them in a general shrinking from any form of flamboyance that is not clearly associated with masculinity. The urban variables are the only ones that boys, and particularly burnout boys, can use with impunity. They are the only ones that clearly indicate an urban stance, and hence are associated with toughness, autonomy, and urban know-how – a kind of ownership of the local area. Variables that are more of a generally expressive resource, on the other hand, detract from a cool image, and conflict with the more inexpressive demeanor associated with both physical and technical masculinity (Sattel 1983). Lesley Milroy (1998) has noted that men's patterns of variation in general are extremely constrained, and has related this to the male value of inexpressivity.

Within this sequence of events, it appears that in the early stages, the use of advanced variants depends on class, or engagement in the local market, with those engaged in the local market leading. Gender at this stage is related to speakers' linguistic participation within the market, with girls and women leading in the use of forms appropriate to that market. Thus burnout girls lead in the use of advanced variants, while jock girls lag in their use. As the changes age, and begin to lose their urban associations, as in the case of (oh), the class difference remains but women across the board begin to make greater use of advanced variants. Finally, when the change becomes sufficiently old that it is no longer locally associated, girls make the greater use of it across the board, while boys in the local market shy away from it. But in addition, as variables that are widespread with respect to both age and geography, they cease to be the symbolic property of some adolescent group or category, and become a more general resource – possibly a kind of intensifier.

8.4   The Meaning of Stigma and Prestige

The common practice in variation studies of reducing the social meaning of variation to an opposition between prestige and stigma derives from, and suits, a study of variation based on an abstract socioeconomic hierarachy. But the notions of prestige and stigma themselves are as abstracted from local social reality as are the class categories; at the same time, they stand for critical aspects of this reality, and at times they are foregrounded in local reality as well. Critics of the association of prestige with standard language (e.g. L. Milroy 1980, J. Milroy 1982, Romaine 1982) argue that prestige is a matter of point of view and may be differentially assigned in diverse speech communities. The notion "covert prestige" (Trudgill 1972) goes part of the way towards recognizing the local desirability of the vernacular, but retains the recognition of the overarching power structure within which local communities function. While vernacular speakers know that their speech is stigmatized in the context of a global hierarchy, their day-to-day life unfolds in a place that is in many ways orthogonal to global prestige and stigma. And linguistic variables that are prestigious or stigmatized in the abstract are full of positive meaning in the concrete everyday. This is perhaps easier to see in the adolescent context than among adults. Belten High students certainly know that the jocks have institutional prestige, and that prestige is linked to an adult global class system. They also know that burnout behavior is institutionally stigmatized and that it is stigmatized in an adult global class system as well. But from an adolescent perspective, subjecting oneself to this adult system carries the potential ultimate stigma of failure to overcome childhood subordination to adults. I have argued in chapter 1 that childhood subordination to adults and adult class subordination are not entirely separate, certainly to the extent that the initial association of "proper" language with power and with institutions begins in the former. But the crucial dynamic is not so much the construction of prestige and stigma as the construction of identities, all of which are positive, and while they are aligned with class they have other lives. The jocks are no doubt trying to construct an institutional persona by developing a preppy speech style – they are making a positive statement rather than simply avoiding forms that are more stigmatized. The burnouts are no doubt courting global stigma in their use of negative concord, but in the interests of building a joint non-institutional persona.

The importance of adolescence for the study of sociolinguistic variation lies in its transitional status between childhood and adulthood, in which adult power and authority are appropriated into the peer social order. It is at this point that speakers begin to connect to the global social order independently of their families, and with reference to their age peers. Placed by adults in school, the institution that is designed both to reproduce class and to offer mobility, adolescents create their social order with respect to this institution. Communities of practice emerge in response to the institution, seeking ways to participate in it, to gain control of it, to avoid it, to find alternatives to it, etc. They embody ideologies that together constitute the social order.

By foregrounding the opposition between institutional and local engagement, the jocks and the burnouts define the dominant extremes of social class for adolescence. Although access to material goods through parents' financial means is clearly important in the adolescent social order, access to parents' income is recognized as involving patronage. Furthermore, burnouts are more likely than jocks to have their own money because athletics does not prevent them from having after school jobs. The primary issues of class center not around material wealth, then, but around institutional and local engagement. These two forms of engagement offer alternative ways of achieving autonomy. These ways are competing as well, for the burnouts' defection from the school threatens the credibility of the jocks' adult-like roles in school, which depends on a sizeable constituency. In turn, the jocks' participation in the social world offered by the school provides peer legitimation of age-group subordination, threatening the burnouts' claim that this subordination is illegitimate.

Together, by marking the extremes, the jocks and the burnouts define the terms of peer ideology. These foregrounded extremes are not along academic lines, but along lines of social engagement, marginalizing intellectual activity in the public sphere. Within each school, the jocks and the burnouts serve as foci in a school-based social landscape, facilitating the organization of social meaning and the stylistic activity that makes this meaning palpable. And as extremes with respect to institutional and local engagement, the jocks and burnouts of the schools across the metropolitan area connect their respective social landscapes to the urban–suburban continuum. There is no mystery, therefore, to how linguistic change spreads systematically from urban centers, and there is no mystery to how each age cohort engages in this process of spread in a seamless fashion. The social meaning of variation is built into the very means by which individual speakers are connected to their closest friends on the one hand, and to the most abstract level of social organization on the other.

References

Andersen, E. S. 1990. *Speaking With Style: The Sociolinguistic Skills of Children.* London: Routledge.

Baltes, P., Reese, W. W., and Lipsitt, L. P. 1980. Life-span developmental psychology. *Annual Review of Psychology* 31: 65–110.

Bauman, R. in press. The ethnography of genre: Form function, Variation. *Stylistic Variation in Language*, ed. P. Eckert and J. Rickford. Cambridge: Cambridge University Press.

Belenky, M. F., Clinchy, B., Goldberger, N., and Tarule, J. 1986. *Women's Ways of Knowing.* New York: Basic Books.

Bell, A. 1984. Language Style as Audience Design. *Language in Society* 13: 145–204.

Bender, E. 1998. Syntactic variation and linguistic competence. Dissertation Proposal, Stanford University.

Biondi, L. 1975. *The Italian-American Child: His Sociolinguistic Acculturation.* Washington DC: Georgetown University Press.

Blom, J.-P. and Gumperz, J. 1972. Social meaning in linguistic structure: Code-switching in Norway. *Directions in Sociolinguistics*, ed. J. Gumperz and D. Hymes. New York: Holt, Rinehart and Winston, 407–34.

Bott, E. 1957. *Family and Social Network.* London: Tavistock.

Bourdieu, P. 1977a. The economics of linguistic exchanges. *Social Science Information* 16(6): 645–68.

Bourdieu, P. 1977b. *Outline of a Theory of Practice.* Cambridge: Cambridge University Press.

Bourdieu, P. and Boltanski, L. 1975. Le fétichisme de la langue. *Actes de la recherche en sciences sociales* 4: 2–32.

Brown, P. and Levinson, S. 1979. Social structure, groups and interaction. *Social Markers in Speech*, ed. K. R. Scherer and H. Giles. Cambridge: Cambridge University Press. 291–342.

California Style Collective. 1993. Variation and personal/group style. *21st Annual Conference on New Ways of Analyzing Variation in English.* Ottawa.

Callary, R. E. 1975. Phonological change and the development of an urban dialect in Illinois. *Language in Society* 4(2): 155–69.

Chambers, J. 1992. Dialect acquisition. *Language* 68: 673–705.

Chambers, J. K. 1995. *Sociolinguistic Theory*. Oxford: Blackwell.

Cheshire, J. 1982. *Variation in an English Dialect*. Cambridge: Cambridge University Press.

Connell, R. 1995. *Masculinities*. Berkeley: University of California Press.

Coupland, N. in press. Language, situation and the relational self: Theorizing dialect-style in sociolinguistics. *Stylistic Variation in Language*, ed. P. Eckert and J. Rickford. Cambridge: Cambridge University Press.

Coupland, N., Coupland, J., and Giles, H. 1991. *Language, Society and the Elderly*. Oxford: Blackwell.

Eckert, P. (1980). Clothing and geography in a suburban high school. *Michigan discussions in anthropology* 6: 45–8. Reprinted in *Researching American Culture*, ed. Conrad Kottak, 1982. Ann Arbor: University of Michigan Press. 139–44.

Eckert, P. 1983. Beyond the statistics of adolescent smoking. *American Journal of Public Health* 73: 439–41.

Eckert, P. 1989. *Jocks and Burnouts: Social Categories and Identity in the High School*. New York: Teachers College Press.

Eckert, P. 1990a. Adolescent social categories, information and science learning: Toward a Scientific Practice of Science Education, ed. M. Gardner, J. Greeno, F. Reif, and A. Schonfeld. Hillsdale NJ: Lawrence Erlbaum. 203–17.

Eckert, P. 1990b. Cooperative competition in adolescent girl talk. *Discourse Processes* 13: 92–122.

Eckert, P. 1994. *Identities of Subordination as a Developmental Imperative*. Palo Alto: Institute for Research on Learning.

Eckert, P. 1996a. (ay) goes to the city: Reminiscences of Martha's Vineyard. *Towards a Social Science of Language: Festschrift for William Labov*, ed. J. Baugh, C. Feagin, G. Guy, and D. Schiffrin. Philadelphia and Amsterdam: John Benjamins, 47–68.

Eckert, P. 1996b. Age as a sociolinguistic variable. *Handbook of Sociolinguistics*, ed. F. Coulmas. Oxford: Blackwell.

Eckert, P. 1997a. Gender and sociolinguistic variation. *Readings in Language and Gender*, ed. J. Coates. Oxford: Blackwell, 64–76.

Eckert, P. 1997b. Gender, race and class in the preadolescent marketplace of identities. *Paper presented at the Annual Meeting of the American Anthropological Association*. Washington, DC.

Eckert, P. 1997c. Vowels and nailpolish. *Gender and Belief Systems: Proceedings for the Third Berkeley Conference on Women and Language*, eds. N. Warner et al. Berkeley: Berkeley Women and Language Group, 183–90.

Eckert, P. and McConnell-Ginet, S. 1992. Think practically and look locally: Language and gender as community-based practice. *Annual Review of Anthropology* 21: 461–90.

Eckert, P. and McConnell-Ginet, S. 1995. Constructing meaning, constructing selves: Snapshots of language, gender and class from Belten High. *Gender Articulated: Language and the socially constructed self*, ed. K. Hall and M. Bucholtz. New York: Routledge. 469–508.

Edwards, W. F. 1991. Sociolinguistic behavior in a Detroit inner-city black neighborhood. *Language in Society* 21: 93–115.

Eisikovits, E. 1987. Sex differences in inter- and intra-group interaction among adolescents. *Women and Language in Australian and New Zealand Society*, ed. A. Pauwels. Australian Professional Publications.

Ferguson, C. A. 1977. Babytalk as a simplified register. *Talking to Children*, ed. C. E. Snow and C. A. Ferguson. Cambridge: Cambridge University Press.

Fischer, J. L. 1958. Social influences on the choice of a linguistic variant. *Word* 14: 47–56.

Foucault, M. 1977. *Discipline and Punish: The Birth of the Prison*. London: Penguin Press.

Gal, S. 1979. *Language Shift: Social Determinants of Linguistic Change in Bilingual Austria*. New York: Academic Press.

Giddens, A. 1979. *Central Problems in Social Theory: Action, Structure and Contradition in Social Analysis*. Berkeley and Los Angeles: University of California Press.

Gleason, J. B. 1973. Code switching in children's language. *Cognitive Development and the Acquisition of Language*, ed. T. Moore. New York: Academic Press.

Goffman, E. 1976. Gender advertisements. *Studies in the Anthropology of Visual Communication* 3(2): 69–154.

Goffman, E. 1977. The arrangement between the sexes. *Theory and Society* 4: 301–32.

Goodwin, C. and Goodwin, M. H. 1992. Assessments and the construction of context. *Rethinking Content*, ed. A. Duranti and C. Goodwin. Cambridge: Cambridge University Press. 147–89.

Gumperz, J. 1962. Types of linguistic communities. *Anthropological Linguistics* 4: 28–40.

Haeri, N. 1997. *The Sociolinguistic Market of Cairo: Gender, Class and Education*. London: Kegan Paul International.

Hade, M. 1962. Phonology in a generative grammar. *Word* 18: 54–72.

Hindle, D. 1979. The social and situational conditioning of phonetic variation. Ph.D. Dissertation, University of Pennsylvania.

Højrup, T. 1983. The concept of life-model: a form-specifying mode of analysis applied to contemporary Europe. *Ethnologia Scandinavica*, 1–50.

Hymes, D. 1972. Models of the interaction of language and social life. *The Ethnography of Communication*, ed. J. Gumperz and D. Hymes. New York: Holt, Rinehart and Winston. 35–71.

Hymes, D. 1974. *Foundations in Sociolinguistics: An Ethnographic Approach*. Philadelphia: University of Pennsylvania Press.

Irvine, J. in press. Style as distinctiveness: The culture and ideology of linguistic differentiation. *Stylistic Variation in Language*, ed. P. Eckert and J. Rickford. Cambridge: Cambridge University Press.

Kanter, R. M. 1977. *Men and Women of the Corporation*. New York: Basic Books.

Knack, R. 1991. Ethnic boundaries in linguistic variation. *New Ways of Analyzing Sound Change*, ed. P. Eckert. New York: Academic Press. 252–72.

Kroch, A. and Small, C. 1978. Grammatical ideology and its effect on speech. *Linguistic Variation: Models and Methods*, ed. D. Sankoff. New York: Academic Press. 45–56.

Kroch, A. S. 1978. Toward a theory of social dialect variation. *Language in Society* 7: 17–36.

Labov, W. 1963. The social motivation of a sound change. *Word* 19: 273–309.

Labov, W. 1964. Stages in the acquisition of Standard English. Social Dialects and Language Learning, ed. R. W. Shuy. Champaign IL: National Council of Teachers of English. 77–103.

Labov, W. 1966. *The Social Stratification of English in New York City*. Washington, DC: Center for Applied Linguistics.

Labov, W. 1972a. *Language in the Inner City*. Philadelphia: University of Pennsylvania Press.

Labov, W. 1972b. *Sociolinguistic Patterns*. Philadelphia: University of Pennsylvania Press.

Labov, W. 1981. Resolving the Neogrammarian controversy. *Language* 57: 267–309.

Labov, W. 1989. The child as linguistic historian. *Language Variation and Change* 1: 85–94.

Labov, W. 1990. The intersection of sex and social class in the course of linguistic change. *Language Variation and Change* 2(2): 205–51.

Labov, W. 1991. The three dialects of English. *New Ways of Analyzing Sound Change*, ed. P. Eckert. San Diego: Academic Press. 1–44.

Labov, W. 1994. *Principles of Linguistic Change: Internal Factors*. Oxford: Basil Blackwell.

Labov, W. in press. The anatomy of style shifting. *Stylistic Variation in Language*, ed. P. Eckert and J. Rickford. Cambridge: Cambridge University Press.

Labov, W., Yaeger, M. and Steiner, R. 1972. *A Quantitative Study of Sound Change in Progress*. Philadelphia: US Regional Survey.

Lambert, W., Hodgson, R., Gardner, R., and Fillenbaum, S. 1960. Evaluative reactions to spoken language. *Journal of Abnormal and Social Psychology* 60: 44–51.

Lave, J. and Wenger, E. 1991. *Situated Learning: Legitimate Peripheral Participation*. Cambridge: Cambridge University Press.

Lockwood, D. 1989. *The Blackcoated Worker: A Study in Class Consciousness*, 2nd edn. Oxford: Clarendon.

MacAulay, R. K. S. 1977. *Language, Social Class and Education: a Glasgow Study*. Edinburgh: University of Edinburgh Press.

Maltz, D. N. and Borker, R. A. 1982. A cultural approach to male–female miscommunication. *Language and Social Identity*, ed J. J. Gumperz. Cambridge: Cambridge University Press. 196–216.

Mayer, A. 1975. The lower middle class as historical problem. *Journal of Modern History* 47: 409–36.

Mendoza-Denton, N. 1997. Chicana/Menicana identity and linguistic variation. An ethnographic and sociolinguistic study of gang affiliation in an urban high school. PhD dissertation, Stanford University.

Milroy, J. 1982. Probing under the tip of the iceberg: phonological 'normalization' and the shape of speech communities. *Sociolinguistic Variation in Speech Communities*, ed. S. Romaine. London: Edward Arnold. 26–48.

Milroy, J. and Milroy, L. 1985. Linguistic change, social network and speaker innovation. *Journal of Linguistics* 21: 339–84.

Milroy, L. 1980. *Language and Social Networks*. Oxford: Blackwell.

Milroy, L. 1998. Women as innovators and norm-creators: The sociolinguistics of dialect leveling in a northern English city. *Paper presented at Fifth Biennial Women and Language Conference*, Berkeley.

Milory, L. and Milroy, J. 1992. Social netowrk and social class: Toward an integrated sociolinguistic model. *Language in Society* 21(1): 1–26.

Mitchell, J. C. 1986. Network procedures. *The Quality of Urban Life*, ed. D. Frick. Berlin: de Gruyter. 73–92.

Ochs, E. 1991. Indexing gender. *Rethinking Context*, eds. A. Duranti and C. Goodwin. Cambridge: Cambridge University Press.

Payne, A. 1980. Factors controlling the acquisition of the Philadelphia dialect by out-of-state children. *Locating Language in Time and Space*, ed. W. Labov. New York: Academic Press. 143–78.

Reid, E. 1978. Social and stylistic variation in the speech of children: Some evidence from Edinburgh. *Sociolinguistic Patterns in British English*, ed. P. Trudgill. London: Edward Arnold. 158–71.

Rickford, J. 1986. Concord and contrast in the characterization of the speech community. *Proceedings of the Fourteenth Annual Conference on New Ways of Analyzing Variation*, ed. R. W. Fasold. Washington, DC: Georgetown University Press.

Rickford, J. and McNair-Knox, F. 1994. Addressee- and topic-influenced style shift: A quantitative sociolinguistic study. *Sociolinguistic Perspectives on Register*, ed. D. Biber and E. Finegan. New York: Oxford University Press. 235–76.

Roberts, J. and Labov, W. 1992. Acquisition of a dialect. *Paper presented at the Twenty-First Conference on New Ways of Analyzing Variation*. Ann Arbor.

Romaine, S. 1982. What is a speech community? *Sociolinguistic Variation in Speech Communities*, ed. S. Romaine. London: Edward Arnold. 13–24.

Romaine, S. 1984. *The Language of Children and Adolescents*. Oxford: Basil Blackwell.

Sankoff, D. 1987. Variable rules. *International Handbook of the Science of Language and Society*, ed. U. Anmow, N: Dittmar and K. Mattheier. Berlin: Walter de Gruyter.

Sankoff, D., Cedergren, H., Kemp, W., Thibault, P., and Vincent, D. 1989. Montreal French: Language, class, and ideology. *Language Change and Variation*, ed. W. Fasold and D. Schiffrin. Amsterdam: John Benjamins. 107–18.

Sankoff, D. and Laberge, S. 1978. The linguistic market and the statistical explanation of variability. *Linguistic Variation: Models and Methods*, ed. D. Sankoff. New York: Academic Press. 239–50.

Sattel, J. 1983. Men, inexpressiveness, and power. *Language, Gender and Society*, ed. B. Thorne, C. Kramarae, and N. Henley. Rowley, MA: Newbury House. 118–24.

Schilling Estes, N. 1996. The linguistic and sociolinguistic status of /ay/ in outer banks English. PhD dissertation, University of North Carolina.

Shuy, R. W., Wolfram, W. A., and Riley, W. K. 1967. Linguistic correlates of social stratification in Detroit speech. *Final Report, Research Project No. MH 15048-01*. National Institute of Mental Health.

Thorne, B. 1993. *Gender Play*. New Brunswick, NJ: Rutgers University Press.

Traweek, S. 1988. Beamtimes and Lifetimes. Cambridge, MA: Harvard University Press.

Trudgill, P. 1972. Sex, covert prestige and linguistic change in the urban British English of Norwich. *Language in Society* 1: 179–95.

Trudgill, P. 1974. *The Social Differentiation of English in Norwich*. Cambridge: Cambridge University Press.

Tway, P. 1975. Workplace isoglosses: Lexical variation and change in a factory setting. *Language in Society* 4: 171–83.

Wenger, E. 1998. *Communities of Practice*. New York: Cambridge University Press.

Wolfram, W. 1969. *A Sociolinguistic Description of Detroit Negro Speech*. Washington, DC: Center for Applied Linguistics.

Wolfram, W. 1989. Structural variability in phonological development: Final nasals in vernacular black English. *Language Change and Variation*, ed. R. Fasold and D. Schiffrin. Amsterdam: John Benjamin.

Wolfson, N. 1976. Speech events and natural speech: some implications for sociolinguistic methodology. *Language in Society* 5(2): 189–210.

Woolard, K. 1985. Language variation and cultural hegemony. *American Ethnologist* 12: 738–48.

Zhang, Q. 1995. Variation and the linguistic market in Tianjing. *Paper Presented at Conference on New Ways of Analyzing Variation in English*. University of Pennsylvania.

Index